JOHN BUNYAN
AND ENGLISH NONCONFORMITY

JOHN BUNYAN
AND
ENGLISH NONCONFORMITY

RICHARD GREAVES

THE HAMBLEDON PRESS
LONDON AND RIO GRANDE

Published by The Hambledon Press, 1992

102 Gloucester Avenue, London NW1 8HX (U.K.)

P.O. Box 162, Rio Grande, Ohio 45674 (U.S.A.)

ISBN 1 85285 072 8

A description of this book is available from
The British Library and from The Library of Congress.

Phototypeset by The Midlands Book Typesetting Company, Loughborough
Printed on acid-free paper and bound in
Great Britain by Cambridge University Press

Contents

Preface   vii

Acknowledgements   ix

Abbreviations   x

1 'To Be Found Faithful': The Nonconformist Tradition in England, 1660–1700   1

2 The State of Historical Scholarship   37

3 Conscience, Liberty, and the Spirit: Bunyan and Nonconformity   51

4 The Organizational Response of Nonconformity to Repression and Indulgence: The Case of Bedfordshire   71

5 Bunyan and Nonconformity in the Midlands and East Anglia   89

6 The Spirit and the Sword: Bunyan and the Stuart State   101

7 Bunyan and the Changing Face of Popery   127

8 Bunyan and the Fifth Monarchists   141

9 *The Holy War* and London Nonconformity   155

10 Amid the *Holy War*: Bunyan and the Ethic of Suffering   169

11 The Authorship of *Reprobation Asserted*   185

12 Tercentenary Reflections   193

13 Conventicles, Sedition, and the Toleration Act of 1689   207

Index   223

Preface

Thirty years ago, as a doctoral student at the University of London, I began my studies of John Bunyan, never dreaming how much of my life would be devoted to someone most Americans erroneously associate with Babe and the Blue Ox. In the mid-1980s several Bunyan scholars and Stuart specialists, including James Forrest and Ted Underwood, urged me to write a biography of Bunyan. By the time I could give serious consideration to such a project, Christopher Hill was working on his brilliant study of Bunyan, making it prudent to postpone a biography. Shortly thereafter, Michael Mullett began writing what promises to be an excellent biography. With the encouragement of Martin Sheppard, I have therefore opted to bring together the essays I have written on Bunyan over the past three decades. I have taken the liberty to make modest revisions, both substantive and stylistic. Because of the nature of such a collection, some overlapping remains, for which I beg the readers' indulgence.

The Bunyan to whom I was introduced in the 1960s has changed rather dramatically in the ensuing years. Despite the provocative work of William York Tindall, Bunyan was still depicted by many writers at that time more as a Victorian evangelical than as a vigorous Stuart Nonconformist. Scholarly interest in Bunyan has increased considerably in recent decades on the part of both literary scholars and historians. This renaissance of Bunyan scholarship, the significance of which was underscored in 1988 with the founding of the journal *Bunyan Studies*, has replaced the prudish, pious Victorian preacher with the Bunyan of history.

In the early 1960s Roger Sharrock was already at work placing Bunyan in his proper literary context, but the historical Bunyan remained in the shadows and Nonconformity was still coloured in hagiographical hues. The historiographical picture changed substantially in the 1970s and 1980s, thanks in large measure to Christopher Hill's probing studies of mid-century radicals in *The World Turned*

Upside Down, of Milton in *Milton and the English Revolution*, and finally
of Bunyan in *A Turbulent Seditious and Factious People*. In the meantime
scholars such as Sears McGee, Bob Owens, and Aileen Ross were
exploring Bunyan's millenarianism; Vera Camden and Roger Pooley
his psychology; Dayton Haskin the impact of Luther on Bunyan; and
Barrie White and Anne Laurence his early life. Neil Keeble, Nigel
Smith, and many others have contributed sophisticated, provocative
literary studies. We can no longer divorce Bunyan from a sometimes
radical historical context, nor can we depict Stuart Nonconformity in
quiescent, hagiographical terms. A robust writer deeply immersed in
the colloquial speech of his contemporaries, Bunyan was a staunch,
sometimes vitriolic critic of his society.

I have chosen to frame this collection of Bunyan essays with two
pieces covering broad but closely related themes: the first attempts to
illustrate a Nonconformist tradition that was much more active and
vigourous than has often been thought; this was Bunyan's world. To
elevate him above it, as a figure of solitary literary splendour and
saintly piety, is to misunderstand him and his works. The closing essay
attempts to explain the 1689 Act of Toleration against the background
of Nonconformist activity in the preceding three decades. Although
Bunyan did not live to see the passage of this statute, he was very much
a part of the movement that ultimately achieved limited toleration.
The 1689 Act of Toleration would have been unthinkable without the
determined efforts of dissidents such as Bunyan.

Acknowledgements

During the course of my work on Bunyan in the past three decades I have been singularly fortunate to have had the advice and encouragement of numerous scholars. My debt is especially great to Geoffrey F. Nuttall, my earliest guide, and to Roger Sharrock, who graciously invited me to join the editorial team that produced the Oxford *Miscellaneous Works*. It is also a pleasure to thank Vera Camden, Robert G. Collmer, James F. Forrest, Joyce Godber, Dayton Haskin, Christopher Hill, Neil H. Keeble, Anne Laurence, J. Sears McGee, Michael Mullett, W.R. Owens, Roger Pooley, Aileen Ross, Paul Seaver, Stuart Sim, Gordon Tibbutt, Ted L. Underwood, and Robert Zaller. I am grateful as well to Dr. Williams's Library for permission to use its manuscripts.

The articles collected here (and now revised) were originally published in the following places and are reprinted by the kind permission of the original publishers:

1 *Bunyan Studies: John Bunyan and his Times*, 4 (Spring 1991), pp. 37–65.
2 *Bunyan in England and Abroad: Papers Delivered at the John Bunyan Tercentenary Symposium, Vrije Universiteit Amsterdam, 1988*, ed. M. van Os and G.J. Schutte (Amsterdam: VU University Press, 1990), pp. 29–43.
3 *John Bunyan: Conventicle and Parnassus. Tercentenary Essays*, ed. N. H. Keeble (Oxford: Clarendon Press, 1988), pp. 21–43.
4 *Church History*, 44 (December 1975), pp. 472–84.
5 *Journal of the United Reformed Church History Society*, 1 (April 1976), pp. 186–96.
6 *Bunyan in Our Time*, ed. Robert G. Collmer (Kent, Ohio: Kent State University Press, 1989), pp. 138–60.
7 *Bunyan Studies: John Bunyan and his Times*, 1 (Autumn 1988), pp. 15–25.
8 *Albion*, 13 (Summer 1981), pp. 83–95.

9   *The Baptist Quarterly*, 26 (October 1975), pp. 158–68.
10 *John Bunyan and His England, 1628–1688*, ed. Anne Laurence, W.R. Owens, and Stuart Sim (London: Hambledon Press, 1990), pp. 63–75.
11 *The Baptist Quarterly*, 21 (July 1965), pp. 126–31.
12 *American Baptist Quarterly*, 7 (December 1988), pp. 496–508.
13 *Eighteenth-Century Life*, 12, n.s. (November 1988), pp. 1–13.

Abbreviations

Add. MSS	Additional Manuscripts
BDBR	*Biographical Dictionary of British Radicals in the Seventeenth Century*, ed. Richard L. Greaves and Robert Zaller, 3 vols. (Brighton, Sussex, 1982–84)
BL	British Library
Brown	John Brown, *John Bunyan (1628–1688): His Life, Times, and Work*, rev. Frank Mott Harrison (London, 1928)
CR	A.G. Matthews, *Calamy Revised* (Oxford, 1934)
CSPD	*Calendar of State Papers, Domestic*
DNB	*Dictionary of National Biography*
Doe	*The Works of That Eminent Servant of Christ, Mr. John Bunyan*, ed. Charles Doe (London, 1692)
DWL	Dr. Williams's Library, London
GA	John Bunyan, *Grace Abounding to the Chief of Sinners*, ed. Roger Sharrock (Oxford, 1962)
Greaves, *DUFE*	Richard L. Greaves, *Deliver Us from Evil: The Radical Underground in Britain, 1660–1663* (New York, 1986)
Greaves, *EUHF*	Richard L. Greaves, *Enemies Under His Feet: Radicals and Nonconformists in Britain, 1664–1677* (Stanford, Cal., 1990)
Greaves, *SAR*	Richard L. Greaves, *Saints and Rebels: Seven Nonconformists in Stuart England* (Macon, Ga.,1985)
Greaves, *SOK*	Richard L. Greaves, *Secrets of the Kingdom: British Radicals from the Popish Plot to the Revolution of 1688–1689* (Stanford, Cal., 1992)
Hill, *JB*	Christopher Hill, *A Turbulent Seditious and Factious People: John Bunyan and His Church* (Oxford, 1988)
HW	John Bunyan, *The Holy War*, ed. Roger Sharrock and James F. Forrest (Oxford, 1980)

Keeble, *JB*	N.H. Keeble, ed., *John Bunyan: Conventicle and Parnassus, Tercentenary Essays* (Oxford, 1988)
Laurence	Anne Laurence, W.R. Owens, and Stuart Sim, *John Bunyan and His England, 1628–88* (London, 1990)
Minutes	*The Minutes of the First Independent Church (now Bunyan Meeting) at Bedford 1656–1766*, ed. H.G. Tibbutt (Publications of the Bedfordshire Historical Record Society, vol. 55)
MW	*The Miscellaneous Works of John Bunyan*, general ed. Roger Sharrock, 12 vols. (Oxford, 1976–)
Offor	*The Works of John Bunyan*, ed. George Offor, 3 vols. (Glasgow, 1852–53)
PP	John Bunyan, *The Pilgrim's Progress*, ed. James Blanton Wharey and Roger Sharrock (Oxford, 1960)
PRO SP	Public Record Office, State Papers
Rel. Bax.	Richard Baxter, *Reliquiae Baxterianae*, ed. Matthew Sylvester (London, 1696)
Sharrock, *JB*	Roger Sharrock, *John Bunyan* (London, 1968)
Tindall	William York Tindall, *John Bunyan: Mechanick Preacher* (New York, 1934)
Turner	*Original Records of Early Nonconformity*, ed. G. Lyon Turner, 3 vols. (London, 1911–14)
Wigfield	W.M. Wigfield, *Recusancy and Nonconformity in Bedfordshire: Illustrated by Select Documents Between 1622 and 1842* (Publications of the Bedfordshire Historical Record Society, vol. 20: 145–249)

To

James and Ann Forrest

and the memory of

Roger Ian Sharrock

'To Be Found Faithful': The Nonconformist Tradition in England, 1660–1700[1]

Traditionally, historians have depicted Restoration Nonconformity largely in terms of persecution, defeatism, the death of 'militant Puritanism', and the espousal of a detached pietism freed from the shackles of political entanglement and preoccupied with otherworldly pursuits. This warped view is based on a faulty historical methodology that neglects the rich archival sources for the period, an excessive reliance on printed sermons and devotional literature, insufficient attention to the laity, and a preoccupation with partisan denominational history. The result has been an almost hagiographical treatment of Dissenters, framed in the context of defeat and survival rather than vitality, with undue stress on denominational distinctiveness and a failure to appreciate the rich and subtle tapestry that Restoration Nonconformity was. Yet to deny the reality of persecution, the growth of denominational identities, or the pronounced evangelical core at the root of Protestant Nonconformity would result in an erroneous view of Dissent.

Nonconformity never commanded the allegiance of a majority of the English nation, and in fact throughout the late seventeenth century the number of Dissenters was surprisingly small. Not until 1718 were reasonably accurate figures for Dissent compiled, by which point — with the benefit of legal toleration — they numbered approximately 338,000 in England and 18,000 in Wales, or some 6 percent of the population. A survey ordered in 1669 by Gilbert Sheldon, archbishop of Canterbury, recorded at least 120,000 Dissenters, including 1,138 ministers, but no returns were made for four dioceses (Bristol, Gloucester, Hereford, and Rochester), and information from others is incomplete. Under the Declaration of Indulgence issued in 1672, the government granted 1,610 licences

1. The quoted phrase is from a letter of Matthew Henry to his father. BL Add. MSS 42,849, fol. 14r.

to ministers (down from the approximately 2,000 ejected between 1660 and 1662), which might suggest that Sheldon's figures were 25 to 30 percent too low, especially since Quakers (who had no traditional ministers) were not licensed in 1672. Perhaps a figure of roughly 180,000 would approximate the strength of Dissent in 1669, thereby indicating that they amounted to perhaps 4 percent of the population. Numerically, the Presbyterians were the largest Nonconformist group, being roughly three times the size of the Congregationalists, and four times that of the Baptists. By 1715, when Dissenters were more than 6 percent of the population, there were approximately 179,000 Presbyterians, 60,000 Congregationalists, 40,000 Particular Baptists, 19,000 General Baptists, and 39,500 Quakers.[2]

By the early eighteenth century Nonconformists exceeded 10 percent of the population only in Devon, Essex, Lancashire, Monmouthshire, Hertfordshire, and Bristol. The last had the greatest concentration of Dissenters in England (19.6 percent). Numerically, however, most Nonconformists were in Middlesex and London (33,220), Devon (25,610), Lancashire (20,270), Yorkshire (18,460), Essex (18,080), and Somerset (17,280). Dissent was least successful in much of the west, Cornwall, and Lincolnshire.

The prevailing view that Nonconformity was strongest in the towns and appealed especially to the middling sort of people is probably accurate for the late seventeenth century. William Penn suggested that 'a chief part' of the nation's merchants, shopkeepers, and clothiers were Dissenters. It was, then, only natural that business and trade metaphors appealed to Nonconformist authors. The Congregationalist Bartholomew Ashwood candidly directed his treatise, *The Heavenly Trade, or the Best Merchandizing*, to merchants, one of whom, Jeremy Holwey of Bristol, was the recipient of the epistle dedicatory. The godly were depicted as 'Saints Adventure[r]s', whose safe return was assured by Christ's work as a surety, and as factors who traded with the stock of Christ and obeyed his 'Letters of Advice' with respect to the disposition of his goods. Ashwood's readers must have favoured free trade, for of grace and salvation he wrote: 'Here are no Monopolies, or hard impositions upon this trade: no restraint from setting up, or selling out of Wisdome's goods, in any parts of the world'.[3]

2. Turner, iii, pp. 69–70, 105–39; Michael R. Watts, *The Dissenters: From the Reformation to the French Revolution* (Oxford, 1978), pp. 269–70, 491–510.
3. William Penn, *Considerations Moving to a Toleration and Liberty of Conscience* (London, 1685), p. 4; Bartholomew Ashwood, *The Heavenly Trade* (London, 1679), sig. A7r; pp. 29, 36, 352–53, 357; cf. pp. 67, 206, 248, 288, 293, 358; Vavasor Powell, *The Bird in the Cage* (London, 1661), pp. 65–66.

The Presbyterian George Swinnock managed to stretch the business metaphor to nearly 1,900 pages in *The Christian Man's Calling: or, a Treatise of Making Religion Ones Business*. In the first of three volumes he praised his gentry patrons, Richard and Letitia Hampden of Hampden, Buckinghamshire, for acting like wise merchants in their spiritual concerns; 'you return your riches into the other world by Bills of Exchange', and Swinnock's readers were urged to follow their example. 'The duty of every Christian to make Religion his business' was later the theme of one of Thomas Watson's Cripplegate lectures. As a City preacher, Watson was especially fond of commercial imagery.[4] In contrast, the Quakers turned the metaphor against their orthodox opponents, castigating the professional clergy for making 'merchandize of souls for dishonest gain'.[5] Too much should not be made of the use of mercantile metaphors in Nonconformist literature, for Dissenters, in their efforts to drive their message home, also had frequent recourse to analogies from the world of husbandmen, mariners, attorneys, masters, and servants.

Nothing was more important in shaping the character of Restoration Nonconformity than the failure of the Presbyterians to attain comprehension in the established church. Apart from roughly doubling the number of Dissenters, the exclusion of the Presbyterians generally moderated the Nonconformist movement. Although Presbyterians such as Colonel Thomas Blood and William Lecky engaged in militant activity against the regime, most eschewed such endeavours and were generally 'respectable' men and women. Nonconformist strength in Parliament was also greatly enhanced by the fact that Presbyterians were not comprehended. Of the fifty-one members of the House of Commons between 1661 and 1689 whom Douglas Lacey was reasonably certain could be identified as Nonconformists, no less than thirty-four were Presbyterians, compared to two Congregationalists and one Baptist.[6] Of the six Nonconformist peers, four were unmistakably

4. George Swinnock, *The Christian Man's Calling*, 3 vols. (London, 1660–65), i, sigs. Blr, D3v; p. 7; iii, p. 863; Thomas Watson, *Religion Our Business* (London, 1682), p. 453. Cf. Watson, in *The London-Ministers Legacy to their Several Congregations*, 2nd ed. ([London], 1662), p. 31; Watson, *Heaven Taken by Storm* (London, 1669), p. 136; Watson, *A Divine Cordial* (London, 1663), p. 32; Watson, *The Godly Mans Picture* (London, 1666), p. 291. Other ministers in the London area found the metaphor appropriate; cf. e.g. Edmund Calamy, *The Righteous Mans Death Lamented* (London, 1662), p. 12; James Janeway, *Heaven upon Earth*, 3rd ed. (London, 1671), pp. 198, 231–32.

5. Richard Hubberthorn, *The Light of Christ Within* (London, 1660), p. 23; William Simpson, *A Discovery of the Priests and Professors* (London, 1660), p. 1.

6. Douglas R. Lacey, *Dissent and Parliamentary Politics in England, 1661–1689* (New Brunswick, N.J., 1969), pp. 374–459.

Presbyterian, and Philip Lord Wharton probably was as well. In addition to strengthening Dissent numerically and politically, the exclusion of the Presbyterians from the Church of England also enhanced the possibility of ties to the Scottish Covenanters, as in fact materialized to a modest degree during the Rye House plotting and the Argyll and Monmouth rebellions.

The inevitable recourse to denominational labels must not be allowed to obscure the fact that throughout the late seventeenth century substantial fluidity existed within the Nonconformist movement. In retrospect, ecumenical endeavours had only minimal success and failed to achieve unification. At the Savoy Conference in 1661 Episcopalian and Presbyterian efforts to reach an accord foundered, setting a negative tone for all subsequent discussions of comprehension. In 1690, Presbyterians and Congregationalists in London founded the Common Fund to assist ministers, churches, and ministerial students, and the following year they produced a blueprint for union, the *Heads of Agreement*, in which they proclaimed that 'in all substantials we are fully of one mind'. They envisioned a union of visible saints bound together by a common allegiance to the Bible as the Word of God and the sole basis of faith and practice, and either the doctrinal provisions of the Thirty-nine Articles, or the Westminster Confession and Catechisms, or the Savoy Declaration of 1658. But the union collapsed in 1695.[7] There had been cooperation at other levels, such as the influential Merchants' Lectures at Pinners' Hall in London, established in 1672 by the Congregationalists and Presbyterians. The ministerial associations of the 1650s, in which Richard Baxter and numerous other future Nonconformists had participated, were victims of the Restoration, but some sense of community remained, and was reinforced by joint lectureships and worship services, shared prison cells, and reunions at funerals. Yet the divisions were real enough; for instance, nearly 120 ministers attended the funeral of John Burgess in 1671, 'part staying [during] the office for the dead, part going out'. Although the common fear of Catholics during the Popish Plot was potent enough to inspire discussions about Protestant unity, they were still-born.[8]

7. *Heads of Agreement Assented to by the United Ministers in and about London* (London, 1691), sig. A3v; pp. 2–3, 14–15. For the collapse of the Union, see Edmund Calamy, *Memoirs of the Life of the Late Revd. Mr. John Howe* (London, 1724), pp. 180–82; Roger Thomas, in *The Beginnings of Nonconformity* (London, 1964), pp. 37–48.

8. William Bates, *A Funeral-Sermon for . . . Richard Baxter*, 2nd ed. (London, 1692), p. 94; PRO SP 29/56/1; 29/100/107; (cf. SP 29/44/69; 29/126/13); Philip Henry, *Diaries and Letters of Philip Henry, M.A.*, ed. Matthew Henry Lee (London, 1882), p. 242; Calamy, *Memoirs*, p. 70.

Of the numerous proposals for the attainment of unity, two of the boldest were espoused by the Congregationalist minister Stephen Lobb and the layman Henry Care. Lobb accepted the need for a national church government based not on the Bible but on the civil magistrate's right to regulate religion in order to prevent disorders in the state. Subscription would be required only to the doctrinal tenets of the Thirty-nine Articles and to the Oaths of Allegiance and Supremacy. With an eye to Dissenters, Lobb proposed that each parish church be accorded the right to determine how it would administer the sacraments and impose discipline, and whether or not it would use the liturgy. Bishops would continue as officers of the crown, appointed by letters patent, and would be consecrated only in districts where a majority of the clergy favoured it. Even then, any parish church which objected to episcopacy would be exempted from the bishop's authority. Care's proposal was similar, granting each parish the right to impose its own discipline and determine its form of worship. Bishops would be appointed only with the consent of the clergy, and congregations would have the right to approve or reject prospective ministers. Apart from a test against Popery, mandatory subscriptions would be required only to tenets expressed solely in the words of Scripture.[9] These visionary schemes produced no results.

At the practical level, denominational loyalty appears to have been relatively unimportant to many, especially the laity. Captain Thomas Walcott variously regarded himself as a Baptist and a Congregationalist; perhaps he, like John Bunyan, was an open-membership, open-communion Baptist. The Rye House plotter William Hone, who 'heard sometimes *Baptists*, sometimes *Independents*, and sometimes *Presbyterians*', was probably typical of many Nonconformists who were more interested in a good sermon than the theological or ecclesiastical issues that divided Dissenting groups. Arthur Annesley, earl of Anglesey, attended Church of England services on Sunday mornings, but listened to both Anglican and Nonconformist preachers in his chapel on Sunday afternoons. Most of his chaplains were Presbyterians, but he was closely associated with Congregationalists and his wife belonged to John Owen's church. Philip Lord Wharton too was closely linked to Owen and other Congregationalists, though most clerics in his employ were Presbyterians.[10] Nor was the line

9. [Stephen Lobb], *The True Dissenter* (1685), pp. 134–41; [George Care], *Liberty of Conscience Asserted and Vindicated* (London, 1689), pp. 22–24. Cf. *The Weekly Pacquet of Advice from Rome* (1680–81), iii, p. 544.

10. PRO SP 63/332/43.1, 53.1; BL Stowe MSS 213, fol. 196r; *The History of the Whiggish-Plot* (London, 1684), p. 21; Lacey, *Dissent*, pp. 459–62, 473–74.

between Conformist and Nonconformist always clearly demarcated. James Holloway of Bristol, for instance, 'professed himself neither a *Dissenter* from the *Church of England*, nor joyn'd with them altogether'. Philip Henry was undoubtedly typical of most Nonconformists in maintaining friendships with persons who conformed.[11] Bunyan received a licence as a Congregationalist in 1672, called himself a Baptist, but really preferred to be known simply as a Christian. Baxter similarly insisted that he was 'a Meer Christian, . . . a Catholick Christian', firmly rejecting the label Presbyterian except in the general sense that it referred to anyone who was 'for a Spiritual serious way of Worship (though he were for moderate Episcopacy and Liturgy), and that lived according to his Profession' without joining a sect.[12]

Historians have tended to regard such statements as idle posturing, but ecumenical concerns ran deep throughout the period. In his last speech before his execution in 1683, William Lord Russell wished that 'all our unhappy Differences were removed, and that all sincere Protestants would so far consider the Danger of Popery, as to lay aside their Heats, and agree against the Common Enemy; and that the Church-men would be less severe, and the Dissenters less scrupulous'. Similar feelings had been expressed to members of Parliament by the gentry and freeholders of various counties and by townsfolk early in 1681.[13] The book of devotions of the London layman John Gould included a prayer against evils in the church, including doctrinal disputes and 'languishing about vayne & fruitlesse questions, endlesse dispensations and controversyes'. Divisions among Protestants, opined the Whig author Thomas Hunt, were the result of 'some old peevish and stiff Church-men' opposed to an accommodation and 'some crafty Statesmen' who thought a schism would be useful in undermining the country's ancient constitution.[14]

Prominent Dissenting clerics regularly pressed the case for unity.

    11. *History of the Whiggish-Plot*, p. 68; Henry, *Diaries*, p. 169. Cf. [John Hickes], *A True and Faithful Narrative* (1671), p. 3.
    12. Turner, ii, p. 855; *MW*, iv, p. 270; *MW*, v, p. 153; Richard Baxter, *Church-History of the Government of Bishops* (London, 1680), sigs. a4r, b1r; *Rel. Bax.*, pt. 2, § 112 (p. 278). Cf. Baxter, *The Cure of Church-Divisions* (London, 1670), sig. A2r; Baxter, *Fair-Warning* (London, 1663), p. 23; Sir Charles Wolseley, epistle to *A Faithful Narrative of the Life and Death of . . . John Machin* (London, 1671), sig. A6r.
    13. *The Last Speech & Behaviour of William Late Lord Russel* (London, 1683), p. 2; *Vox Patriae* (London, 1681), pp. 11–20.
    14. John Gould, 'Book of Devotions', DWL MSS 24.147, fol. 49; Thomas Hunt, *Postscript*, ad cal. *An Argument for the Bishops Right* (London, 1682), pp. 7–8. Cf. Hunt, *A Defence of the Charter* (London, [1682]), p. 11. Although sympathetic to the Dissenters, Hunt was not one himself.

Reflecting on Baxter's career, William Bates recalled 'how ardently he endeavour'd to cement the breaches among us, which others widen and keep open'.[15] Baxter's *Cure of Church-Divisions* was an eloquent plea for unity, love, and peace, based on the conviction that divisions among Protestants were nothing but 'a heap of sins'. The key to unity, he concluded, was being of one mind, heart, and life, and on that basis he urged individual congregations not to revile each other but to preserve a unity of faith, love, and practice.[16] Baxter, the architect of compromise, thought differences over such issues as polity, ordination, and baptism could be overcome through love, and he sought a compromise between those who insisted on a church composed only of visible saints and those who viewed it as a school for Christ to teach the way of regeneration. The only condition of membership in the church, he insisted, was belief in the triune God and devotion to him in a covenant that renounced the devil, the world, and the flesh. In short, union is part of the church's 'very *essence*, without which it can be *no Church*, and without which we can be *no members* of it'.[17] Disunity in the church, added John Howe, signaled a decay of the spirit and a growth of carnality. Too much stress, he claimed, was placed on the things that divided Christians, when in fact they agreed on 'one common, new, spiritual, divine nature and principle of life'.[18] Proponents of union focused on their common adherence to the doctrinal tenets of the Thirty-nine Articles.[19]

Even the groups on the left of the religious spectrum wrestled with the question of unity. The Particular Baptist Benjamin Keach urged less division among those who agreed on the fundamentals of divinity, but the General Baptist Thomas Grantham was careful to distinguish between a common fellowship among Christians based on love, and church communion, which required unity in doctrine and

15. Bates, *Funeral-Sermon*, p. 120. Similar comments were made about others, including Joseph Alleine and John Machin. *The Life & Death of That Excellent Minister of Christ, Mr. Joseph Alleine* (London, 1672), p. 40; *Faithful Narrative*, p. 69.

16. Baxter, *Cure*, sigs. A2v, A4v, B4v; p. 296. Cf. John Owen, *The Church of Rome No Safe Guide* (London, 1679), pp. 2–3; Robert Hearne, *Loyalties Severe Summons to the Bar of Conscience* (London, 1681), p. 45 (Hearne was an Anglican); Ashwood, *The Best Treasure* (London, 1681), pp. 211–12.

17. Baxter, *Cure*, pp. 45–47, 50–51 (cf. sig. C2r), 67–68.

18. John Howe, *The Works of the Rev. John Howe, M.A.*, 2 vols. (New York, 1838), i, pp. 526–27; cf. i, pp. 472–82; Calamy, *Memoirs*, p. 36.

19. Owen, *A Peace-Offering in an Apology and Humble Plea for Indulgence and Libertie of Conscience* (London, 1667), pp. 12–13; James Jones, *A Plea for Liberty of Conscience* (London, 1684), pp. 4–5; John Corbet, *An Account Given of the Principles & Practises of Several Nonconformists* (London, 1682), p. 7; Bates, *Funeral-Sermon*, p. 120.

practice concerning everything essential 'to the true Constitution and
Government of the Church of Christ', including believers' baptism.[20]
The latter practice not only engendered some of the fiercest debates
among Nonconformists but effectively precluded ecumenical union.
The Quakers were even more isolated by their distinctive tenets, yet
George Fox virtually echoed his nemesis Baxter in averring that
'Spiritual Men should not wrangle one with another about Religion, but
they should obey Christs Command, love one another, love enemies,
and love doth edifie'. But as Isaac Penington the younger pointed
out, any attempt to achieve unity before there was 'one heart and
one mind' contravened both the nature of religion and the Spirit of
God.[21] Union achieved through a policy of compulsion was foreign to
the entire Dissenting community, and at least on that principle they
were one.

Although the Restoration meant a defeat for those who subsequently
chose the path of Dissent, Nonconformists quickly dispelled any mood
of defeatism and demonstrated a striking vitality and resiliency. This
strength was manifested in at least six fundamental areas, including a
vibrant literary tradition brilliantly examined by Neil Keeble. Milton,
Bunyan, and Baxter were the giants of this tradition, and to this trinity
should be appended the name of Andrew Marvell, whose sympathies
were clearly with the Dissenters. The literary culture of Nonconformity,
in Keeble's judgment, 'was rather creative, positive and salutary in its
demotic realism, its subjective authenticity, its metaphorical richness
and its sensitivity to the numinous'.[22]

Nonconformist vitality is reflected too in the vigorous debates
between rival Dissenting groups and with Anglicans. No debate was
more crucial than that launched by the publication in 1669 of Samuel
Parker's *Discourse of Ecclesiastical Polity*, which asserted that Nonconformists must be silenced as irrational opponents of the absolute power
of monarchs and subverters of the state. Among the Dissenters who
entered the lists against this challenge to their right to exist were
John Owen, John Humfrey, Slingsby Bethel, and Robert Ferguson.

---

20. [Benjamin Keath], *Sion in Distress*, [2nd ed.] (London, 1681), pp. 30–31;
Thomas Grantham, *The Loyal Baptist* (London, 1684), p. 15. Cf. Grantham, *Hear
the Church* (London, 1687), p. 39. The Presbyterian John Corbet said virtually the
same thing; *Account*, p. 23.

21. [George Fox], *Something in Answer to the Old Common-Prayer-Book* (London,
1660), p. 16; Isaac Penington the younger, *Concerning Persecution* (London, 1661),
p. 19.

22. N. H. Keeble, *The Literary Culture of Nonconformity in Later Seventeenth-Century
England* (Leicester, 1987), p. 283.

Understandably, as the debate unfolded it embraced a discussion of the right to organize and take up arms in self-defence, a tenet put into practice in the explosive 1680s.[23] Other debates ranged over such issues as the ministry, sacraments, and ecclesiastical polity. The proper subjects of baptism as well as the question of whether or not it was necessary for church membership were fiercely disputed in the 1670s. Bunyan's contention that baptism was not essential was repudiated by the Particular Baptist Thomas Paul and the General Baptist John Denne, and when Bunyan defended himself he was attacked in 'A Postscript' to Henry Danvers' *Treatise of Baptism* (1673). The latter work was refuted by the Congregationalists Obadiah Wills (with Baxter's blessing) and Richard Blinman. Others entered the fray, including the Presbyterian Joseph Whiston and no less than nine other Baptists, including William Kiffin and John Tombes. A running debate throughout the period also occurred between the Quakers and the rest of the Nonconformists; Baxter at one point disputed with William Penn for seven hours.[24] In general, the debates reveal a depth of commitment and a command of sources, but the vehemency with which many of the disputations were conducted also underscores the fact that the participants, clergy and laity alike, were competing with each other for a tiny segment of the population and were in a real sense fighting for their very survival.

The vitality of Nonconformity was also manifest in its organizational ability. The Quakers were particularly adept organizers, with an intelligence network that spanned much of the country, and with yearly and (county) monthly meetings. From time to time the government seized Quaker records and thus gained some appreciation of the Friends' organization. In 1670, for instance, Yorkshire officials confiscated a register book containing the names of 500 heads and principal teachers in the county, records of the monthly and quarterly meetings, and a comprehensive index.[25] Other Nonconformists used organizational skills to establish academies to train future ministers; some of them exposed their students to the preaching of leading divines.[26] Organization was sufficient to ordain ministers, collect and administer funds to relieve the needy, facilitate the transfer of members between

23. Richard Ashcraft, *Revolutionary Politics & Locke's Two Treatises of Government* (Princeton, N.J., 1986), chap. 2.

24. Greaves, *SAR*, pp. 169–72; Geoffrey F. Nuttall, *Richard Baxter* (London, 1965), pp. 105–106.

25. PRO SP 29/277/174.1.

26. See e.g. BL Add. MSS 54,185 for notes of sermons by Nonconformist ministers preached at an academy near Sheffield.

churches, and support the publication and distribution of Nonconformist literature.

One of the most crucial organizational efforts was made at the
congregational level, where discipline was administered to maintain the
integrity and distinctiveness of the local church as a society of visible
saints. Insufficient attention to discipline had, of course, long been a
charge levelled against both the Catholic Church and the Church of
England, whose courts imposed 'purse-penalties' and persecuted the
innocent

> . . . cause they cannot sleep
> With thee in Errour. . . .

John Howe refused to conform in part because of the absence of
effective discipline in the state church, and John Corbet complained
that discipline was directed against those who refused to conform
to the liturgy and canons, not, as in the primitive church, against
propagators of heresy or transgressors of the rules of godly living.
Discipline was tantamount to spiritual enclosure: 'The Church being
the Lord's heritage and portion ought not to lye common, but must
be fenced with Christ's Spiritual Discipline, that it be not laid wast[e]
and lost'.[27]

As voluntary societies, the Nonconformist churches were limited in
the imposition of discipline to admonition and excommunication. In
the case of public offences, the guilty were openly admonished before
the congregation, a variant of the traditional custom of shaming sexual
offenders and others. Various leading Dissenters cautioned against the
over-zealous use of discipline, suggesting that some churches were too
rigid in not distinguishing between the repentant offender and the
obstinately impenitent. 'No sin', Baxter said, 'will warrant you to cast
out the sinner, unless it be seconded with Impenitency', and then 'only
impenitency after the Churches admonition.'[28]

The church books record the punishment of a wide variety of
offences, including such obvious ones as failure to attend services,
inebriety, adultery and fornication, violating the sabbath, swearing and
lying, marital disputes and spousal abuse, and even dancing. There

---

27. Grantham, *The Prisoner Against the Prelate* [1662], pp. 45, 48–49, 53; Calamy,
Memoirs, p. 32; Corbet, *The Remains of the Reverend and Learned Mr John Corbet*
(London, 1684), p. 133; Corbet, *Account*, p. 5.

28. Baxter, *Cure*, p. 86 (cf. pp. 80, 84); Grantham, *Hear the Church*, p. 14; *Heads
of Agreement*, pp. 8–9.

was obvious concern about those who defected to the Friends or, less often, to the Catholics. The General Baptist church at Fenstanton, Cambridgeshire, disciplined one of its members for attending an Anglican service.[29] One of the most serious offenses was the failure to marry 'in the Lord'. As Thomas Watson explained, the saint has an obligation 'to graft upon a Religious stock; he is not so ambitious of *Parentage* as *Piety*; nor is his care so much to espouse dowry as virtue: In a word, he seeks for a *meet* help, one that may help him up the hill to Heaven'. The seriousness with which this duty was viewed, especially by the groups on the left of the religious spectrum, is evident in the disciplinary records. At Amersham, Buckinghamshire, the General Baptists subscribed to an article 'not to have Any Communion with thos[e] that Marry out of the Lord'. In policing moral behaviour, the Dissenters insisted on respect and deference. One Fenstanton Baptist was admonished because 'he would not give an account of his actions, nor suffer himself to be so lorded over [by the church]; which was adjudged a great evil' by the congregation.[30] Although the Dissenters had no difficulty adducing Biblical support for their imposition of discipline, in practical terms discipline was also a factor in maintaining the control over members that was essential for survival. Nonconformist congregations were cells of disciplined 'saints'.

The remaining areas that illustrate the vigour of Nonconformity should be viewed as responses to persecution, a subject that requires the historian to navigate between the extremes of hagiography and the dismissal of repression as insignificant. Throughout the reign of Charles II the enforcement of laws to repress Nonconformity varied from place to place and from period to period, with the courts themselves having no consistent policy. The mid-1670s and the years after 1685 were generally free of serious repression, but even at other times persecution was inconstant and often depended on the attitude of local magistrates.[31] Sometimes they were genuinely uncertain of their

29. *Records of the Churches of Christ, Gathered at Fenstanton, Warboys, and Hexham, 1644–1720*, ed. Edward Bean Underhill (London, 1854), pp. 257–58, 278–79, 299–300; *The Church Book of Ford or Cuddington and Amersham in the County of Bucks*, ed. W. T. Whitley (London, 1912), pp. 2, 5, 9, 12, 18, 27–28, 30–33; *Minutes*, pp. 36–122.

30. Watson, *How Must We Make Religion Our Business?*, in *The Morning-Exercise at Cripple-Gate*, 4th ed. (London, 1677), p. 459; *Church Book*, ed. Whitley, pp. 23, 25–28, 30, 33, 202, 219, 224, 227; *Records*, ed. Underhill, pp. 259, 263–64.

31. Hickes, *Narrative*, p. 10; PRO SP 29/94/126; 29/125/50; 29/127/7, 47; 29/225/132; 29/416/173.1; 29/418/110; 29/436/144; *Calendar of the Clarendon State Papers Preserved in the Bodleian Library*, vol. v: 1660–1726, ed. F. J. Routledge (Oxford, 1970), p. 589.

responsibilities because of Nonconformist claims that the statutes were directed only against Catholics (especially 35 Eliz. I, c. 1) or *seditious* sectaries, or that warrants could not be served on Sundays.[32]

Periods of long incarceration, such as those imposed on Bunyan and Francis Bampfield (twelve and nine years respectively), were rare, but many were jailed for brief periods, and fines and the seizure of possessions were commonplace.[33] Occasionally overzealous magistrates and their assistants resorted to physical violence, probably in retaliation to the Dissenters' recourse to barred doors, defiant language, and refusal to obey the officials. Most of the violence was directed against the Quakers, whose disdain for various social customs and spiritual radicalism riled conservatives. Many, including women, were beaten, some with pikes and muskets. At Cirencester, Friends were thrown down a staircase, killing an elderly woman, while at Bristol Quaker women were stripped and subjected to indignities. Dissenters were also beaten and pushed down staircases at Salisbury and London, and stoned in Cambridge. In the early 1680s Nonconformist meeting-houses were not only closed down but sometimes stripped of their furnishings or even dismantled.[34] Persecution was real enough, though hardly of the intensity experienced during Mary Tudor's reign.

Recourse to imprisonment as a means of controlling Nonconformists was a bankrupt policy for a variety of reasons. Some of the more humane gaolers allowed their charges brief periods of liberty, which could be used to hold conventicles, and the laity often gathered outside gaol windows to hear imprisoned clerics preach. Prison space was woefully inadequate to contain more than a small number of Dissenters, hence preachers were the obvious target of magistrates. Because they had no formal clergy, the Quakers therefore posed a special problem. Bristol officials responded with mass arrests, until in one gaol Friends were 'pil'd up as men do Faggots'. At one point in early 1682, some eighty-five Quakers shared a Bristol gaol with forty

32. *Observator Observ'd*, no. 1 (6 May 1681), p. 2; *The Impartial Protestant Mercury*, no. 59 (11–15 Nov. 1681); *The Case of Protestant Dissenters* (London, 1682); [Edward Whitaker], *The Ignoramus Justices* (London, 1681), pp. 11–18.

33. Cf. e.g. *A True and Impartial Narrative of Some Illegal and Arbitrary Proceedings . . . in and near the Town of Bedford* (1670); Nottingham University Library, MSS PwV 95, fol. 293.

34. *A Short Relation of Some Part of the Sad Sufferings* (1670), pp. 7–9, 30, 32, 39–41; *Impartial Protestant Mercury*, no. 70 (20–23 Dec. 1681); no. 71 (23–27 Dec. 1681); no. 76 (10–13 Jan. 1682); no. 82 (31 Jan.–3 Feb. 1682); no. 106 (25–28 April 1682); *The True Protestant Mercury*, no. 101 (21–24 Dec. 1681); no. 180 (23–27 Sept. 1682); no. 182 (30 Sept.–4 Oct. 1682); *CSPD, Add. 1660–85*, pp. 402–403.

other inmates in conditions so cramped that prisoners could not lie down to sleep at the same time.[35] Such treatment only gave its victims a powerful propaganda tool with which to berate the established order. 'You . . . have not counted it enough to take away all outward supplies', thundered the Quaker William Pooley, 'but after you have stripped of all, to cast into Prison; you . . . have not Compassionated the Condition of the Fatherless, nor Widdows, nor yet spared to Spoil the Goods of the Motherless Child! O Merciless Cruelty'![36] While virtually all Nonconformists devoted some attention to the ethic of suffering, none surpassed the Friends in depicting themselves as godly sufferers for the cause of Christ.

Although the threat of incarceration undoubtedly daunted the timid, imprisonment hardened the convictions of others and provided them with an opportunity to reinforce their convictions and plan future moves in gaolhouse seminars. Prior to his release in 1672, Bunyan and his colleagues used their time in a Bedford gaol to map out an organizational structure for their region that could withstand future periods of persecution. The Congregationalist John Maidwell shared the Leicester gaol with some forty other Dissenting ministers and lay people, and every day they preached, prayed, and sang. 'Did our enemies know', he candidly wrote, 'what kindness they have shewn us in sending us hither, they would soon release us'. Consciously inspired by the example of the Marian martyrs, the Nonconformists espoused an ethic that made suffering a Christian duty as well as a means to acquire spiritual benefits. 'He that will live godly in Christ Jesus', advised Sarah Cheevers, 'must suffer Persecution; it is an evident token' of one's faith. The sentiment was shared by many clergy and laity, such as those at Warboys, Huntingdonshire, who continued to meet despite the crackdown on conventicles in 1683 because 'we are content to suffer for Christ, knowing it is the lot of the righteous not only to believe, but also to suffer for His sake'.[37] The history of

35. PRO SP 29/92/110; 29/436/144; *Impartial Protestant Mercury*, no. 89 (24–28 Feb. 1682); no. 96 (21–24 March 1682); no. 98 (28–31 March 1682).

36. William Pooley, *Part of the Sufferings of Leicestershire & North-hamptonshire* (London, 1683), p. 9. See F[rancis] H[owgill], *A Testimony Concerning the Life . . . of Edward Burroughs* (London, 1662), p. 14, who compares the Church of England to the Catholic Church because of its policy of persecution. Cf. John Chandler, *A True Relation of the Unjust Proceedings* (1662), p. 13; Samuel Bold, *A Sermon Against Persecution* (London, 1682), p. 36. Bold was an Anglican who favoured toleration.

37. DWL MSS 12.63.(22); John Griffith, *Some Prison-Meditations and Experiences* (1663), pp. 4–5; Sarah Cheevers, in [Daniel Baker], *This is a Short Relation of Some of the Cruel Sufferings* (London, 1662), p. 87; *Records*, ed. Underhill, p. 280. For Bunyan's organizational activities, see chap. 4, infra.

Restoration Nonconformity has tended to read like hagiography in large measure because the Dissenters commonly viewed themselves in this light. The ethic of suffering is, in fact, one of the most pervasive themes in Nonconformist literature.

The ability to withstand the repressive campaign of the state is further corroboration of Nonconformity's vitality. The responses were creative, flexible, and resolute. The notorious field conventicles in Scotland attended by thousands of worshippers, some of them armed, were rarely imitated in England, except along the northern border and in the southwest. The Quakers met on the beaches in Cornwall and sometimes in city streets when their meeting-houses were closed, but generally most English Dissenters held their conventicles in homes, barns, or other buildings, virtually defying the magistrates to stop them. Despite a proclamation prohibiting conventicles, Bristol Friends met three times a week in a house across the street from the mayor's home.[38] When officials were determined to prosecute, Dissenters sometimes met at night; in London some gathered at 4 a.m. Others posted sentries to enable them to disperse before a magistrate could arrive, especially since most Dissenters preferred to escape rather than face prisons or fines. Only a small minority courted even a mild form of martyrdom. At Taunton, Somersetshire, one of the hotbeds of Dissent, the Presbyterians brazenly posted sixteen sentries in each street leading to their meeting-house in 1682. The building used by Nathaniel Vincent's Presbyterian congregation in London was constructed to facilitate escape: 'almost every seat that adjoins to the Sides of the Conventicle has a door like the Sally Port of a Fire ship to make escape by. And in each door, a smal Peep-hole like to Taverns & Alehouses door, to Ken the person before they let them in'.[39]

Magistrates who reached a conventicle before it dispersed sometimes found the doors barred and the congregants defiant, either refusing to leave or willing to use force to help their minister escape. According to Sir John Trevor, at three huge Presbyterian meetings in London in 1670 the doors were defended by 3,000 to 4,000 people. Vincent got away in December 1681, but his followers stayed behind to resist the authorities; 'the more the Justices talk[ed] to them, and required them to dispers themselv's the louder they sang'.[40] When magistrates

38. PRO SP 29/92/110; 29/98/152; 29/115/44; 29/277/29, 95, 204, 204.1; 29/278/158; 29/387/41; 44/62, p. 125.

39. John Cosin, *The Correspondence of John Cosin, D.D., Lord Bishop of Durham* (Surtees Society, vol. 55, 1872), ii, p. 243; PRO SP 29/56/48, 77; 29/418/43, 89; 29/419/19; 29/421/127; 29/441/1.

40. PRO Sp 29/179/95; 29/275/174; 29/417/156; 29/421/127; *CSPD 1680–81*, p. 640; *True Protestant Mercury*, no. 100 (17–21 Dec. 1681).

padlocked meeting-houses, the Dissenters broke in and continued their services. Lay conventiclers as well as their ministers contended that the Conventicle Act was contrary to divine law, to which they owed their ultimate obedience. In 1676 a Huntingdonshire layman went so far as to tear up a copy of the Conventicle Act, adding that 'I am not to obey a wicked Kings Lawes upon Earth . . . but I am to obey the King of heaven'. A London Baptist was no less defiant in the face of the same statute, insisting that he would be hanged at his own door before he would alter his religious convictions. Friends at Pakefield, Suffolk, embraced the tactics of passive resistance, forcing a constable and his assistants to pile them in a cart like logs and dump them unceremoniously before a justice's door. Quakers also protested against religious holidays by keeping their shops open, while Baptists in Devon closed theirs after magistrates dispersed their conventicles.[41]

Resistance to conventicle legislation sometimes turned violent, an aspect of Nonconformist history virtually ignored in traditional accounts. In 1664, Presbyterians from Whitchurch and Beaminster, Dorset, 'Riotously & Rebelliously' left a conventicle 'Armed with Pikes, staves & other weapons, [and] did Assault, [and] wound . . . Officers & Soldiers', shedding 'much blood' and breaking a soldier's arm. When George Alsop, on the instructions of the bishop of London, tried to read the liturgy in the Quakers' meeting-house in Gracechurch Street, London, in 1670, the Friends manoeuvered him away from his guard of soldiers, pulled him by the neck, and bruised his chest and a knee. The same year a Quaker assaulted a constable at Whitby, Yorkshire, when the latter arrested another Friend as he preached, and Westmorland Quakers blatantly threatened those who disrupted their meetings. In Bristol the attorney Nathaniel Wade not only encouraged the Nonconformists to arm themselves but twice resisted justices attempting to break up conventicles. Two or three hundred Londoners attacked a party of soldiers in February 1683 after they had arrested a conventicle preacher.[42]

Violence took other forms as well. The people of Guernsey were so angry at the use of the sign of the cross in baptism that the dean could travel between parishes only in the company of soldiers. On several occasions opponents of the restored church ripped up the Book of Common Prayer, and in Winchester an incarcerated Dissenter stabbed

41. PRO SP 29/140/9; 29/216/133; 29/275/134.1, 134.2; 29/277/112; 29/278/163; 29/287/171; 29/292/27; 29/294/224; 29/378/165, 166; 29/386/218; 29/417/144; 29/421/175; 29/424/16.
42. PRO SP 29/93/8; 29/276/82; 29/277/14; 29/281/97; 29/414/54; 29/422/79.

a jailer who had whipped his wife for her Nonconformity. At Newbury, Berkshire, Nonconformists threatened to prevent parishioners from taking communion in the established church, invaded the vestry to demand the election of churchwardens by all the parishioners, and tried to rescue their leader when he was arrested.[43]

Some of the violence was directed against informers. In East Anglia they were stoned at Yarmouth, 'violently asaulted, beaten & troden upon' at Norwich, and pummelled and dragged 'through a foul hogsty & from thence through a pond of water' at Wrentham; one of the latter informers died as a result of his injuries. Dissenters in Wiltshire and Somerset drew weapons to threaten informers and used staves to keep them away from their preacher, while informers were physically assaulted in London. On other occasions Nonconformists harassed informers and magistrates with specious lawsuits as retaliation.[44] Many Dissenters were anything but passive sufferers under Stuart repression.

Perhaps the most dramatic manifestation of Nonconformist zeal was the militancy of some Dissenters. From the Fifth Monarchist uprising in London under Thomas Venner in January 1661 until the Revolution of 1688-89 there was a steady stream of militant activity ranging from conspiracies to attempted assassinations and open rebellion. In all this, Dissenters played a crucial role. The 1662 Tong conspiracy to seize the Tower of London, Windsor Castle, and Whitehall Palace reportedly had the support of several Nonconformist ministers, and aimed not only to restore the Commonwealth but to establish freedom of conscience for Protestants and abolish episcopacy and the Book of Common Prayer. The alleged architect of the abortive 1663 Dublin plot to preserve Protestant and English interests in Ireland was the Presbyterian Thomas Blood, whose close associates included the Presbyterian ministers Robert Chambers, William Lecky, and Andrew McCormack. Among those who planned or participated in the ill-fated northern rebellion of 1663 were the Congregationalist minister Edward Richardson, who drafted a declaration that called for a reform of ecclesiastical polity to conform with Scripture and the practice of the best Reformed churches, and his fellow cleric Jeremiah Marsden, also a Congregationalist. Other Congregationalist ministers recruited support among the exiles in the Netherlands, but the rising was something of

43. *Calendar of the Clarendon State Papers*, v, p. 253; PRO SP 29/96/110, 110.1, 114, 114.1, 129; 29/146/68; *CSPD 1665–66*, p. 300; *Gazette*, no. 518 (31 Oct.–3 Nov. 1670); *Intelligencer*, no. 31 (18 April 1664), pp. 251–52.

44. PRO SP 29/277/204, 204.1; 29/287/63; 29/335/302; 29/362/67; 29/363/53, 71; 29/383/74; 29/386/16; 29/436/55, 111, 144; *CSPD 1682*, p. 272; *True Protestant Mercury*, no. 158 (8–12 July 1682).

an ecumenical affair with the participation as well of Presbyterians, Baptists, and even Quakers.[45] Colonel John Rathbone, after whom a 1665 plot to seize the Tower and execute the king was named, was a Fifth Monarchist. The Particular Baptist Henry Danvers, thought to be an associate of Rathbone's, was linked to numerous conspiracies against the government. The core of the small gang of radicals who tried to kidnap and assassinate the duke of Ormond in 1670 was Nonconformist and included Blood and the Fifth Monarchists Richard Halliwell and William Smith. Dissenters also played a major role in the Rye House plotting and the Argyll and Monmouth invasions.[46] The evidence for Nonconformist militancy is irrefutable, though it does not implicate the majority of Dissenters.

A final example of Nonconformist vitality is the existence throughout the period of a thriving underground press, most of whose themes were religious in nature. Although the state enjoyed limited success in curtailing the Nonconformist pulpit, the publications of the underground press kept up a barrage of criticism against religious persecution, corrupt prelates, the alleged dregs of Popery in the state church, and an idolatrous liturgy. Despite the sustained efforts of Roger L'Estrange, who was appointed surveyor of the press in February 1662, illegal publishing thrived. Early in 1664 a conservative author estimated that more than 300 treasonous and schismatic works had appeared since Charles' return, and in April of that year the number was revised to 460. Press runs were in the hundreds and sometimes the thousands, and copies were smuggled throughout the kingdom. Other works were printed in the Netherlands and smuggled into England and Scotland. In addition to its attacks on a persecuting government and a corrupt ecclesiastical establishment, the press played a major role in fanning anti-Catholic hysteria. Rumours of a Popish plot were propagated as early as 1662, intensified after the Fire of London in 1666, and reached a climax in the late 1670s, providing Whigs and Nonconformists with ammunition in the exclusion controversy. Beginning in the late 1670s, the underground printers, virtually all of whom were Dissenters, published political works by the earl of Shaftesbury and his colleagues that were highly critical of the Stuart regime. These printers also issued the revolutionary manifestoes produced by the militants. Thus the underground press, which was so

45. Greaves, *DUFE*, pp. 112–29, 140–50, 176–201.

46. *BDBR*, s.v. John Rathbone; Greaves, *SAR*, pp. 164–68, 172–75; Greaves, *EUHF*, chap. 6; Greaves, *SOK*, chaps. 3–7; Ashcraft, *Revolutionary Politics*, chaps. 8–10; Peter Earle, *Monmouth's Rebels: The Road to Sedgemoor 1685* (New York, 1977), pp. 5–17.

closely tied to the Nonconformists, not only helped maintain the fidelity of Dissenters to their convictions but kept them abreast of current developments, instructed them in political and religious principles, and painted a stridently critical picture of the Stuart regime and the state church.[47]

It remains to assess the source of Nonconformist vitality, the key to which was the bedrock spiritual experience that provided the fundamental continuity of Nonconformity. At the core of this experience was a firm conviction of spiritual regeneration, a thorough transformation wrought by the Holy Spirit, the end result of which was 'a *Moral Reformation* of Life'. Regeneration, explained John Owen, entails 'the infusion of a *new real Spiritual* Principle into the Soul and its Faculties, of Spiritual Life, Light, Holiness, and Righteousness, disposed unto, and suited for the Destruction or Expulsion of a contrary inbred habitual Principle of sin and enmity against God, enabling unto all Acts of Holy Obedience'.[48] Regeneration made possible the attainment of union with God, a goal shared by all Nonconformists, but explained especially by Friends virtually in a mystical sense. 'What I *am*', said John Perrot, 'I *am* not of *my self*, and my standing in what *I am* brought unto is neither *of my self*, but of the *Almighty power of* God, and I never desire to be *any thing* but in *his Spirit* the *Eternal Sust[en]ance* which was *Life*.'[49]

Having once established the principle that regeneration is properly the work of the Spirit, the Dissenters then wrestled with the question of what they could do to be ready for this transforming experience. Like their New England counterparts, they were confronted on the one hand with the implications of the Calvinist doctrine of election and on the other with the evangelical impulse to encourage people to *do* something to prepare for the Spirit's regenerative work. For the Quakers the most crucial act was the acceptance of a truly passive state, or what William Smith called 'a true waiting for the appearance of Christ in you'. Waiting, in fact, became a distinctive part of the Friends' total religious experience, whether it entailed waiting for the Spirit's leading in a meeting or waiting in a more private sense for

47. Greaves, *DUFE*, chap. 7; Greaves, *EUHF*, chap. 5.

48. Owen, *A Discourse Concerning the Holy Spirit* (London, 1674), p. 182. Cf. John Audland, *The Suffering Condition of the Servants of the Lord* (London, 1662), p. 16.

49. John Perrot, *The Mistery of Baptism and the Lord's Supper* (London, 1662), p. 4. Cf. Watson, DWL MSS 24.13, fol. 5v; John Maidwell, DWL MSS 12.63.(20)

'Gods searching hand . . . [to] try thy wound, and fetch out that which hath oppressed thee, and powr in fresh Oyl to heal thee'.[50]

Mainline Restoration Nonconformists developed the notion of preparation for regeneration to the point of making it a duty and urging others to endeavour to be godly. In his lecture *What Must, and Can, Persons Do Towards Their Own Conversion*, William Greenhill denied any necessary connection between preparatory activities and the infusion of grace, but he was also adamant that all human efforts undertaken before conversion were not fruitless or purposeless. These endevours included subjecting oneself to a powerful minister, heeding chastisement, forsaking sin, hoping for mercy, and observing the effects of regeneration in the lives of others. Theologically, divine sovereignty in the soteriological process was maintained by crediting these efforts to 'preventing' (i.e. enabling) or 'exciting' grace. 'A mans continued making use of that Moral Power, which he hath towards Conversion, from one degree of Preparatory Grace to another', explained John Corbet, 'will at length terminate in Grace immediately sufficient [for salvation] if he live.'[51] Owen laid out an eightfold path to salvation: conviction of sin, accompanied by a deep sense of eternal danger; 'disquieting and perplexing *Affections*' and an unsuccessful search for salvation; prayers for deliverance, abstinence from sin, and moral reformation; fear of God; conviction of sin and recognition that deliverance is only possible as spelled out in the Gospel; acceptance of the obligation to seek the revelation and righteousness of Christ; and finally 'the ingenerating and acting of Faith in God by Jesus Christ', that is, the moment of spiritual rebirth. Mainline Nonconformists were thus able to satisfy their theological scruples about salvation stemming solely from divine agency and yet provide their audience with a regular diet of exhortation to prepare for the climactic infusion of regenerating grace.[52]

The notion of preparation made it possible to map out schema such as that offered by Owen, the practical effect of which might

50. William Smith, *Sweet Oyle Poured Forth Through the Horn of Salvation* (London, 1661), pp. 6, 8. For a non-Quaker view of waiting, see [Thomas Goodwin], *Patience and Its Perfect Work* (London, 1666), pp. 87–89.

51. William Greenhill, *What Must, and Can, Persons Do Towards Their Own Conversion*, in *Morning-Exercise at Cripple-Gate*, pp. 31, 33–39; Corbet, *A Humble Endeavour of Some Plain and Brief Explication* (London, 1683), p. 49.

52. Owen, *Holy Spirit*, pp. 305–309; Richard Frankland, BL Add. MSS 54,185, fol. 3v; Matthew Meade, *The Good of Early Obedience* (London, 1683), pp. 57–62; R[ichard] A[lleine], *Godly-Gear* (London, 1674), pp. 201–208; Zachary Crofton, *The Hard Way to Heaven* (London, 1662), p. 5; Janeway, *Heaven*, p. 370; Ashwood, *Best Treasure*, p. 395.

seem to provide a standardized pattern for the conversion process. The growing numbers of spiritual autobiographies reinforced this idea by presenting concrete illustrations, or at least what purported to be historical accounts of spiritual crisis and resolution. But such tendencies toward the development of a uniform pattern of religious experience were explicitly countered by assertions that God worked in different ways with different people. God, Owen declared, 'is pleased to exercise a *Prerogative* and *Sovereignty* in this whole Matter, and deals with the Souls of Men in unspeakable variety. Some he leads by the Gates of Death and Hell unto Rest in his Love', while others are guided down 'plain and easie' paths; for some the process is lengthy, for others not. The historian, therefore, must not overgeneralize Puritan and Nonconformist piety; as readers of *The Pilgrim's Progress* know, the experience of Christiana is strikingly different from that of Christian. Unfortunately this variety tends to be obscured by the fact that most metaphors used by Dissenters to depict the Christian life are dramatic: many are of pilgrimages and warfare.[53] Zachary Crofton imaginatively depicted the way to heaven as 'a red Sea passage, in which there is no possibility of motion unto safety and life, but by going forward; for enemies are behind, and walls of water doe on each side enclose us'. Nicholas Lockyer similarly used the image of a narrow way, on one side of which were devils and on the other a rebuking, frowning God. How different was Nathaniel Vincent's depiction of the world as an inn where the godly lodge, or Richard Alleine's blunt admission that the commencement of the Christian life could be very tedious.[54]

Nonconformists who recorded their spiritual experience in any detail were more likely to have undergone (or to have imagined themselves to have undergone) a stormy rather than a calm passage. A comparison of the spiritual diaries of Owen Stockton, Elias Pledger, and one of Matthew Henry's relatives reveals something of the range of religious experiences, though none of these reflects the calmest path. The closest to this is the experience of Stockton, whose diary often notes how comforting meditations were; he did not undergo the emotional extremes of doubt and ecstasy reflected in some diaries. Typical of his more troublesome moments was the time 'I saw the plaug of my

53. Owen, *Holy Spirit*, p. 306; Owen Stockton, DWL MSS 24.7, fol. 7r; William Brend, *A Loving Salutation to All Friends Every Where* (London, 1662), p. 6; Nathaniel Vincent, *Israels Lamentation* (London, 1677), p. 10; Keach, *War with the Devil* (London, 1673); Bunyan, *HW*.

54. Crofton, *Hard Way*, p. 18; Nicholas Lockyer, *A Memorial of God's Judgments, Spiritual and Temporal* (London, 1671), pp. 168–69; Vincent, *A Funeral Sermon* (London, 1679), p. 11; R. Alleine, *Godly-Fear*, p. 386.

heart breaking out; I argued against my corruption yet it overcame me & lead me captive; it wounded me that I should still sin against God even whilst under his correcting hand'. On a day of humiliation he found himself indisposed by a sense of guilt to perform his religious duties, but all it took to improve his mood was a discussion with his wife that evening and some reflection on Isaiah 64:6-8.[55] By way of contrast, Pledger's diary records a rollercoaster of spiritual emotions, though never to extremes. With monotonous regularity Pledger noted whether or not he had been faithful to his duties or whether he had returned to his 'old lukewarmnes again'. The religious zeal tended to diminish with age: 'I was wont at my first conversion to have God & heaven much in my thoughts even in my worldly busines, but now I find a great decay & worldly & proud thoughts take up your room; this makes me frequently suspect my Sincerity'. At times he was troubled by temptations 'to Indecent action', but these he seems to have resisted; more problematical were the 'distrustful worldly thoughts' that crowded his mind. In general, he was hypersensitive and possibly conscientious to an unhealthy degree.[56]

The diary of a member of the Henry family suggests a tortured soul and a dizzy seesawing of spiritual emotions. In the space of a few days in 1686, the diarist had 'some Extraordinary Sense of Sin', but the impression lasted only briefly and then returned at night. The author prevailed, confirming an intense hatred of sin, yet 'I dread to think what it will at last bring me if Reigning in me'. Again, unbelief prevailed; hence on the ensuing sabbath there were 'many fears concerning my State, how it is with me. I know not'. Before long, the author took a spiritual inventory and discovered that the 'special' sins were pride, security, sensuality, impenitency, and despising others. This paved the way for 'a willingness to be the Lords wholly', and occasionally to a feeling of loving God.[57] What this tortured soul underwent is not to be confused with that type of experience in which the road to regeneration was tumultuous, but the subsequent Christian life apparently calm. This appears to have been the case with Bunyan and George Trosse. 'God was pleas'd', the latter recalled, 'by the Terrours of my Conscience, by my dreadful Convictions, by the Streamings, as it were, of the *Lake of Fire and Brimstone* thro' my Soul, to drive me from Sin and Hell.'[58]

55. Stockton, DWL MSS 24.7, fols. 1r, 10r, 47r, 63r, 72r.

56. Elias Pledger, DWL MSS 28.4, fols. 6r, 12r, 14r, 29v, 42r.

57. BL Add. MSS 42,849, fols. 78r–80v.

58. George Trosse, *The Life of the Reverend Mr. George Trosse*, ed. A. W. Brink (Montreal, 1974), pp. 112–13. Cf. Meade, *The Good*, p. 56.

Dissenting clerics recognized that their followers were likely to struggle with temptation and guilt; indeed some conflict was a sign of Christian vitality, and believers were repeatedly urged to beware of evil creeping into their lives. The problem was to do this without pushing sensitive disciples into neuroses. Thus Samuel Slater the elder instructed his congregation not to exist habitually 'in a fluctuating state; . . . come to some well grounded confidence; that you may be able to say, We know that this and that is our condition, and this and that is our dignified priviledge'.[59] But Owen told his followers that in the conflict with sin there could be no peace, only the assurance that if they relied on God they would prevail in their faith. Others held out more hope, at least with respect to the possibility of acquiring a sense of tranquility about being securely among the children of God. Ann Henry Hulton was able to tell her mother that 'I have experienced much of the goodness of God in being better to mee then my fears, and shaming my distrustful apprehensions'. The key to such comfort depended on one's ability to grasp the idea that salvation was a wholly unmerited gift, a promise, and only to a much lesser degree that the pursuit of a holy life was evidence of election.[60]

To the extent that Nonconformists experienced a good deal of spiritual turmoil in their lives, the culprit was the intense emphasis placed on the duty of self-examination. The importance of this responsibility was underscored not only by the frequency with which it was repeated in Nonconformist literature but by the fervency with which it was exhorted. To Thomas Watson self-examination was nothing less than a spiritual inquisition in which the believer placed herself or himself on trial in the court of conscience. 'It is the duty of a Christian', insisted Vavasor Powell, 'to *suspect* and *search* himself', and that responsibility, added William Dyer, was more important than any obligation to know the state of the nation. 'Observe your hearts *inclinations*', Baxter advised; 'if [you detect] any inordinate inclination after any thing, set a special guard; mark which way your *thoughts*

59. Ashwood, *Best Treasure*, p. 122; Owen, *Holy Spirit*, p. 352; Lockyer, *Memorial*, p. 206; Owen, *The Nature, Deceit, and Prevalency of the Remainders of Indwelling-Sin in Believers* (London, 1675), p. 19; Stockton, *Consolation in Life and Death* (London, 1681), p. 101; Penington, *Persecution*, p. 12; Slater, in *London-Ministers Legacy*, p. 53. Cf. Edmund Calamy, *Old Mr. Edmund Calamy's Former and Latter Sayings* (London, 1674).

60. Owen, *Nature*, pp. 38, 55; BL Add. MSS 42,849, fol. 18r; Samuel Petto, *The Difference Between the Old and New Covenant* (London, 1674), pp. 295–98, 325; Thomas Doolittle, *If We Must Aim at Assurance*, in *Morning-Exercise at Cripple-Gate*, pp. 241–43, 259–64; Stockton, *Consolation*, pp. 100–101; Meade, *The Good*, pp. 60–62; Hurst, *Servant*, p. 15; Bates, *Funeral-Sermon*, pp. 57–58.

go, that you may know your *inclinations* by your *thoughts*'.[61] The Quakers shared this concern with self-interrogation; Katherine Evans, for example, exhorted her husband and children to watch diligently over their thoughts, words, and actions, and Margaret Fell urged all Friends to search themselves.[62] The Dissenter was thus expected to be the inquisitor and policeman of his or her thoughts on a daily basis. To aid in this duty, broadsheets replete with appropriate questions were prepared so that they could be affixed to a wall for ease of use. Christopher Jelinger's had twelve queries, Joseph Alleine's a staggering twenty-nine. Typical of the latter were these questions: 'Wherein have I denied my self this day for God? Have I been diligent in the Duties of my Calling? Am I a Mourner for the sins of the Land?' Alleine offered another five questions for morning interrogation, one of which included instructions to ask any of the twenty-nine inquiries omitted the previous evening. If literally implemented, such examinations must have produced inordinately introspective personalities and probably neurotic behaviour.[63]

How much autoinquisition Dissenters engaged in is difficult to ascertain. Claims that Joseph Alleine 'delight[ed] in Self-examination', and that John Machin 'was a great Observer of the frame and bent of his heart *at all times*' were undoubtedly hyperbole of the sort commonly expressed in funeral paeans. The Monmouth rebel William Hewling had clearly been engaging in self-examination when he told his sister Hannah that he found himself 'very hard, and dead, and proud, and too apt to relish the things of this world', but in the face of execution introspection was normal. The diary of Eleanor Stockton, Owen's wife, not only provides an example of one Dissenter who took this duty seriously, but underscores the way in which introspection could

61. Watson, *Heaven Taken*, pp. 55–63; Powell, *Bird*, p. 54; William Dyer, *Christs Famous Titles* (Cambridge, 1672), pp. 54, 114–15; Baxter, in *London-Ministers Legacy*, p. 180. See also Timothy Cruso, DWL MSS 12.63.(8); BL Add. MSS 54,185, fols. 34r, 51v; R. Alleine, *Godly-Fear*, pp. 292–93, 296–97; Watson, *Divine Cordial*, p. 91; Watson, in *London-Ministers Legacy*, p. 29; Pledger, *Of the Cause of Inward Trouble*, in *Morning-Exercise at Cripple-Gate*, pp. 300, 318; Stockton, *Consolation*, pp. 84, 109; Owen, *An Humble Testimony unto the Goodness and Severity of God* (London, 1681), pp. 135–40; Owen, *Holy Spirit*, p. 351; Owen, *Nature*, pp. 135, 139; Owen, *The Grace and Duty of Being Spiritually-Minded* (London, 1681), p. 29.

62. Evans, in Baker, *Short Relation*, p. 53; Margaret Fell, *An Evident Demonstration to Gods Elect* (London, 1660), p. 11.

63. Watson, DWL MSS 24.13, fol. 5v; Joseph Alleine, *Christian Letters* (1672), pp. 44–46; Christopher Jelinger, *The Resolution-Table* (London, 1676); J. Alleine, *Mr. Joseph Alleines Directions, for Covenanting with God* (London, 1674); *Life and Death of J. Alleine*, pp. 58–61.

unsettle the mind. One morning as she 'was takeing som account of my selfe', she began to worry if God would be merciful 'to shuch a vile wretched unholy creature that have so dishonoured him as I have don'. One New Year's morning she launched upon 'the worke of selfe examination' to ascertain 'what my present state and condition was, namely wheither I was still in the state of nature or in a lapst and backsliding condition'. When the answer was not readily apparent, she became very dejected, though in both cases the crises were resolved by meditating on Scriptural passages.[64]

Some ministers encouraged their people to keep a diary to record their spiritual inquisitions. Watson, in fact, suggested the keeping of two books, one to record sins, the other to note divine mercies. In the beginning Owen Stockton was uncertain as to whether his diary would be conducive to the glory of God, but he soon decided it was. The diaries and other personal books took varied forms. Whereas Bunyan's *Grace Abounding to the Chief of Sinners* concentrated almost entirely on his experience of regeneration, John Machin's diary was a record of his self-examination over the years.[65] In addition to keeping an account of her spiritual progress, Eleanor Stockton copied Biblical passages for special needs, such as 'helps against frowardnes', aids to recover from 'back slideing', and 'som evidenses of saveing faith', to which she added quotations from favourite religious works, including Joseph Caryl's commentary on Job. In effect, she combined a spiritual diary with a commonplace book. Lady Ann Waller kept a large folio volume in which she recorded the sermons she heard as well as her own observations on the Bible and other religious works; although obviously serious about her religion, she seems not to have been caught up in the deeply introspective task of daily examination. Even less personal is John Mould's book of devotions, a collection of Bible verses, prayers, and confessions of faith and sin.[66] Clearly we must think in terms of varieties of Nonconformist religious experience.

Having once recognized such varied experience, certain shared characteristics and ideals can be denoted. One of the most distinctive features of Nonconformist piety was its zeal and intensity, or what Baxter called the 'heat of internal affection'. Saints, the preachers

---

64. *Life and Death of J. Alleine*, p. 120; *Faithful Narrative*, pp. 63–64; Hewling, quoted in *Remarkable Passages in the Life of William Kiffin*, ed. William Orme (London, 1823), p. 145; DWL MSS 24.8, fols. 12r, 13r.

65. Powell, *Bird*, p. 120; Watson, *Religion*, p. 149; DWL MSS 24.7, fol. 1r; *Faithful Narrative*, p. 65.

66. DWL MSS 24.8, fols. 6r, 8r–11r, 17r, 22r; Calamy, *The Happinesse of Those Who Sleep in Jesus* (London, 1662), p. 28; DWL MSS 24.147.

demanded, must obey every command of God, driving relentlessly toward perfection. 'Go on towards *perfection*', exhorted Bartholomew Ashwood, 'press after *nearer* and more *compleat* Conformity to the *Nature* and *Will* of *Christ* every day.'[67] Assessing his own performance against this standard, Elias Pledger incredibly wrote, 'I did not allow my self I thank god in any known sin, from November [1683?] to August 87'. A member of the Henry family was no less resolute: 'I have renewed my Covenant more solemnly than ordinary to leave evry Sin or else I shall be never the better for him & I will hold to my Bargain in his Strength'.[68]

In the quest for godliness, Nonconformists denounced moderation as a sign of indifference. 'When the iron is red hot', observed Watson, 'it enters best; and when our services are red hot with zeal, they soonest pierce heaven.' The road to heaven demanded a highly active, diligent effort — a resoluteness Watson described as violence because of the vigour of affection and strength of endeavour that was demanded. There could be no neglect of spiritual duties, no sloth, no formalism, a danger to which Dissenting clergy were particularly sensitive.[69] 'The Formalist he is all for outward action, and for nothing of inward sincerity', warned Dyer; the bane of every serious Nonconformist was the hypocrite. The latter had none of the zealous commitment of the truly godly, none of the dedication so crucial for the survival of Dissent, but thrived on self-interest and a 'Notional knowledge' or religion that could only bring disrepute on Nonconformists struggling to maintain their rationale for the church as an institution of visible saints.[70]

To convey their zeal and intensity the Nonconformists repeatedly had recourse to sensual imagery. Believers have a taste for God that

67. Baxter, in *London-Ministers Legacy*, p. 191; Ashwood, *Heavenly Trade*, sig. a4r; R. Alleine, *Godly-Fear*, p. 313; R[ichard] A[lleine], *Vindiciae Pietatis* (London, 1663), p. 338; Watson, *Picture*, p. 238; Robert Seddon, BL Add. MSS 54,185, fol. 64v; Calamy, *The Art of Divine Meditation* (London, 1680), p. 43.

68. Pledger, DWL MSS 28.4, fol. 9v; BL Add. MSS 42,849, fol. 79v.

69. Watson, *Picture*, pp. 159–60, 164; Meade, *The Vision of the Wheels* (London, 1689), p. 48; Baxter, *Cure*, p. 123; Watson, *Heaven Taken*, pp. 8–9, 14; Crofton, *Hard Way*, p. 5; Owen, *Holy Spirit*, pp. 167, 350; Meade, *The Good*, p. 194; Thomas Manton, *How May We Cure Distractions in Holy Duties?*, in *Morning-Exercise at Cripple-Gate*, p. 392; Howe, in Calamy, *Memoirs*, p. 125; Owen, *Grace and Duty*, pp. 148–49; Baxter, in *London-Ministers Legacy*, p. 182; Bunyan, *PP*, pp. 39–41.

70. Dyer, *Titles*, p. 183; Keach, *A Golden Mine Opened* (London, 1694), pp. 8, 60, 488; Keach, *Sion in Distress*, pp. 9–21; Dyer, *A Cabinet of Jewels* (London, 1676 ed.), pp. 55, 100; Dyer, *Christs Voice to London* (London, 1666), pp. 73–74; Dyer, *Mount Sion* (London, 1689), sigs. A5r, A6r; Baxter, *The Vain Religion of the Formal Hypocrite* (London, 1660); Ashwood, *Heavenly Trade*, sig. A4r; Meade, *The Good*, p. 229; Watson, *Picture*, pp. 138–39, 239, 244–45; Powell, *Bird*, p. 67.

arises from spiritual hunger; they taste, eat, and digest the Word and thereby receive spiritual nourishment. 'A *meditating Christian*', mused Calamy, '*is one that chews the cud*, that chews on the Truths of Jesus Christ.'[71] The godly listen to the voice of the Spirit, see with the eye of faith, and feel the internal working of the Spirit. Howe exhorted the saints to 'feel the fire burn within, and find it refining us, consuming our dross, melting and mollifying us, new moulding us'.[72] In openly sensual terms, Matthew Henry wrote to his mother about enjoying God and tasting covenant love. Perhaps the best summation of Dissenting piety in sensual imagery was provided by Thomas Bromley:

> For by the *Exercise of the Internal Senses*, we see Spiritual Objects, as the Internal Light-World, Visions of Angels, and Visions of Representation. In this state we likewise hear the Songs, Voices, and Harmony of Angels . . . : We smell the Perfumes of Christ's Garments, and are oft entertained with Paradisical Odours. We touch and feel the powerful tincture of Christ's Body which many times strongly affects the Heart with powerful delight: We also oft taste the Heavenly Manna, and those Dews of Paradise which are sweeter than Honey.[73]

The positive outlook of these sensual passages provided a healthy corrective to the stress on personal evil and autoinquisition.[74]

Nonconformist zeal was expected to have a practical manifestation in a discernibly holy life, a reflection of the theological doctrine of sanctification. All Christians, of course, were expected to live a holy life, but what distinguished the Dissenters was the emphasis accorded to this ideal. Sanctification, defined as the Spirit's purification of the soul from corruption and its enabling of the Christian to fulfil the obligations of the new covenant, was supposed to result in holy living. As Sir Charles Wolseley remarked, 'practical Sanctity is the great End

---

71. Calamy, *Art*, pp. 24, 29; Keach, *Golden Mine*, pp. 130–31, 134–36, 338, 340–42; Owen, *Grace and Duty*, p. 6; Owen, *Eshcol, a Cluster of the Fruit of Canaan* (London, 1684), p. 91; Ashwood, *Heavenly Trade*, p. 141; Kiffin, *Passages*, p. 89; Keach, *A Summons to the Grave* (London, 1676), sigs. a4r, b2r.

72. Howe, *Works*, i, p. 582; Keach, *Golden Mine*, pp. 80–84, 86; Henry Scudder, *The Christian's Daily Walk*, 11th ed. (London, 1674), p. 445; R. Alleine, *A Companion for Prayer* (London, 1680), p. 9; Dyer, *Titles*, sig. A3r; Ashwood, *Heavenly Trade*, p. 131; Calamy, *Art*, p. 25; [Nathaniel Vincent, et al.], *The Morning-Exercise Against Popery* (London, 1675), p. 642.

73. BL Add. MSS 42,849, fol. 19r; Thomas Bromley, *The Way to the Sabbath of Rest*, 2nd ed. (London, 1692), pp. 14–15. Cf. Calamy, *Art*, p. 15.

74. Cruso, DWL MSS 12.63.(5); Mould, DWL MSS 24.147, fol. 27; Trosse, *Life*, p. 130; BL Add. MSS 54,185, fol. 62v; Howe, in Calamy, *Memoirs*, p. 63.

of Religion while we live here'.[75] This entailed, in the first place, a dedication to things of the Spirit, or what Owen called 'the Constant Contemplation of things Spiritual and heavenly'. This was supposed to entail a keen sense of self-denial, of the 'Mortification' of a desire for earthly pleasures.[76] Sanctification also involved a commitment to obey both 'tables' of the Ten Commandments, including the second table duties to other people. As Owen pointedly observed, 'he, all whose Religion lyes in Prayer and Hearing, hath none at all'. Nonconformist piety was not so narrowly evangelical that it focused on matters of the heart to the exclusion of social responsibility.[77]

The ideal of the sanctified life, as espoused by Dissenters, could place an almost intolerable psychological burden on those who took their religion seriously. Simply to eschew the pleasures of drink or sex, to attend church regularly, and to aid the needy was not enough. There was a fundamental responsibility to see that neither time nor thought was wasted, even in idle discourse or the discussion of religious affairs designed not to glorify God but to revel in one's religiosity.[78] What to most people were harmless pastimes caused spiritual distress among the more sensitive Dissenters. Pledger was sorely tempted to walk in the fields, but was grateful when he overcame the urge. He was not always so strong, for he expressed remorse for indulging himself 'in unnecessary ease and sleep' in the mornings. After hearing both morning and afternoon sermons on an August Sunday in 1672, the earl of Anglesey spent the rest of the day engaged in spiritual 'dutyes', though 'with some diversion', for which he felt compelled to ask God's pardon. A member of the Henry family confessed to being 'unprofitable, formal, [and] very Proud, to punish which God has left me to commit a great tongue Sin, a rash untrue word. Conscience quickly Smote'. Philip Henry likewise succumbed to being 'unskilful in redeeming time'. The Dissenting conscience was expected to operate in a supercharged state, sensitive to every nuance of spiritual

75. Wolseley, epistle to *Faithful Narrative*, sig. A3r; Owen, *Holy Spirit*, pp. 153, 338, 347, 351, 376, 503–504, 512, 516–17, 573; Baxter, *Cure*, p. 333; Ashwood, *Best Treasure*, p. 74.

76. Owen, *Nature*, p. 169; Owen, *Grace and Duty*, sigs. A3v–A4r; pp. 45, 54, 91, 121; Crofton, *Hard Way*, p. 15; Calamy, *Art*, p. 50; Howe, *Works*, i, pp. 570, 572; Richard Frankland, BL Add. MSS 54,185, fol. 2r; William Penn, *No Cross, No Crown* (1669), p. 35. Cf. Henry, *Diaries*, p. 169.

77. Owen, *Grace and Duty*, p. 43; Owen, *Nature*, p. 7; *Life and Death of J. Alleine*, pp. 111–13; Swinnock, *Calling*, i, p. 7.

78. BL Add. MSS 54,185, fol. 93r; Henry, *Diaries*, p. 239; Keach, *Sion in Distress*, p. 28; Watson, *Religion*, p. 85; Owen, *Grace and Duty*, p. 59; Dyer, *Titles*, p. 194; Thomas Case, in *London-Ministers Legacy*, p. 125.

responsibility, to every wasted opportunity, to the cause of godliness in one's soul and in society.[79]

No picture of Restoration Nonconformity would be complete without recognition of the domineering emphasis of the Holy Spirit on belief and action. Virtually every aspect of the Christian life was linked to the work of the Spirit; perhaps the best example is Owen's mammoth tome on the Spirit, which is virtually a summa of Nonconformist theology.[80] In 1677–78 Howe preached no less than thirty-four sermons on the Spirit at Cordwainers' Hall in London. Lay interest in this topic seems to have been inexhaustible judging from the attention given to it in contemporary publications and sermons. Yet the doctrine of the Holy Spirit was tantamount to the proverbial loose cannon on the deck of a ship, for it could be used to justify virtually any practice or tenet. It was, of course, the primary justification for the Friends' repudiation of traditional sacraments and a professional, ordained clergy. Quakers appealed to the Baptists, their near cousins on the radical end of the religious spectrum, to leave 'the Shaddows, and Watry Element, and . . . come to Christ the Substance' by following the Inner Light. Baptists and Quakers argued furiously over the meaning of that Light, as each group sought not only to distinguish itself from the other but to demonstrate its rival's fundamental unsoundness. The Friends, in fact, indicted all other religions as lies because they purportedly had not been instituted by the Spirit.[81]

While Nonconformists of all persuasions placed substantial emphasis on the Spirit, those of a moderate bent, keenly aware of mid-century enthusiasm, sought to limit claims that could be made on the Spirit's behalf. Most Nonconformists felt the Quakers had gone too far in their use of the Spirit to repudiate alleged forms of godliness. The Friends, claimed John Swinton, 'being in Union with the Spirit of Truth, *it leads them into all Truth*', but to other Nonconformists the danger in this position was the opening it provided for endless fresh revelations — for subjectivity unbounded by objective authority.[82] The General Baptist

79. Pledger, DWL MSS 28.4, fol. 41r; BL Add. MSS 40,860, fol. 34r; Add. MSS 42,849, fol. 81r; Henry, *Diaries*, p. 185; Pledger, *Of the Cause*, p. 300; Watson, *Heaven Taken*, p. 99.

80. Owen, *Holy Spirit*. Cf. Howe, *Works*, i, pp. 507–508.

81. Howe, *Works*, i, pp. 503–607; Perrot, *Mistery*, p. 8; Richard Crane, *The Hue and Cry After Bloodshed* (1662); Fox, *The Protestant Christian-Quaker or Sufferer* (London, 1680), p. 19.

82. John Swinton, *A Testimony for the Lord* [1662?], p. 2. Cf. William Smith, *A Message from the Spirit of Truth into All the World* (London, 1663), pp. 6, 11; Swinton, *Testimony*, p. 4; Fox, *A Paper Sent Forth into the World* (London, 1654), p. 7; Baxter, *Cure*, pp. 165–67.

Thomas Grantham contended that the Spirit could introduce no new ordinances nor annul any imposed by Christ. In effect, this restricted the Spirit's operations within Biblical parameters, a solution acceptable to Presbyterians, Congregationalists, and Baptists. 'The Spirit works according to rule, or agreeable unto the word, in what it does for the maintaining of this [spiritual] life', explained Howe. The Word and the Spirit were partners, with the latter's responsibility being the revelation of the hidden things of the Gospel and the work of regeneration and sanctification. 'For although the Letter of the Scripture, and the sense of all the Propositions are equally exposed to the Reason of mankind; yet', asserted Owen, 'the real spiritual Knowledg of the Things themselves, is not communicated unto any but by the especial Operations of the Holy Spirit.' This solution enabled most Dissenters to use Scripture to fence the Spirit's activities and yet to insist that a mere recitation of the Bible without the illumining work of the Spirit rendered the reading spiritually ineffectual.[83]

Using the Bible to define the parameters of the Spirit's work left the Dissenter with practical questions concerning the relationship of the Spirit to reason, and the nature of the Biblical record itself. Both the enthusiastic excesses of the 1650s and the Quaker challenge rendered it imperative to address the long-standing epistemological issue. The Friends unabashedly asserted that 'the lowest Persuasion of *Faith*', which is derived from 'the Evidence and Demonstration of the Spirit', is superior to 'the highest Perswasion of *Reason*'. This, I suspect, is what most Dissenters would like to have argued had it not been for the necessity to protect their flank from the more radical sectaries. Dyer, for instance, in an unguarded moment commented that the person who would 'clearly see with the *eye* of *Faith*, must shut the *eye* of *Reason*'.[84] But the normal approach was to make reason subservient to faith while averring that things revealed through faith, such as the Trinity or the Incarnation, were not contrary to but 'above' reason. Enlightened reason — reason illumined by the Holy Spirit, suggested Owen — could prevent the excesses of enthusiasm and serve as 'the only Judg of the Sense and Truth of Propositions drawn from the Scripture or proposed therein'. Even this was not sufficient for Nonconformists such as Wolseley and Ferguson, who reflected the century's growing

83. Grantham, *St. Paul's Catechism* (London, 1687), p. 14; Howe, *Works*, i, p. 533; Congregationalist confession of faith, DWL MSS 24.13, fol. 15r; Ashwood, *Best Treasure*, pp. 305, 312; Owen, *Holy Spirit*, sigs. A2r–v, C1v–C2r; Watson, *Picture*, p. 90; Thomas Walcott, *A True Copy of a Paper* (London, 1683), p. 1.

84. Penington, in John Crook, *Truth's Principles* (London, 1662), p. 21; Penington, *Persecution*, p. 29; Dyer, *Titles*, sig. A3r.

preoccupation with rationalism by contending that religion must be established on rational grounds. Revelation in this view presupposed the prior use of intellectual faculties; before there can be an act of faith, reason must be convinced that the claim to belief is itself divine. 'There is', explained Ferguson, 'no Conviction begot by the Holy Ghost in the Hearts of men, otherwise than by rational Evidence satisfying our Understandings.'[85] Those who espoused this view were much closer to the Latitudinarians of the established church than to the Friends and other enthusiasts.

Protestantism in general and the Puritan-Nonconformist tradition in particular were strongly orientated toward the Bible as the source of belief and practice. The commitment to the preeminence of the Word, both spoken and written, brought the Dissenters several important advantages, not least among them the ease with which they could conduct services outside traditional churches. The emphasis on the Word made their faith simpler to understand than Catholicism, with its prominent element of mystery. But to make the Bible the authoritative source of religion did not solve the problem of how it should be interpreted, especially its relationship to reason and experience.

In practice, most Nonconformists treated Scripture as if it were infallible, though without formally addressing this issue. For the most part they were content to think of the Bible as the perfect rule of faith and obedience, the authorship of which was divine, at least to the extent that the Spirit suggested the words and aided the authors in expressing their thoughts.[86] As the writers' 'Minds were under that full assurance of Divine Inspiration', Owen declared, 'so their *words which they wrote* were under the especial care of the same Spirit, and were of his Suggestion or Indicting'.[87] Wolseley explicitly asserted that the Scriptures were not only divine but inerrant, each part being written 'by the infallible direction of the Holy Ghost'. In contrast, several Dissenters enunciated a view closer to that expressed in our

85. Seddon, BL Add. MSS 54,185, fols. 5v–6r; Watson, *The Duty of Self-Denial* (London, 1675), pp. 5, 9–46; Corbet, *Remains*, p. 255; Owen, *Holy Spirit*, sigs. C1v–C2r; p. 186; *Rel. Bax.*, pt. 2, § 285 (p. 387); Robert Ferguson, *The Interest of Reason in Religion* (London, 1675), pp. 20–21; Wolseley, *The Reasonablenes of Scripture-Belief* (London, 1672), sigs. A4v–A5v; pp. 86, 184–85.

86. BL Add. MSS 54,185, fols. 14r, 32v; Corbet, *Account*, p. 3; Bates, *Funeral-Sermon*, p. 106; Vincent, et al., *Morning-Exercise Against Popery*, pp. 149, 160; Walcott, *True Copy*, p. 1.

87. Owen, *Holy Spirit*, pp. 113–14; Owen, *Church of Rome*, p. 8; Owen, *The Principles of the Doctrine of Christ* (London, 1684), p. 8; Watson, *Heaven Taken*, pp. 23–27; Corbet, *Remains*, pp. 93–94; Calamy, *Art*, p. 140; Vincent, et al., *Morning-Exercise Against Popery*, pp. 160, 314–15, 318.

own century by such neo-orthodox theologians as Karl Barth and Emil Brunner. Ferguson, for instance, distinguished between the letters of the Bible and God's speaking in it, though he also contended that the words themselves were inspired. Grantham too posited that the Word of God was 'delivered' in the Bible, but also acknowledged that over time minor alterations probably had crept into the text. These, however, did not trouble him, because he was convinced that even with the changes the Bible continued to contain its holy message.[88]

While Nonconformists believed that a 'saving' knowledge of Scripture was only possible through the enlightening work of the Spirit, all but the Quakers were unwilling to use experience as the key to Scriptural interpretation. On the contrary, despite the difficulties inherent in understanding some parts of the Bible, the prevailing tendency was to insist that it be interpreted rationally. 'An interpretation of Scripture repugnant to the common reason of mankind, and to sense rightly circumstantiated, is impossible to be true', Corbet thought. The sense of the Bible, especially with respect to the fundamentals of the Christian faith, was said to be plainly evident for anyone to read and understand.[89] Because of that plainness and the general agreement that the Bible was to be understood rationally, the duty of Bible reading could be stressed. This obviously implied a degree of literacy on the part of Nonconformists, at least among heads of households. Owen Stockton, in fact, went so far as to make illiteracy a sin, and reinforced this notion with the observation that 'the want of ability to read, is usually accompanied with very gross ignorance of God, and the mysteries of salvation'. Nonconformity thus helped to spearhead the expansion of literacy, and Neil Keeble is undoubtedly correct in concluding that the percentage of literate Dissenters was greater than that of the population as a whole (about 50 percent compared to approximately 33 percent).[90]

Fired by their belief in the primacy of the Word, Nonconformists eloquently campaigned to obtain liberty of conscience for Protestants, the achievement of which in 1689 was their greatest historical contribution. Their key tenet in this campaign was the principle that

---

88. Wolseley, *Reasonablenes*, pp. 405, 422; Ferguson, *Interest*, pp. 118–19, 129, 131–32; Grantham, *Hear the Church*, pp. 34, 42–43.

89. Scudder, *Daily Walk*, p. 170; G. Care, *Liberty*, pp. 8–9; Wolseley, *Reasonablenes*, p. 426; Thomas Jolly, BL Add. MSS 54,185, fol. 25r; Owen, *Holy Spirit*, p. 11; Corbet, *Account*, p. 19; Corbet, *Remains*, p. 95, Vincent, et al., *Morning-Exercise Against Popery*, p. 318; Ferguson, *Interest*, pp. 138, 144–45.

90. Stockton, *A Treatise of Family Instruction* (London, 1672), pp. 207–209; Swinnock, *Calling*, iii, p. 503; Keeble, *Literary Culture*, pp. 136–39.

each person must be free to obey the dictates of her or his conscience, the sovereignty over which was vested in God alone. 'Without all Exceptions', proclaimed the Quaker Edward Burrough, 'every man . . . [should] be permitted in the free exercise of Conscience, without any kind of Force put upon him . . . , to follow that Religion, and to live in such Faith, and perform such Worship to God, as he does trust his own Soul withal, and give account thereof before God in the day of dreadful Judgement'.[91] Concomitant with this argument for individual responsibility was a ringing declaration that consciences cannot be compelled by force. Compulsion, they insisted, creates hypocrites by forcing people to act against their consciences. It is impossible, argued the earl of Anglesey, 'for *Men* to impose any necessity upon things which God hath left *free*, as mens *Consciences* are, which ought to be *as free* in a State as their *Thoughts*'. Consciences must be persuaded, not coerced, a point the Quaker William Caton reinforced with an impressive range of citations from historical personages as diverse as Luther and Calvin, the Emperors Constantine and Maximilian, Chrysostom and Augustine, Erasmus and William Tyndale, and Caspar von Schwenckfeld and Poland's King Stephen.[92]

Historical arguments buttressed the case for toleration, beginning with the conviction that compulsion was contrary to the nature of the Gospel itself. Isaac Penington the younger summed this up nicely: 'The Gospel makes meek, tender, gentle, peaceable, fills with love and sweetness of spirit, teacheth to love, to forgive, to pray for and bless enemies: and how shall this man persecute?'[93] Apologists for freedom of conscience also pointed to the early centuries of church history, arguing that the apostolic church rejected persecution and concerned

91. Edward Burrough, Epistle to the Reader, in William Caton, *The Testimony of a Cloud of Witnesses* (1662), sig. B1v; Burrough, *The Case of Free Liberty of Conscience* (London, 1661), pp. 5, 8; Crook, *The Cry of the Innocent for Justice* ([London], 1662), pp. 21, 34; George Bishop, *To the King and His Both Houses of Parliament* (1663); Meade, *Vision*, pp. 98–99; Calamy, *Memoirs*, p. 111; Owen, *Indulgence and Toleration Considered* (London, 1667), p. 14; Owen, *Peace-Offering*, p. 41; Wolseley, *Liberty of Conscience* (London, 1668), p. 42.

92. Arthur Annesley, earl of Anglesey, *The King's Right of Indulgence in Spiritual Matters* (London, 1688), p. 11; Wolseley, *Liberty*, pp. 10, 28–30, 36, 39–40; Grantham, *Prisoner*, p. 72; G. Care, *Liberty*, pp. 13, 15; Owen, *Indulgence*, p. 22; Burrough, *Case*, p. 9; Burrough, Epistle to Caton, *Testimony*, sigs. A3v–A4v; Audland, *Suffering Condition*, pp. 5–9; Jones, *Plea*, pp. 5–6. For a sympathetic Anglican view see Bold, *Sermon*, p. 30.

93. Penington, *Persecution*, p. 21; Owen, *Peace-Offering*, p. 23; Wolseley, *Liberty*, p. 30. Cf. Bold, *Sermon*, sig. A2r.

itself only with maintaining unity in the fundamentals of the faith, not external rites of worship. They also noted that historically the policy of persecution had always failed, and that the principal use of such a policy had been, in Owen's words, 'to drive Truth, and the purity of the Gospel, out of the World, and to force all men to centre in a Profession and Worship, framed to the Interest of some few men, who made no small advantage of it'. Instead of persuading people to alter their beliefs, persecution reinforced their convictions. The Quakers in particular defiantly proclaimed their intention to meet regardless of the consequences.[94]

Although most of the arguments put forth in defence of religious liberty logically mandated the inclusion of Catholics, Nonconformist enmity against them was so intense that most Dissenters claimed liberty only for Protestants.[95] As George Care summarized the case against toleration for Catholics, they were gross idolaters who represented a foreign power, they would deny liberty to Protestants if they exercised authority, and they exceeded the pagans in their cruelty.[96] Nonconformists cited the threat of Catholicism as another reason why Protestants should not persecute each other. 'We are', Owen lamented, 'some of the first who ever any where in the World, from the Foundation of it, thought of ruining and destroying Persons of the SAME RELIGION with our selves, meerly upon the choice of some *Peculiar Ways of Worship* in that Religion.'[97]

Appeals for toleration were also made on practical grounds. The Quakers pointedly noted that persecutors would favour toleration if rulers of a different religion came to power. 'I am *not for knocking*

---

94. Owen, *Peace-Offering*, pp. 26, 31; Owen, *Indulgence*, pp. 11, 22; G. Care, *Liberty*, pp. 15, 17–18; Wolseley, *Liberty*, pp. 40, 45; Fox, *Protestant Christian-Quaker*, pp. 7, 9, 11; Fox, *Something in Answer*, p. 15; Burrough, *Case*, p. 11; Burrough, *A Testimony Concerning the Book of Common-Prayer*, ad cal. Fox, *Something in Answer*, p. 38; Jones, *Plea*, p. 6; Crook, *Apology*, pp. 2–5.

95. For the anti-Catholicism of Dissenters and their supporters see e.g. Owen, *Church of Rome*; William Dell, *The Increase of Popery in England* (London, 1681); Ferguson, *The Third Part of No Protestant Plot* (London, 1682); Baxter, *Fair-Warning*; [Elkanah Settle], *The Character of a Popish Successour* (London, 1681); Keach, *Sion in Distress*; 'Popish Courant', appended to each issue of the *Weekly Pacquet*; [Henry Care], *The Character of a Turbulent . . . Romish Priest* (London, 1678); Andrew Marvell, *An Account of the Growth of Popery* (Amsterdam, [1677]); [Charles Blount], *An Appeal from the Country to the City* (London, 1679).

96. G. Care, *Liberty*, p. 23. Cf. [Owen?], *An Account of the Grounds and Reasons* [1680], p. 2.

97. Jones, *Plea*, pp. 4–6; Owen, *Indulgence*, pp. 12, 23; Annesley, *King's Right*, p. 63; G. Care, *Liberty*, sig. A2r.

men down and taking their Purses, because their eyes are not so good as mine', the radical Edmund Hickeringill reflected, 'for fear that the next man I meet (who may happen to *out-see me* as well as *out-stare me*) should . . . serve me with the same sawce.'[98] More common was the argument that toleration for Protestants was conducive to the maintenance of civil order, and that Dissenters had earned freedom by their peaceful deportment, a claim the government could rightly dispute.[99] Persecution, it was also asserted, was impractical because of its negative impact on trade. In Owen's words, 'an *attempt* for the pretended Conformity . . . is scarce due Compensation for his *Majesties* loss in the diminishing of his *Subjects* and their Wealth'. Anglesey painted a dismal picture of industrious artisans fleeing the country to avoid religious repression; the resulting decline in trade would adversely affect both the aristocracy by reducing rents and the king by declining revenue, thereby weakening England's ability to withstand foreign invaders.[100] To these pragmatic arguments, Dissenters added frank warnings that persecutors' actions rendered them subject to divine wrath.[101]

The Nonconformists' campaign for toleration merged with the broader movement for the assertion of political liberty and opposition to tyrannical government. The basic right of magistrates to suppress evil and encourage good was not contested, but questions were raised concerning the state's authority to involve itself in strictly theological matters, specifically any attempt to define and enforce orthodoxy and punish heresy. The province of the state included the regulation of behaviour and, for most Nonconformists, support for Protestantism, so long as matters of conscience were left to the individual.[102] By arguing these principles, the Dissenters, though only a tiny minority

98. Edmund Hickeringill, *The Test or, Tryal of the Goodness & Value of Spiritual-Courts* (London, 1683), pt. 2, p. 17; Penington, *Persecution*, p. 21; Burrough, *Case*, p. 9. Cf. Baxter, *Cure*, sig. B4r. For Hickeringill's radical views, see *BDBR*, s.v.

99. Annesley, *King's Right*, pp. 4–7, 9; Owen, *Indulgence*, p. 21; [Edward Whitaker], *The Second Part of the Ignoramus Justices* (London, 1682), pp. 4–5, 9; Burrough, *Case*, pp. 8, 12. Cf. Hunt, *Postscript*, p. 100.

100. Owen, *Indulgence*, p. 23; Annesley, *King's Right*, pp. 7–8; G. Care, *Liberty*, p. 16; *True and Impartial Narrative*, p. 3; Owen, *Indulgence*, pp. 8, 23; *Short Relation of Sad Sufferings*, p. 74; Jones, *Plea*, p. 4; Caton, *Testimony*, pp. 50–51; Burrough, *Case*, pp. 7, 11–12.

101. Annesley, *King's Right*, p. 62; Henry, *Diaries*, p. 193; Audland, *Suffering Condition*, p. 12; Caton, *Testimony*, p. 51.

102. G. Care, *Liberty*, pp. 3–4, 9–10; Bates, *Funeral-Sermon*, p. 109; Whitaker, *Second Part*, p. 22; Owen, *Indulgence*, p.17; Wolseley, *Liberty*, pp. 24–27; Burrough, *Case*, pp. 3, 6; John Moon, in [William Smith], *A Real Demonstration of the True Order* (London, 1663), p. 5.

of the nation, contributed not only to the shape of the 1689 Settlement but to the broader heritage of a political tradition that embraced liberty of conscience. This achievement was made possible by their ability to withstand the repressive campaigns of the Stuart state, an ability rooted in a religious experience characterized by intense piety, the primacy of the Word, a keen awareness of the indwelling Spirit, and a strong sense of responsibility.

2

The State of Historical Scholarship

Much of the crescendo of interest in John Bunyan in the decade 1978–88 involved literary rather than historical concerns, although in the latter area growing attention has been paid to what Samuel Taylor Coleridge once called 'the Bunyan of the conventicle', particularly his relationship to the radical tradition in England. No scholar has done more to affirm the importance of that tradition than Christopher Hill, and it was therefore fitting that his brilliantly provocative 'social biography' of Bunyan appeared in the year commemorating the tercentenary of Bunyan's death. All modern Bunyan scholars also salute Roger Sharrock, whose inspiration and tireless labours were responsible for Oxford University Press' critical edition of Bunyan's works, the indispensable foundation for all recent and future studies, both literary and historical.

In assessing the state of Bunyan scholarship, I would like to focus on four themes: *Grace Abounding* as an historical source; the enigma of the Ranters; Bunyan's attitude toward the social order; and his place in the radical tradition, with special attention to his views on resistance and the millennium.

Because of the relative paucity of biographical data for Bunyan, scholars have a natural tendency to treat *Grace Abounding* as a reliable source of information about his life and psyche. Whereas the book indisputably contains valuable historical facts, it is not a document that can bear the psychological and biographical interpretations often built on it. *Grace Abounding* is an example of a literary genre with specifically pastoral intentions, and thus, as Hill argues, 'we are not therefore necessarily bound to accept everything in Grace Abounding as autobiographical truth'.[1]

1. Hill, *JB*, p. 65.

Writing more than a decade after the events he purportedly describes, Bunyan can hardly have recalled with complete accuracy the
precisely detailed episodes that fill the pages of his book. Indeed, he
was obviously unable to remember the timing and apparently even
the sequence of some events. Such phrases as 'upon a time', 'at
another time', 'one day', 'upon a day', 'about this time', 'once I was
walking', 'once I was much troubled', and 'as I remember' indicate
imprecise times and sequences.[2] Moreover, most of the events in
the book occurred over a span of roughly six years (c. 1650–1656),
so that the reader's impression of almost unremitting spiritual crisis
is misleading; Bunyan must have experienced substantial periods of
relative calm when religious concerns were not at the forefront of his
attention.

Given the fact that Bunyan had not received formal ministerial
training, *Grace Abounding* served as de facto credentials to demonstrate
his qualifications to preach. The length and intensity of the spiritual
struggle had a tripartite purpose: to establish him as one of the truly
great sinners who, like Paul, was converted to preach the Gospel;
secondly, to persuade others who might doubt or struggle that they
too could persevere; and finally, to reassure himself that the cause
for which he was imprisoned was indeed just. Throughout the book,
Bunyan projects the confidence of a man assured of God's support.
As Peter Carlton has demonstrated, Bunyan used disclaiming locutions
to give his writing an air of divine authority. He does not think of
Biblical verses; they fall or dart in on him, as God bombards him
with ammunition to withstand the onslaught of the Tempter, who in
fact is a projection of Bunyan's personal doubts.[3] *Grace Abounding* thus
prefigures the internal struggle allegorically developed in *The Pilgrim's
Progress* and *The Holy War*. The passages in *Grace Abounding* that depict
a microcosm of the struggle being waged between the cosmic forces
of good and evil manifest an inventive quality. Robert Bell has aptly
remarked that as Bunyan 'recast and revised Grace Abounding six
times between 1666 and 1688, he . . . [shaped] his life-story to
conform roughly to that of his savior. And he specifically recalls, or
invents, other small details to underscore this implicit parallel'.[4] Thus
extreme caution must be used when employing this work to reconstruct
Bunyan's life and religious experience.

2. *GA*, §§ 20, 37, 44, 71, 77, 94, 115–16, 122, 161, 174, 180, 203, 212, 255,
260–61.

3. Peter J. Carlton, 'Bunyan: Language, Convention, Authority', *Journal of English
Literary History* 51 (April 1984): 17–32.

4. Robert Bell, 'Metamorphoses of Spiritual Autobiography', *Journal of English
Literary History* 44 (Spring 1977): 109.

Unlike a spiritual diary, which records events such as temptations and mystical experiences as they happen, *Grace Abounding* is less likely to be historically accurate because of the circumstances under which Bunyan wrote it and the substantial amount of time that elapsed between its composition and the highly detailed events it purportedly describes. This realization should be a salutary caution not to use *Grace Abounding* as evidence that Bunyan apparently 'suffered from . . . [a] deep neurosis or psychopathic trauma',[5] or, like some Puritans, 'took on the appearance of a modern-day manic-depressive'[6] — views expressed by T. Wilson Hayes and Lynn Sadler respectively. Anne Hawkins has argued that Bunyan's conversion was of the dyadic *lysis* type — a gradual process, unlike the crisis experience of Paul, and dyadic because it followed a pattern of conversion, relapse, and reconversion.[7] Theologically, the doctrines of election and perseverence to which Bunyan subscribed, as a strict Calvinist, rendered the notion of reconversion impossible. The fact that similar experiences are recounted in other seventeenth-century works does not support the theory of double conversion, as Hawkins argues, but reflects the fact that most Calvinists seem to have gone through a period of serious doubting in which they were unsure of their election — a process which in theological terms underscored the fact that sanctification, unlike justification, was a life-long process that was never completed in this life. Bunyan's adherence to 'a stock pattern of conversion' — a point made by both Bell and Hawkins — should serve as a warning that Bunyan composed his account with an eye to what his readers might expect, not necessarily to a balanced account of what had actually transpired.

Evidence of Bunyan's tendency to exaggerate is mounting in another area: his recurring claims, to quote but one passage, that 'my Bible and Concordance are my only Library in my writings'.[8] Not so, says Gordon Campbell: 'Bunyan was a piscatory poacher' who 'fished in other men's waters'. Campbell and B.R. White have rightly stressed the importance of John Gifford's Bedford congregation in shaping Bunyan's beliefs, most obviously his open-membership views, but also, as Campbell

5. T. Wilson Hayes, *Winstanley the Digger* (Cambridge, Mass., 1979), p. 34.

6. Lynn Veach Sadler, *John Bunyan* (Boston, 1979), p. 39. Cf. Sharrock, *JB*, p. 57.

7. Anne Hawkins, 'The Double-Conversion in Bunyan's *Grace Abounding*', *Philosophical Quarterly* 61 (Summer 1982): 259–76. Cf. the criticism by Vincent Newey, ' "With the eyes of my understanding": Bunyan, Experience, and Acts of Interpretation', in Keeble, *JB*, p. 202.

8. *MW*, vii, p. 9.

demonstrates, such tenets as the Trinity and double predestination.[9] Dayton Haskin has explored Martin Luther's influence on Bunyan in depth, and Campbell has shown Bunyan's familiarity with William Perkins' *A Golden Chaine: or the Description of Theology* (1616).[10] Perkins may also have been one of the sources of Bunyan's views on covenant theology, which were highly developed by 1659; another was certainly John Dod and Robert Cleaver's *A Plain and Familiar Exposition of the Ten Commandements* (1603).[11] Other evidence indicates that Bunyan read Thomas Grantham's *St. Paul's Catechism*.[12] We know that he refuted works by Edward Burrough, Edward Fowler, William Penn, Thomas Paul, William Kiffin, Henry Danvers, and Edmund Campion. Ted L. Underwood has, in fact, identified the source of Campion's views quoted by Bunyan.[13] Moreover, *The Advocateship of Jesus Christ* includes a story from the life of Bruno of Cologne (d. 1101), founder of the Carthusians. The *Vita di S. Bruno* by Giacomo Desiderio was published in 1657, but Bunyan could not read Italian. The story had also been incorporated in the Roman Breviary, but the papacy had deleted it in the early seventeenth century. Bunyan claimed he could not remember where he had read the account, but it was obviously not in the Bible and probably came from another Protestant work.[14] W.R. Owens has pointed out that Bunyan's exposition of the slaying and resurrection of the two witnesses in Revelation 11 — namely that the account refers to the future persecution of Protestants — broadly conforms to the views of Joseph Mede (1586–1638). As Owens notes, direct evidence that Bunyan read Mede is lacking, but Bunyan's claim that he had not seen the works of others on this subject rings false, a

9. Gordon Campbell, 'Fishing in Other Men's Waters: Bunyan and the Theologians', in Keeble, *JB*, pp. 137–51 (p. 140 quoted); B. R. White, 'The Fellowship of Believers: Bunyan and Puritanism', in Keeble, *JB*, pp. 7–9.

10. Dayton Haskin, 'Bunyan, Luther, and the Struggle with Belatedness in *Grace Abounding*', *University of Toronto Quarterly* 50 (Spring 1981): 300–13; Campbell, 'The Source of Bunyan's *Mapp of Salvation*', *Journal of the Warburg and Courtauld Institutes* 44 (1981): 240–41.

11. *MW*, ii, pp. xix–xx.

12. Richard L. Greaves, 'A John Bunyan Signature', *The Baptist Quarterly* 25 (1974): 379.

13. *MW*, iv, p. 397. Bunyan probably learned of Campion's views from *A True Report of the Disputation or Rather Private Conference Had in the Tower of London, with Ed. Campion Jesuite* (1583); Campion disputed with William Charke, former fellow of Peterhouse, Cambridge, and John Walker, prebendary of St. Paul's.

14. *MW*, xi, p. xxxvi.

conclusion endorsed by J. Sears McGee.[15] Bunyan was less than candid when he claimed to have relied solely on the Bible.

In one of the best known passages in *Grace Abounding*, Bunyan recounts his acquaintance with Ranter books and the conversion of a friend to Ranter ways.[16] No student of Bunyan has attributed more significance to his Ranter associations than Christopher Hill, who suggests that Bunyan found the Ranters attractive less because of their libertinism than because of their political views, especially Lawrence Clarkson's hostility to the rule of the gentry and Abiezer Coppe's condemnation of the wealthy. Despite meeting many Ranters on his travels, Bunyan eventually came to hate them because they, like the Quakers, says Hill, had so nearly convinced him they were right. Bunyan criticized the Ranters in *The Holy City* (1665) and *The Resurrection of the Dead* (1665?), and, Hill contends, in some of his major works. '*Mr. Badman* has many Ranter qualities; Carnal Security and Atheism in *The Holy War* appear to be Ranters. So perhaps are the Doubters.' In the second part of *The Pilgrim's Progress* Bunyan attacks the Ranter view that matter is eternal; and Hopeful, says Hill, 'seems to have had Ranter tendencies'.[17]

Given the importance Hill attaches to Ranters in Bunyan's England, it is worth noting that Colin Davis has contended that Ranters are a myth invented and perpetrated in the seventeenth century by persons as disparate as Royalists, Presbyterians, Baptists, and Quakers to condemn those who espoused unacceptable tenets and reputedly engaged in licentious conduct. The sectaries, according to Davis, used the myth to establish boundaries within which the Holy Spirit could work and to justify the imposition of discipline to control behaviour and belief. The re-emergence of the Ranters in recent historiography, according to Davis, is the work of Marxist historians determined 'to create the history of a popular democratic tradition in English history and culture', a tradition hostile to capitalist culture and the Protestant ethic.[18]

The core of Davis' argument is his attempt to demonstrate that there is no evidence of a Ranter organization, no proof of close links between alleged Ranter leaders, and no shared Ranter ideology — not even the reputed key tenets of pantheism and antinomianism. The problem

15. William Robert Owens, 'A Critical Edition of John Bunyan's Posthumously Published Treatise *Of Antichrist, and His Ruine*' (Ph.D. diss., Open University, 1983–84), pp. lxxxviii–lxxxix; *MW*, iii, pp. xxxv–xxxvi.

16. *GA*, § 44.

17. Hill, *JB*, pp. 58, 75, 78, 207. For Clarkson and Coppe see *BDBR*, s.vv.

18. J. C. Davis, *Fear, Myth and History: The Ranters and the Historians* (Cambridge, 1986); the quotation is on p. 130.

of demonstrating the existence of the Ranters is complicated by the fact that the term was indiscriminately used in a pejorative sense, as when Edward Fowler called Bunyan himself a Ranter. By using Davis' methodology, Hill asserts that historians could prove Baptists and Quakers did not exist.[19] However, those groups professed distinctive, positive tenets: the Baptists insisted on believers' baptism, and the Quakers relied on the Inner Light rather than external ordinances. In contrast, Ranter notions were expressed in almost entirely negative terms — opposition to traditional morality, to the Bible as authoritative, to the orthodox understanding of sin, and so forth. The Ranters Bunyan met as a young man condemned him as 'legal and dark, pretending they only had attained to perfection that could do what they would and not sin'.[20] They were, as Bunyan described them, extreme Antinomians whose views were not compatible with those of pious Antinomians such as Bunyan's friend William Dell.[21]

Frank McGregor's forthcoming study of the Ranters may resolve the enigma by positing a core of distinctive Ranter tenets. He is already on record as referring to Ranter prophets as 'mystical antinomians: mystical in their claim to have become one with God; antinomian in denying the reality of sin to the believer'.[22] Perhaps we may be closest to Bunyan and his contemporaries if we think of Ranters as eccentric dissidents who disputed traditional assumptions about sin, hell, and the Bible, and yet did not belong to extant sectarian groups. This is to say rather less than Byron Nelson, who posits 'a coalition of radical antinomians who did accept a central if highly flexible core of Ranter doctrines', and substantially less than Jerome Friedman, who identifies at least five subgroups of Ranters.[23] Yet most of those whom Bunyan called Ranters were probably only people of loose morals who espoused antipathy toward Christianity rather than principled objectors to orthodoxy. In short, Bunyan normally used the term pejoratively and polemically, not accurately.

In the 1930s William York Tindall and Jack Lindsay depicted Bunyan as a preacher who detested the wealthy and spoke eloquently for the

19. Hill, *JB*, p. 381.

20. *GA*, § 45.

21. For Dell see Eric C. Walker, *William Dell, Master Puritan* (Cambridge, 1970).

22. J. F. McGregor, 'Seekers and Ranters', *Radical Religion in the English Revolution*, ed. McGregor and B. Reay (Oxford, 1984), p. 129.

23. Byron Nelson, 'Bunyan and the Ranters', Conference on Bunyan and Puritanism, Durham University (March 1988); Jerome Friedman, *Blasphemy, Immorality, and Anarchy: The Ranters and the English Revolution* (Athens, Ohio, 1987). Friedman's principal categories are Philosophical Ranters, Sexual Litertines, Revolutionary Ranters, Divine Ranters, and Gentleman Ranters.

masses.[24] This interpretation has been forcefully restated by Hill, who amassed considerable evidence to illustrate Bunyan's apparent hostility to the rich as well as to tyrants and persecutors. His piety, avers Hill, was class-conscious. Hill notes a crucial turning point in *A Few Sighs from Hell*, when Bunyan veered from the popular attack on the Quakers and took aim instead at the rich, most of whom were deemed especially susceptible to the Devil's temptations. Bunyan subjected the gentry and the Anglican clergy to withering criticism for their covetousness and materialism, and then warned them that the saints would wash their feet in the blood of the wicked. From this demonstration of class hatred, Hill asserts, Bunyan never retreated. The humility he stressed was humbleness in the eyes of God, not a sense of worthlessness in the face of social superiors.[25]

The strong sense of class in Bunyan's writings to which Hill rightly calls our attention is, of course, blatant in the allegories. *The Pilgrim's Progress* and *The Holy War* are populated with enough evil peers to fill the House of Lords. From his Bedford prison in the late 1660s, as he wrote the great trial episode, Bunyan must have relished the opportunity to add the provocative marginal comment, 'Sins are all Lords and Great ones'.[26] Indeed they were, but Lords Hategood, Lechery, Turn-about, and their sordid friends hardly exhausted Bunyan's inspired invective. An even greater contingent populates the pages of *The Holy War*, ranging from such personified vices as Lords Adultery and Lustings to the satanic figures of Lords Apollyon and Beelzebub. If the gentry are less prominent, they are at least present; one thinks of Sir Having Greedy in *The Pilgrim's Progress* and the gentleman Carnal Security, son of Lady Fear-nothing in *The Holy War*.

But if Dr. Hill is right to insist on a strong sense of class-awareness in Bunyan, we err if we push this too far. The New Testament itself is, after all, the source of substantial radical social comment, particularly in its criticism of the wealthy, yet no New Testament author condemns an entire social class to damnation. Nor did Bunyan. In the 1660s it was more difficult for Bunyan to think kindly of peers than in the early 1680s; Great-heart's master, however, was a peer, and Christ himself was described as Lord of the Hill. All peers were not necessarily evil. That point became more evident in *The Holy War*, written in the context of the exclusion controversy, when peers such as the earls of Shaftesbury and Essex fought for the godly cause. The

24. Tindall; Jack Lindsay, *John Bunyan: Maker of Myths* (London, 1937).
25. Hill, *JB*, pp. 87–89, 277.
26. *PP*, p. 94.

forces of righteousness in *The Holy War* were strictly monarchical and traditionally hierarchical: King Shaddai, Prince Emanuel, and Lords Innocent, Understanding, and Willbewill, although the latter's path was rocky. Self-denial, a virtue to which Bunyan attached great importance, was ennobled.

Bunyan held out hope for the godly rich and great, few though they might be. This position, after all, simply reflected the political realities of late Stuart England, when the Nonconformists received crucial support from a friendly minority in both houses of Parliament. Bunyan's friend, John Owen, was close to some of these parliamentary supporters, including the earl of Anglesey, Philip Lord Wharton, Sir John Hartopp, and Richard Hampden. Prominent Nonconformist aristocrats attended Owen's services at Moorfields, where Bunyan sometimes preached; he surely met some of them and thus knew at first-hand that the ranks of the rich and powerful included at least a sprinkling of saints.[27]

The significance of Bunyan's association with John Owen is only now beginning to be appreciated. Owen had ties to a group of conspirators centring around the earl of Shaftesbury and the duke of Monmouth who, in 1682, were plotting a general insurrection to force Charles II to exclude James, duke of York, from the line of succession. A key figure in this cabal was Owen's assistant, the Scottish minister Robert Ferguson, who also had links to the Rye House conspirators and their scheme to assassinate the royal brothers in 1683. Although Bunyan had no ties to the latter group, some awareness of the projected insurrection is not inconceivable, given the fact that Monmouth himself cited not only Owen but George Griffith and Matthew Meade as co-conspirators.[28]

The focus of most literary specialists on the great epics has obscured the need to establish a definitive chronology of Bunyan's lesser writings. Hill is unquestionably correct in his contention that 'it is likely that Bunyan revealed more of his mind in his posthumous treatises than in those which he published himself'. All but three of the unpublished works, according to Hill, contain matter the censor would have found objectionable: the three inoffensive works are *The Desire of the Righteous Granted*; *Justification by an Imputed Righteousness*; and *The Acceptable*

27. Hill, *JB*, p. 167; Douglas R. Lacey, *Dissent and Parliamentary Politics in England, 1661–1689* (New Brunswick, N.J., 1969), pp. 403, 409, 448, 460, 473.

28. See chap. 10, infra; Greaves, 'The Rye House Plotting, Nonconformist Clergy, and Calvin's Resistance Theory', in *Later Calvinism: A Geography*, ed. W. Fred Graham (St. Louis, forthcoming).

Sacrifice (which Bunyan had given to the printer before his death).[29] The very important millenarian treatise, *Of Antichrist, and His Ruine*, was probably written in mid or late 1682 and is thus contemporary with the plotting of Monmouth and his associates for an insurrection.[30] The equally revealing *Seasonable Counsel* of 1684 was written shortly after the government learned of the conspiracy. When subjected to a close reading in proper historical context, such works can contribute to our knowledge about Bunyan. The same might be said of *The Holy War*, which Bunyan composed in 1681 at or immediately after the climax of the exclusion controversy in the abortive Oxford Parliament. That he could have written such a substantive work, with obviously militant imagery, in total isolation from contemporary events does not fit the emerging picture of a Bunyan sensitive to political developments, though ordinarily cautious in the expression of his views.

Caution may help to explain why he failed to complete his commentary on Genesis, a work Tindall once called an 'exercise in veiled sedition'.[31] Although Hill is more circumspect in assessing its contents, he appropriately notes that 'the treatise is certainly designed to convey points to which the censor might have objected if put directly'.[32] The commentary attacks absolute monarchy, idolatry, and persecution — a formula primarily applicable to the later years of Charles II and the reign of James II before the latter's Declaration of Indulgence in April 1687. The commentary thus may be unfinished not because of Bunyan's death (the typical explanation) but because changed political circumstances rendered his political attack imprudent. He was writing at a time when the church was 'upon the waves of affliction',[33] which would seem to rule out the final sixteen months of his life. Persecution is a theme also found in most of the other posthumous works, apparently suggesting that they too were composed during those periods when state repression was most active and Nonconformists were most likely to agitate against the state.

Bunyan's position on the crucial question of resistance was fundamentally consistent throughout his career, at least judging from his writings. His fundamental principle was the assertion of passive disobedience to state decrees that opposed divine precepts. He was not afraid to criticize or even condemn the government, as in *The*

29. Hill, *JB*, pp. 327–28, 333.
30. Owens, 'The Date of Bunyan's Treatise *Of Antichrist*', *The Seventeenth Century* 1 (July 1986): 153–57; *MW*, ix, p. xxiii; chap. 10, infra.
31. Tindall, p. 134.
32. Hill, *JB*, p. 323.
33. Offor, ii, p. 483.

Holy War, where the castigation of Diabolus as a 'rebellious Tyrant' must have evoked an image of Charles II in Bunyan's readers, particularly those recently incensed by the king's repeated dismissals of Parliament and his refusal to support an exclusion bill. The commentary on Genesis links persecuting rulers to Nimrod, perhaps reflecting Bunyan's reading of the marginal note to Genesis 10:8 in the Geneva Bible, where Nimrod is denounced as 'a cruel oppressor & tyrant'. As victims of persecution, the saints, said Bunyan, are descendants of Abel, whereas the offspring of Cain include rulers and lords who have 'tyranically afflict[ed] and persecute[d]'.[34]

Despite his willingness to castigate persecuting rulers, Bunyan did not argue for a commonwealth polity. Indeed, he envisaged an apocalyptic role for kings, particularly in his treatise *Of Antichrist*, in which he insisted that some monarchs would help to overthrow the Antichrist. Neither did he espouse the legitimacy of active resistance against an ungodly government. The duty of the saints was to suffer and bear witness to the Gospel. Hill suspects that 'Bunyan's advocacy of non-resistance was not as absolute as it appears; the unpublished writings make this clear'.[35] Bunyan indisputably endorsed the use of violence against the Antichrist by monarchs, and such a doctrine could have been utilized to support William of Orange's planned invasion of England. But a doctrine of active resistance is customarily understood to mean popular rebellion or an insurrection led by lesser magistrates. Hill points to one passage — found in *The House of the Forest of Lebanon* — in which Bunyan seems to be tolerant of those who take up arms: 'Suppose they were the truly godly that made the first assault, can they be blamed'? Yet only two sentences earlier, Bunyan explicitly stated that 'the War is not carnal but spiritual, [and] it must be made by way of *controversie, contention, disputation, argument, reasonings,* &c.'[36] The arms, then, must be of the spiritual sort.

Hill cites one other key passage in which he thinks Bunyan may have been endorsing a doctrine of active resistance. Commenting on Genesis 8, Bunyan likened the raven that left the ark and ate carcasses to worldly professors in the church, who would, in the apocalyptic context of Revelation 16, devour the flesh of the kings and the mighty — 'the kingdoms and estates of the Antichristian party'. Bunyan is somewhat ambiguous about the status of the raven as a type: although it was 'in the ark' — in the church — it 'was not a type of the most spiritual Christian', though seemingly a Christian nevertheless. Yet the raven

34. See chap. 6, infra.
35. Hill, *JB*, p. 332.
36. *MW*, vii, p. 139.

left the ark, never to return, just as the worldly professor leaves the church after having attained 'some worldly honour'.[37] Bunyan seems to be saying that such people will engage in the work of toppling the Antichrist, presumably with divine blessing. But throughout the commentary the appropriate role for the saints is to suffer steadfastly, not rebel: 'It is the lot of Cain's brood, to be lords and rulers first, while Abel and his generation have their necks under persecution; yet while they lord it, and thus tyranically afflict and persecute, our very desire is towards them, wishing their salvation; and while they persecute, we pray'.[38]

Bunyan did not, therefore, endorse active resistance for the saints, yet he was willing, at least in the commentary on Genesis, to consider the possibility that some of those who professed to be Nonconformists would eventually revolt against the forces of the Antichrist — and he was not about to discourage them in this endeavour. Just as he was willing to cooperate with James II when the latter implemented a policy of toleration,[39] so he was prepared to accept the prospect that God could sanction active resistance by the more worldly Nonconformists against an antichristian regime — by his definition, a regime that persecuted the saints. But was he thinking of Shaftesbury's proposed insurrection in 1682, or Monmouth's futile rebellion in 1685, or, as Hill suggests, perhaps even the growing aristocratic support for William of Orange?[40] Again, we are reminded of the crucial problem of dating the posthumous works. Hill is surely correct in calling attention to the importance of these writings. Given their proper place in the Bunyan canon, they will be invaluable in interpreting the allegories, especially *The Holy War*. Aileen Ross has already pointed the way by using the posthumous works to explain the heavily millenarian content of *The Holy War*.[41]

'Allegory', Hill reminds us, 'was traditionally a way of circumventing the censor'; a Biblical commentary was another means to accomplish the same end.[42] If most of the posthumous works remained unpublished in Bunyan's lifetime because of censorship concerns, they share a degree of common ground with the allegories, notably *The Holy War*,

37. Offor, ii, pp. 478–79.
38. Ibid., ii, p. 445.
39. *MW*, xi, pp. xv–xix.
40. Hill, *JB*, p. 325.
41. Aileen MacLeod Sinton [Ross], 'Millenarianism in the Works of John Bunyan' (Ph.D diss., University of Alberta, 1986), chaps. 5–6; Ross, 'Paradise Regained: The Development of John Bunyan's Millenarianism', in *Bunyan in England and Abroad*, ed. M. van Os and G. J. Schutte (Amsterdam, 1990), pp. 84–87.
42. Hill, *JB*, pp. 201, 323.

and that fact is surely crucial to an accurate reading of them. To say, as Vincent Newey does, that this epic 'is not so much a war, either inward or cosmic, or even of words, as a topography of concept, tenet, and instruction', robs Bunyan's writing of historical relevancy. 'The same holy war, individual and now also collective', postulates Newey, can 'be lived through over and over again, until the end of time'.[43] This approach, so evocative of many earlier interpretations of Bunyan's allegories, launders his thought and life, rendering them innocuous to readers of all persuasions — a Gospel devoid of relevance to the problems of those contemporary Nonconformists who struggled against a government they deemed both tyrannical and idolatrous. As Isabel Rivers sagely notes, 'for Bunyan religious language and religious narrative involve drawing distinctions, defining opposites, and identifying enemies'.[44]

Bunyan's ties to his printers underscore his radical leanings. As I have argued elsewhere, a lively underground press existed after 1660. The best efforts of the government's leading censor, Roger L'Estrange — Bunyan's Mr. Filth — were inadequate to curb the illegal publications.[45] Bunyan published two of his books without the acknowledged assistance of a bookseller: *I Will Pray with the Spirit*, an uncompromising attack on the *Book of Common Prayer* that breathed a spirit of defiance, and *The Holy City*, which, although it claimed that the church was not rebellious, nevertheless castigated most sovereigns for their adherence to Mistress Babylon. Few kings or 'great ones', Bunyan insisted, would have a role in building the New Jerusalem, which was 'very near'. 'Throughout the book', observes J. Sears McGee, 'a throbbing organ continuo line of denunciation of the Roman Antichrist is heard'.[46] Because Bunyan associated persecutors with the Antichrist, and because he was at this moment in prison and a victim of persecution, can the implications of his work have been anything but seditious? *The Holy City* was hardly a work that could be described as 'politically innocuous'.[47] Both books were thus too controversial for a bookseller to handle in the early 1660s.

Sharrock and especially Hill have underscored the extent to which most of Bunyan's publishers were radicals. Matthias Cowley was

43. Newey, ' "With the eyes of my understanding" ', p. 215.

44. Isabel Rivers, 'Grace, Holiness, and the Pursuit of Happiness: Bunyan and Restoration Latitudinarianism', in Keeble, *JB*, p. 69. Cf. Keeble, *The Literary Culture of Nonconformity in Later Seventeenth-Century England* (Leicester, 1987), pp. 119–20.

45. Greaves, *DUFE*, chap. 7; Greaves, *EUHF*, chap. 5.

46. *MW*, iii, p. xxxviii.

47. Sharrock, ' "When at the first I took my Pen in hand": Bunyan and the Book', in Keeble, *JB*, p. 77.

probably a Baptist. Francis Smith was frequently in trouble with the government for illegal printing and was a prominent Whig propagandist; one of his apprentices was Stephen College, the Whig 'martyr'. George Larkin and Benjamin Harris, both of whom were closely associated with the Whigs, printed unlicensed works. The printer of *The Holy City* was almost certainly Joan Dover, whose husband Simon had died while imprisoned for seditious libel. Nathaniel Ponder was incarcerated several times for illegal printing, including Andrew Marvell's *The Rehearsal Transpros'd*, and Benjamin Alsop joined the Monmouth rebels. Hill, I think, is correct in concluding that 'Bunyan chose his printers *because* of their radicalism'.[48]

It is, then, important to remember that Bunyan, as Hill argues, was very much a part of the radical tradition in England. Recent work by other scholars, including James Turner and Robert Owens, confirms this.[49] There are, of course, degrees of radicalism, and Bunyan was never as extreme as militants who advocated unmistakably violent courses of action, or who were unyielding in their defence of commonwealth polity. Sharrock has suggested that 'Bunyan's relation to radical Puritanism is ambiguous, at least on the evidence of publication'. While his ecclesiastical polity had radical political implications, Sharrock observes, Bunyan did not advocate the overthrow of the social order. 'The test case', according to Sharrock, 'is his millenarianism'.[50]

Although the use of such a narrow lithmus test to determine radicalism can be disputed, W.R. Owens' examination of Bunyan's millenarian thought places him in the radical camp, though not its more militant wing, particularly in his early years. Owens' work is especially significant in highlighting changes in Bunyan's millenarian thought as it evolved. In *A Vindication of Some Gospel-Truths Opened* (1657), Bunyan embraced the view of 'more radical interpreters . . . that Christ would rule with the saints for the entire period of the thousand years'. Although Bunyan eschewed attempts to date the coming millennium, Owens plausibly argues that the anticipatory tone of *The Holy City* (1665) suggests he expected it very soon, perhaps in 1666, as did many radicals. But in this work he altered his position on *how* the millennium would be inaugurated; previously he had thought it would commence with Christ's personal return, but now he embraced

---

48. Ibid., pp. 80–81; Hill, *JB*, pp. 283–91. For Alsop, College, Harris, Ponder, and Smith see *BDBR*, s.vv.

49. James Turner, 'Bunyan's Sense of Place', *The Pilgrim's Progress: Critical and Historical Views*, ed. Newey (Totowa, N.J., 1980), pp. 91–110; Owens, 'A Critical Edition', pp. xlvi–cxix; chaps. 6, 7, and 10, infra.

50. Sharrock, ' "When at the first I took my Pen in hand" ', pp. 77–78.

the postmillenial view. Bunyan's refusal to speculate about a date for Antichrist's overthrow was shared by John Owen, and perhaps derived from conversations with him. In any event, Owens suggests that Bunyan's evasiveness about the time in his treatise *Of Antichrist, and His Ruine* probably stemmed from his desire to promote solidarity and instill hope among the saints as a new period of persecution dawned in the early 1680s.[51]

Nothing in Bunyan's millenarianism is incompatible with a radical stance. On the contrary, his insistence that only Protestant monarchs could contribute to the overthrow of the Antichrist, when expressed around 1682, dovetailed beautifully with Whig attempts to bar the duke of York from the throne. When *Of Antichrist* is read in its historical context, its message unequivocally supports radical Whig demands.

That Bunyan should have been so firmly a part of the radical tradition, as recent historical work demonstrates, is hardly surprising. As a young man he lived through the heady days of revolutionary England, served in an army that helped topple monarchy, and joined a congregation dedicated to principles antipathetic to those of the traditional episcopalian state church. As a young man he was probably influenced by Fifth Monarchists,[52] he dueled with Quakers and dissidents he called Ranters, he imbibed a manifest dislike of Catholicism,[53] and for most of his career he was preoccupied with persecution. For a man who equated oppression with the spirit of the Antichrist, and who was persecuted for more than a dozen years by the Stuart state, association with the radical community was only natural.

51. Owens, 'A Critical Edition', pp. xlvii–xlviii, liii, lvi–lvii, lxxxiii, xcv–xcvi. See also Owens, ' "Antichrist must be Pulled Down": Bunyan and the Millennium', in Laurence, pp. 77–94.
52. See chap. 8, infra.
53. See chap. 7, infra.

3

Conscience, Liberty, and the Spirit:
Bunyan and Nonconformity

'I was caught in my present practice and cast into Prison', and thus commenced 'a long and tedious Imprisonment, that thereby I might be frighted from my Service for Christ, and the World terrified, and made afraid to hear me Preach'.[1] Bunyan's candid reflection on his decision to pursue the path of Nonconformity and the consequences of that resolution underscores the relative rapidity with which the determination was made. Unlike ministers ejected in August 1662, Bunyan had little time to ponder the ecclesiological tenets that he would subsequently adduce to justify the separatist way. Those principles were first seriously worked out in his writings only in 1671–72, in *A Confession of My Faith, and a Reason of My Practice*, though a synopsis appeared as early as 1665 in *A Holy City*. Faced with the initial outbreak of persecution that followed the election of the Convention in April 1660 and the return of Charles II in May, Bunyan knew only that conformity would terminate his preaching and force him to worship according to the structured patterns in the Book of Common Prayer. Unwilling to accept either of these conditions, he consciously chose the path of passive resistance, virtually insisting on a confrontation: 'Had I been minded to have played the coward, I could have escaped'.[2]

Of the two considerations that persuaded Bunyan not to conform, the more important was his determination to continue preaching. 'To preach Gods word, it is so good a work, that we shall be well rewarded, if we suffer for that'.[3] The primary goal of his ministry at this time was not the edification of the faithful but the propagation of the Gospel in 'the darkest places in the *Countrey*, even amongst those people that were furthest off of profession'.[4] In this he was a

1. *GA*, §§ 279, 317.
2. 'A Relation of the Imprisonment of Mr. John Bunyan', ad cal. *GA*, p. 105.
3. Ibid., pp. 105–106.
4. *GA*, § 289.

true disciple of the sectarian tradition, as reflected in the 1650s, for example, in the concerted efforts of the Independents and Baptists in particular to preach in the 'dark corners' of the land.[5] Bunyan's hortatory goal was a combination of burning personal conviction and missionary fervour. The man who preached 'as if an Angel of God had stood by at my back to encourage me' found that he inclined 'most after awakening and converting Work'.[6] Conformity would abruptly terminate this preaching, a prospect Bunyan could not accept, given what he believed was the unmistakable evidence that God had blessed his efforts. In fact, he enjoyed so much success in these early years that he constantly battled to curtail feelings of pride.[7] Bunyan's insistence on his right to preach led to his arrest at Lower Samsell, Bedfordshire, on 12 November 1660.

During the first year and a half of his imprisonment Bunyan enjoyed sufficient freedom to continue his 'wonted course of preaching', exhorting the saints to be steadfast in their faith and 'to take heed that they touched not the Common Prayer, &c. but to mind the word of God'.[8] Here, then, was the second principle upon which his Nonconformity was grounded, namely the refusal to worship according to the formal liturgy prescribed in the Book of Common Prayer. His sermons on this theme during his periods of liberty prior to April 1662 became the basis for one of his earliest prison works, *I Will Pray with the Spirit*, the first edition of which probably appeared in 1662. Taking as his text 1 Corinthians 14:15, he defined true prayer as 'a sincere, sensible, affectionate pouring out of the heart or soul to God through Christ, in the strength and assistance of the holy Spirit, for such things as God hath promised, or, according to the Word, for the good of the Church, with submission, in Faith, to the Will of God'.[9] Because the enlightening work of the Spirit was the essential basis of true prayer, the Book of Common Prayer, which Bunyan deemed nothing more than a patchwork quilt of human inventions, was judged valueless. He went so far as to argue that Scripture expressly forbade its use, and that those who mandated its employment were akin to the Marian bishop of London, Edmund Bonner, 'that blood-red Persecutor'.[10] Bunyan clearly regarded the refusal of the 'godly' to accept the Book of Common Prayer as a fundamental basis of Nonconformity.

5. See Christopher Hill, *Change and Continuity in Seventeenth-Century England* (Cambridge, Mass., 1975), chap. 1.
6. *GA*, §§ 282, 289.
7. *GA*, §§ 296–302.
8. 'Relation', p. 129.
9. *MW*, ii, p. 235.
10. *MW*, ii, pp. 249–50, 253.

'Look into the Goals in *England*', he wrote around 1662, 'and into the Alehouses of the same: and I believe, you will find those that plead for the Spirit of Prayer in the Goal, and them that look after the Form of mens Inventions only, in the Alehouse'.[11]

When Bunyan was arrested in 1660, the magistrates were apparently interested only in his insistence on his right to preach, but when he appeared before Sir John Keeling and other justices at the quarter sessions in January 1661, both of the principles that had led him into Nonconformity were challenged. When Keeling pressed Bunyan to explain why he refused to attend services in a parish church, the latter retorted that the Word of God did not command worship according to the Book of Common Prayer, which 'was made by other men, and not by the motions of the Holy Ghost, within our Hearts'.[12] Unable to shake Bunyan's conviction of the necessity of Spirit-prompted extempore prayer, the justices shifted the interrogation to the authority by which he claimed the right to preach. Bunyan retorted with references to 1 Peter 4:10-11 and Acts 18, insisting that all who were the recipients of the Spirit-endowed gift of exhortation had the right to preach.[13] In short, Bunyan's principal justification for Nonconformity was his insistence that the ultimate authority in religious matters was the working of the Holy Spirit through the Bible and in the believer as distinct from the claims of the state to govern religious behaviour. Like Martin Luther, whose commentary on Galatians had been a powerful influence in his conversion, Bunyan rested his case on the sanctity of the conscience duly enlightened by the Spirit. This intensely personal approach to Nonconformity was the hallmark of his first six years in prison.

Not until the eve of his release from the Bedford county gaol in 1672 did Bunyan offer a written exposition of his concept of the church as the communion of visible saints. At root these ecclesiological principles had been worked out well before 1660,[14] subsequent to which they continued to provide the foundation for most of the Nonconformist churches. Even the Presbyterians, once they had been permanently ousted from the state church, embraced these ideals in practice. The true church, for Bunyan, was a fellowship of believers separated from the carnal world and gathered in freedom to pursue the holy life. The traditional concept of a parish church was unacceptable because 'visible Saints by calling' could associate in 'Church communion' only with those

11. *MW*, ii, p. 284.
12. 'Relation', pp. 107–12, 114.
13. Ibid., pp. 117–18.
14. See Geoffrey F. Nuttall, *Visible Saints: The Congregational Way 1640–1660* (Oxford, 1957).

who professed faith and holiness, not with the 'openly prophane'.[15] To ensure the maintenance of a holy community of visible saints required both strict admission requirements and the imposition of discipline to reform wayward members and excommunicate the recalcitrant. A prospective member had to provide a 'relation' of personal faith, undergo examination about her or his religious experience and personal conduct, and declare a willingness to be subject to the laws and government of Christ as exercised in the church. The sacrament or 'ordinance' of baptism was not a requirement for membership in the Bedford congregation.[16] While this concept of the church was manifestly at odds with the principles embodied in the restored Church of England and would have necessitated the pursuit of Nonconformity, Bunyan did not use the idea of the church as the communion of visible saints, separated from the world by its profession of personal faith and holy life, to justify his repudiation of the established church at the Restoration. More pressing to Bunyan in 1660-61 was the right of those imbued with the gifts of the Holy Spirit to preach and of all the 'godly' to pray as the Spirit moved them. Bunyan's crisis at the Restoration was fundamentally personal, not ecclesiological.[17]

The period that extended from Bunyan's arrest in 1660 to the publication of *Grace Abounding* in 1666 was characterized both by a strongly eschatological outlook that culminated with the exposition of millenarian themes in *The Holy City* in 1665, and by substantial spiritual introspection that ranged from his assertion of the sanctity of the individual conscience to the composition of his spiritual autobiography. Apart from writing *Christian Behaviour* (1663), a practical guide to social conduct for the faithful, Bunyan devoted these years to predominantly personal concerns that were a direct outgrowth of his incarceration. Particularly after the strictness of his imprisonment increased in April 1662, his ties with the Nonconformist community were sharply curtailed. He engaged in visitation activities on behalf of the Bedford church in September and October 1661, but his name does not appear again until November 1668, though the records for these years are sparse, and in fact blank for the period between March 1664 and October 1668. Nevertheless, Bunyan's name is not mentioned in connection with either the visitation assignments of November 1661

15. *MW*, iv, p. 154.

16. *MW*, iv, pp. 160–66. See Richard L. Greaves, *John Bunyan* (Appleford, Berks., 1969), pp. 136–44.

17. In *GA*, § 324, Bunyan observes that as he faced imprisonment his major concern was his ability to endure if the incarceration proved to be lengthy and to face death 'should that be here my portion'.

or the selection of Samuel Fenne and John Whiteman as co-pastors in January 1664.[18] Similarly, these years were essentially free of disputes with other Nonconformists. This was a time for Bunyan to ponder his own religious experience, which itself was at the root of the trouble in which he now found himself. He reflected too on God's plan for the future. For Bunyan, what Christopher Hill has called 'the experience of defeat'[19] was largely framed by these considerations.

Contemplating eschatological themes was a direct outgrowth of the fear of death that troubled Bunyan as he faced imprisonment. His first prison work, *Profitable Meditations*, reflected on the day of judgment; as yet his eschatological thinking was highly simplistic compared to the more mature *Holy City* published four years later. In the interval Bunyan clearly did some reading in millenarian literature, at least some of which was replete with citations from the patristics and learned language which he self-consciously lacked.[20] *Profitable Meditations* is significant as an indication of Bunyan's early success in overcoming his fear by affirming the ultimate triumph of the saints:

> I know, O Death, thou maist my body spoil,
> And bring it down: yet I do not thee fear:
> For that shall last with thee no longer while,
> Than my JESUS in the Clouds appear.[21]

Coupled with the certainty of vindication was an assurance that those who persecuted the saints would receive their due chastisement:

> And then he will with Trumpets royal voice
> Raise up his Dead, and gather them on high;
> Then we shall live who have made Him our choice,
> When thou in fiery flames with Hell shalt lie.[22]

The *Prison Meditations* that appeared two years later reinforced the sense of spiritual well-being that stemmed from the conviction of suffering for a righteous cause. Instead of regretting the sermons that got him into trouble, Bunyan rejoyced that he had preached while he had had the opportunity.[23] Now, he reflected, I

18. *Minutes*, pp. 37–39.
19. Christopher Hill, *The Experience of Defeat: Milton and Some Contemporaries* (New York, 1984).
20. *MW*, iii, p. 71.
21. *MW*, vi, p. 26, stanza CXXX.
22. *MW*, vi, p. 26, stanza CXXXI.
23. *MW*, vi, p. 43, stanza 8.

> . . . can with very much content
> For my Profession die,

secure in the knowledge that he had a good conscience.[24] Gaol had
become a school in which 'we learn to dye' with the assurance
of immortality.[25] The intensely personal nature of these poems is
repeatedly revealed, and *Grace Abounding* offers corroboration of the
profound spiritual experience which he underwent in these years.
Traditionally overlooked because of fascination with the earlier spiritual struggles that dominate most of the autobiography, the rich
experience of the early prison years is no less crucial for Bunyan's
later success as a minister. The confidence that he attained in the early
1660s was the basis for the exuberance of his subsequent ministry and
writing. 'I never had in all my life so great an inlet into the Word of
God as now; them Scriptures that I saw nothing in before, are made
in this place to shine upon me; Jesus Christ also was never more real
and apparent then now; here I have seen him and felt him indeed'.[26]
But Bunyan offers us only a tantalizing glimpse — 'a hint or two', he
says — of what transpired,[27] perhaps because the experience was too
mystical to be conveyed in words. From the poetic lines of the *Prison
Meditations* we know that out of this experience came a conviction that
those of 'true Valour' and a 'high and noble Mind' will

> . . . conquer when they thus do fall,
> They kill when they do dye:
> They overcome *then* most of all,
> And get the Victory.[28]

For Bunyan the experience of persecution led in eschatological terms
to the assurance that temporal defeat was in fact the means through
which the spirit triumphed.

Thus persuaded, Bunyan pursued his millenarian studies for two
more years. Although he was not inclined to speculate on a divine
timetable for the inauguration of the millennium, others were,
and excitement mounted in some Nonconformist circles as 1666

24. *MW*, vi, pp. 44–45, stanzas 17, 19.
25. *MW*, vi, pp. 45, 48, stanzas 24, 45.
26. *GA*, § 321.
27. *GA*, § 320.
28. *MW*, vi, p. 50, stanzas 59, 60, 62.

approached. This can only have reinforced Bunyan's predilection to ponder eschatological themes. Indeed, they pervade his 1665 works, including *One Thing Is Needful* and *The Resurrection of the Dead*. The former included a dramatic vision of the returning Christ, resplendent in glorious attire, who would condemn persecutors to their own 'Prison with its locks and bars'.[29] In *The Holy City* Bunyan indicated that Christ would return at the end of the millennium, an interpretation generally espoused by the Fifth Monarchists, to whom Bunyan had perhaps been attracted in the 1650s. The millennium itself, which Bunyan described as a thousand-year period during which the heavenly city — the church — would be constructed, would be instituted when an angel confined the devil to the bottomless pit. Persecution of the church would thereupon cease, the period of tribulation having served its purpose: 'The Church in the fire of Persecution is like *Esther* in the perfuming Chamber, but making fit for the presence of the King'.[30] Thus in the broad context of the divine schema Bunyan visualized a purpose for the suffering of the Nonconformists. He found some consolation too in his belief that such suffering characterized the age that preceded the millennium, whose institution was seemingly imminent: 'It is now towards the end of the world'.[31]

As Bunyan explained his personal affliction in the context of millenarianism, he had to grapple with the role of governments and more precisely of monarchs in the divine plan. On the one hand, the Nonconformists obviously suffered because of state persecution, sanctioned by a sovereign who had failed to honour the promise of liberty to tender consciences made at Breda in 1660. Bunyan must have been tempted to castigate Charles as an agent of the Antichrist. On the other hand, the early 1660s in particular saw a recurring pattern of political activity aimed at the overthrow or substantial modification of the regime. Although the number of overt rebellious acts was few, these were years of unrelieved plotting, with the state's efforts to uncover the conspiracies enormously complicated by widespread and often unsubstantiated rumours.

Like numerous other Nonconformists, Bunyan repudiated the first attempt to overturn the Restoration government; it had been launched in London by a band of Fifth Monarchists led by Thomas Venner in January 1661. 'That practice of theirs, I abhor', Bunyan insisted,

---

29. *MW*, vi, p. 93, stanza 26. *The Resurrection of the Dead* also had an evangelical purpose; see J. Sears McGee's introduction to *MW*, iii, pp. xlv–liv.

30. *MW*, iii, pp. 80–82, 128–29, 139, 169–70.

31. *MW*, iii, p. 165. The best brief overviews of *The Holy City* are found in McGee's introduction to *MW*, iii; and Aileen Macleod Sinton [Ross], 'Millenarianism in the Works of John Bunyan' (Ph.D diss., University of Alberta, 1986), chap. 3.

adding that 'I look upon it as my duty to behave myself under the King's government, both as becomes a man and a christian'.[32] His profession not only rings true but accords with the general tendency of Bedfordshire Nonconformists to shun disruptive political action. An examination of the principal centers of plotting in England in the 1660s in relation to areas of Nonconformist strength reveals discontinuity rather than correlation. This suggests that apart from dissidents in the London area (where Nonconformity was strong), the proclivity to radical political activity was greater among Dissenters in areas where they were heavily outnumbered. Radical activity was at least in part a response to feelings of endangerment and insecurity. In Bedfordshire the number of Nonconformists was substantial enough to undermine the government's hopes of crushing them, thereby permitting Dissenters to follow a more moderate course of passive resistance. The Tong plot of 1662, the northern rebellion in 1663, and the 1665 Rathbone conspiracy, for example, did not involve Bedfordshire.[33]

In *The Holy City* Bunyan admonished monarchs for being enamoured with 'Mistres *Babylon*, the Mother of Harlots, the Mistris of Witchcrafts', but he judiciously cast the blame for this on the Great Whore herself. When 'this Gentlewoman . . . [is] laid in her grave, and all her fat ones gone down to the sides of the pit; these Kings will change their mind, and fall in love with the true and chaste Matron, and with Christ her Lord'.[34] Rather than exhorting his readers to overthrow monarchy, Bunyan tried to teach them that sovereigns would ultimately embrace Christ, even if they were the last ones to do so. This left open the possibility that some would surely perish long before their fellow monarchs turned from their persecutorial ways. In any event, a cosmic struggle would occur before the rulers submitted to Christ: 'They will be shaking the sharp end of their weapons against the Son of God, continually labouring to keep him out of his Throne, and from having that rule in the Church, and in the World as becomes him who is the head of the body, and over all principality and power'.[35] Bunyan sharply tempered this apparent call to arms by insisting that the church is not a rebellious institution bent on destroying either monarchs or their wealth.[36] Incarcerated in a Bedford gaol, he perceived the struggle solely in spiritual terms.

32. 'Relation', p. 120.
33. Greaves, *DUFE*, chaps. 4, 6; Greaves, *EUHF*, chap. 1.
34. *MW*, iii, pp. 167, 169.
35. *MW*, iii, pp. 166–67.
36. *MW*, iii, pp. 96–97.

Bunyan's own spiritual battles in the 1650s were, in his mind, but a part of the greater cosmic encounter against the forces of the Antichrist. For him to culminate this period of introspection by recounting his own spiritual autobiography in the hope that it might sustain others in their religious life was therefore natural. Of the major themes of the early 1660s, he gave little attention in *Grace Abounding* to eschatological concerns apart from the immediate fate of his own soul. However, the work not only marks the culmination of Bunyan's introspection and the affirmation of the sanctity of the individual conscience, but redirects his emphases toward the needs of others. The preface commences with a virtual apology for his recent inability to exhort the saints: '*I being taken from you in presence, and so tied up, . . . I cannot perform that duty that from God doth lie upon me, to you-ward, for your further edifying and building up in Faith and Holiness*'.[37] Here, then, was a work unmistakably directed to the needs of those he had converted in the late 1650s and very early 1660s.

The years from 1666 to 1670 are the most obscure in Bunyan's career. The 1664 Conventicle Act expired on 1 March 1669, and though some religious persecution continued in the interval prior to its re-enactment in April 1670, Nonconformists enjoyed a degree of freedom in this period, in part because of legal uncertainty concerning Nonconformity.[38] In July 1669, however, a judicial opinion stated that the statutes of 13 Eliz. I, c. 12 and 14 Car. II, c. 4 concerning the qualifications of ministers who preached at religious assemblies were still in force.[39] The king thereupon issued a proclamation ordering justices of the peace to enforce these laws.[40] Bunyan benefitted by the confusion. Although Charles did not formally prorogue Parliament until 1 March 1669, it had last met in August 1668 without renewing the Conventicle Act. The following November Bunyan had sufficient freedom to undertake visitation and admonition responsibilities for the Bedford church. The royal proclamation in July apparently curtailed his activities, but between October 1669 and June 1670 he was again active in the congregation's work.[41] As the magistrates began to enforce the 1670 Conventicle Act, he apparently was more closely confined, for the church records do not mention him again until April 1671. From that time until his formal release in March 1672 he enjoyed

37. *GA*, § 38.
38. PRO SP 29/258/43.
39. PRO SP 29/262/115.
40. Frank Bate, *The Declaration of Indulgence 1672: A Study in the Rise of Organised Dissent* (London, 1908), pp. 64–65.
41. *Minutes*, pp. 39–52.

considerable liberty and was extensively involved in the congregation's affairs.[42]

A possible clue to Bunyan's activities in the late 1660s is found in the candid observation of the Bedford church in November 1668 that many of its members had 'in these troublous times withdrawne themselves from close walking with the Church', whereas others were 'guilty of more grosse miscarriages'.[43] Bunyan had written *Grace Abounding* in part to shore up those who wavered, and after its completion he commenced work on a book designed to exhort Nonconformists to persevere in the 'race' for heaven. He tailored the thesis of *The Heavenly Footman* for the conditions of the late 1660s: 'There are but very few that do obtain that ever-to-be-desired Glory: In so much that many Eminent Professors drop short of a welcom from God into his pleasant place'.[44] The analogy of the Christian life as a race was an outgrowth of Bunyan's personal experience and the Biblical foundations on which it rested. In his *Profitable Meditations* he had written:

> I am encourag'd in the heav'nly Race,
> Because Christ dy'd and spilt his Blood for me.[45]

The Heavenly Footman applied this theme to the conditions of Nonconformity in the late 1660s. Although the work itself was not published until 1698, Bunyan composed it relatively early in his career. He refers to 'that little time which I have been a Professor' as well as to two of his earliest works, *A Few Sighs from Hell* (1658) and *The Doctrine of the Law and Grace Unfolded* (1659).[46] A reference to those who run 'a *Quaking*, . . . a *Ranting*; . . . after the *Baptism*, . . . after the *Independency*: . . . for *Free-will*, and . . . for *Presbytery*' suggests the period between the great activity of those sects in the 1650s and Bunyan's concern with sectarian issues beginning in 1671.[47] The references to Ranters in this book may have been sparked by his recollection in *Grace Abounding* of his early encounter with these extreme Antinomians.[48] Allusions to persecution, both past and present, also appear. Bunyan exhorts his readers to bear in mind the punishments inflicted on the saints of old, and he admonishes them not to risk losing an eternal

42. Ibid., pp. 67–72.
43. Ibid., p. 39.
44. *MW*, v, p. 147.
45. *MW*, vi, p. 9, stanza XXVIII.
46. *MW*, v, pp. 152, 153, 178.
47. *MW*, v, p. 152.
48. *MW*, v, pp. 152, 156; *GA*, §§ 44–45.

crown for fear of 'the loss of a few trifles'.[49] The latter was probably a reference to the penalties imposed by the 1664 Conventicle Act, which included both fines and imprisonment.[50] The evidence, then, suggests that Bunyan commenced The *Heavenly Footman* after he completed *Grace Abounding*.

Before he could finish the new work, Bunyan thought of depicting the race for a heavenly crown in allegorical terms as a pilgrimage.

> And thus it was: I writing of the Way
> And Race of Saints in this our Gospel-Day,
> Fell suddenly into an Allegory
> About their Journey, and the way to Glory.[51]

By the time he returned to *The Heavenly Footman*, he was already thinking of the Christian life more as a challenging journey than as a race. Although he carried the race motif through to the conclusion, his new perspective is hinted at various times, as in the mixed metaphor of the closing words: 'Run apace, and hold out to the *end*. And the Lord give thee a prosperous Journey'.[52] As Roger Sharrock has argued, 'the grand central metaphor of *The Pilgrim's Progress*' — the struggle to reach a goal by traversing arduous terrain — was already present in *The Heavenly Footman*.[53] So too were some of the physical images of the allegory: by-paths, quagmires, leaving friends and neighbours, sin as a burden which one carries, and the need of the runner to 'go close by' the cross.[54]

If, then, *The Heavenly Footman* was begun in 1666 or shortly there-after, the first part of *The Pilgrim's Progress* belongs to the same period. Both works reflect the needs of Nonconformists at this time, tempted as they were to drop out of the heavenly race or forsake the pilgrimage because of the threat of persecution. Yet Bunyan claimed he had no intention to publish the allegory, presumably because it seemed somewhat frivolous at a time when persecution was increasing: '*I did it mine own self to gratifie*'.[55] Nevertheless the conditions facing

49. *MW*, v, pp. 164–65, 169–70.
50. See, e.g., Wigfield, pp. 167–71; *A True and Impartial Narrative of Some Illegal and Arbitrary Proceedings . . . in or near the Town of Bedford* (London, 1670), pp. 3–9.
51. *PP*, p. 1.
52. *MW*, v, p. 178; cf. p. 157: 'Take heed that you have not an *Ear open* to every one that calleth after you, as you are in your Journey'. Cf. the similar passage in *PP*, p. 10. Also cf. *MW*, v, p. 166.
53. Sharrock, *JB*, p. 72.
54. *MW*, v, p. 159.
55. *PP*, p. 1.

Nonconformists in the late 1660s provided precisely the milieu that made the theme of a demanding race or a tortuous pilgrimage relevant. So too did the proximity of the completed spiritual autobiography, since *The Pilgrim's Progress* is in its most basic sense an allegorical depiction of Bunyan's spiritual struggles.

The conditions which Dissenters faced in the late 1660s coupled with internal evidence from the allegory provide the opportunity to date the first part of *The Pilgrim's Progress* more precisely. Three-fourths of the way through the allegory Bunyan wrote: 'So I awoke from my Dream. And I slept, and Dreamed again'.[56] Because there is no artistic or thematic reason for this break, some scholars have argued that the awakening signified the end of his imprisonment in 1672 and his completion of the work as a free man.[57] More plausibly, however, the break occurred in either the autumn of 1668 or the autumn of 1669, when Bunyan began periods of relative liberty. The initial draft of the first part must have been completed no later than April 1671, when he received considerable freedom, and possibly as early as October 1669. Two further clues in Bunyan's 'Apology' for the book support this dating: He wrote it, Bunyan admitted, '*to divert my self . . . from worser thoughts*',[58] a probable reference to his fears of dying in prison. Moreover, his statement that he spent only '*vacant seasons*'[59] writing the allegory is compatible both with his need to make 'long Tagg'd laces' to support his family and with his involvement in the serious problems of the Bedford church beginning in 1668. Bunyan's decision to circulate the work among his friends, the time needed for probable revisions, and his reticence to publish the work account for its appearance only in 1678.[60]

In the period from 1670 to 1675 Bunyan's concerns shifted dramatically. At no other time in his career was he so intensely involved in Nonconformist affairs, particularly those concerning the implementation of an effective organizational structure in Bedfordshire and doctrinal and ecclesiological issues important to Dissenters.

The difficulties experienced by the Bedford church in the late 1660s underscored the need for better organization, especially the designation of more local units — virtually cells — and approved preachers (or 'teachers'). On Bunyan's forays from prison beginning

56. *PP*, p. 123.
57. See, e.g., Sharrock's commentary in *PP*, p. 333.
58. *PP*, p. 1.
59. *PP*, p. 1.
60. *PP*, p. 2.

in late 1668, he had ample opportunity to assess the problems at first hand. As we will see in Chapter 4, while he was still in gaol he had the opportunity to develop an organizational structure with fellow Nonconformists. At least nine men who figured prominently in the organizational plan were in the county gaol with Bunyan at some point between about 1666 and 1672. Subsequent to his appointment as a pastor of the Bedford congregation in January 1672 and his release from the county gaol in March, Bunyan and his colleagues took advantage of the Declaration of Indulgence, issued on 15 March, to apply jointly for licences to preach and for places to meet. In addition to Bedford, the application represented the interests of Nonconformist churches at Keysoe, Cranfield, Stevington, and Newport Pagnell, including twenty-one satellite meetings, twelve of which were connected with the Bedford church. In addition to providing closer supervision of and support for church members, such meticulous organization made it extremely unlikely that the revival of persecution could stamp out Nonconformity in Bedfordshire and the contiguous counties.

The organizational efforts brought to the fore such crucial ecclesiological questions as the requirements for church membership and the role of baptism. About 1671 Bunyan dealt with these issues in *A Confession of My Faith*, which he published the following year. Amplifying what he had written in *The Holy City*, he argued, as we have seen, for a church constituted solely of visible saints, without baptism as a condition of membership. Bunyan was thereupon attacked by the General Baptist John Denne in *Truth Outweighing Error* (1673) and the Particular Baptist Thomas Paul in *Some Serious Reflections* (1673), which included an epistle by William Kiffin. Bunyan retorted in *Differences in Judgment About Water-Baptism, No Bar to Communion* (1673), which carried a supportive statement by Henry Jessey, another advocate of open-membership views. In turn the Particular Baptist Henry Danvers repudiated Bunyan in a postscript to his *Treatise of Baptism* (1673), to which Bunyan replied in *Peaceable Principles and True* (1674). Meanwhile, Danvers' *Treatise* sparked an enormous pamphlet war between paedobaptists such as Richard Baxter and Obadiah Wills and Baptists such as John Tombes and Thomas Delaune. Bunyan, however, was not involved in the wider dispute.[61]

In practical terms Bunyan's position on baptism and church membership affected his church's relations with London Nonconformists. When Bedford members desired to transfer to a London congregation,

61. See Greaves, *SAR*, chap. 6. For Denne, Paul, Kiffin, Jessey, and Tombes see *BDBR*, s.vv.

the church took special care to recommend a congregation with compatible views. Those which met their standards included the churches of Henry Jessey, George Griffith, Anthony Palmer, George Cokayne, and John Owen.[62] Of these men, only Jessey considered himself — like Bunyan — to be fundamentally a Baptist. Although Bunyan is rightly regarded as an open-membership Baptist, his closest relations in the Nonconformist community were with the Congregationalists. However, a rupture with the Congregationalist church of Francis Holcroft in Cambridge occurred around 1670 when the Bedford congregation insisted on admitting John Waite of Toft, who had been excommunicated by Holcroft's group. [63]

While Bunyan was sorting out his relations with other Nonconformists, he became embroiled in a doctrinal controversy with the former Puritan Edward Fowler. Regarded by Bunyan as a man who could, 'as to religion, turn and twist like an eel on the angle; or rather like the weather-cock that stands on the steeple', the Latitudinarian Fowler had provoked Bunyan's ire by his book, *The Design of Christianity* (1671). Its thesis — that Christ's work was intended to reform people's lives and restore the righteousness they once possessed in Adam — repudiated the doctrine of justification solely by the imputed righteousness of Christ. Bunyan asserted his position in *A Defence of the Doctrine of Justification, by Faith* (1672), in which he also castigated the Quaker William Penn. Fowler or his curate responded in the vituperative tract, *Dirt Wip't Off* (1672).[64] This, the most argumentative phase of Bunyan's career, came to an end with some parting but oblique shots against Fowler and Penn in *Light for Them That Sit in Darkness* (1675).[65] These doctrinal controversies left Bunyan convinced of 'the Accursed Condition of those among the Religious in these Nations whose notions put them far off from Jesus'.[66]

With the passing of the period of bitter doctrinal and ecclesiological disputes in 1675, Bunyan moved into a serener phase of his career in which his dominant concerns were pastoral in nature. His writings

62. *Minutes*, pp. 66, 71, 79. Cf. p. 92 for a 1690 letter concerning relations with Matthew Meade's church. For all these men see *BDBR*, s.vv. For Owen see also Peter Toon, *God's Statesman: The Life and Work of John Owen* (Exeter, 1971), and for Griffith see Greaves, *SAR*, chap. 3.

63. See chap. 5, infra. The historical controversy over Bunyan's denominational affiliation is surveyed by Joseph D. Ban, 'Was John Bunyan a Baptist? A Case Study in Historiography', *The Baptist Quarterly* 30 (Oct. 1984): 367–76.

64. Greaves, *Bunyan*, pp. 82–85.

65. *MW*, viii, pp. 86, 91, 94, 101, 108, 133ff.

66. *MW*, viii, p. 160.

in this period reflect the evangelical themes of his ministry. *The Strait Gate* (1676), an exposition of Matthew 7:13-14, not only recapitulated the theme of *The Pilgrim's Progress* about the difficulty of attaining heaven but underscored the reorientation of Bunyan's efforts: '*Now we discourse not about things controverted among the godly, but directly about the* saving or damning of the soul'.[67] In this work he insisted that few would be saved, a theme to which he returned in *Saved by Grace* (1676), where attention shifted primarily to the elect and the basis of their redemption. Despite the fact that Bunyan thought the number of the elect was relatively small, the warmth of the Gospel message triumphed over the logical implications of the Calvinist doctrine of predestination in his most popular sermon, the evangelical *Come, & Welcome, to Jesus Christ* (1678). His pastoral preoccupations were similarly reflected in the catechism he wrote for the saints, *Instruction for the Ignorant* (1675). At times reflecting the personal and experiential qualities that are the hallmark of Bunyan's writing, the catechism is unusual in the emphasis it places on self-denial.[68]

Despite the challenges and rewards of the pastoral ministry and opportunities to preach in London to sizeable crowds,[69] these were not trouble-free years for Bunyan. Undoubtedly jealous of his popularity, Church of England officials prosecuted him. Following the revocation of the 1672 licences to preach early in 1675, a warrant for Bunyan's arrest was issued on 4 March on the grounds that he had illegally preached at a conventicle. What effect this had on him is not known; he may have gone into hiding or been fined and even briefly imprisoned under the terms of the 1670 Conventicle Act. By April the church-wardens had presented his name for refusing to attend the parish church and he was excommunicated. When he refused to appear in the archdeacon's court to answer for his conduct, a writ was issued for his arrest. About December 1676 he again entered prison and remained there until the following June. The renewed persecution appears to have prompted him to dust off the manuscript of *The Pilgrim's Progress*, perhaps make some final revisions, and submit it to the printer Nathaniel Ponder. It was entered in the Stationers' Register on 22 December.[70]

The most sensational event in England in 1678 was not the publication of *The Pilgrim's Progress* but the revelations of the Popish Plot. In the climate of fear that ensued, Bunyan — like any good pastor —

67. *MW*, v, p. 69.
68. *MW*, viii, pp. xxx–xlii.
69. Doe, pp. 873–84.
70. *MW*, viii, pp. xix–xxiv. For Ponder see *BDBR*, s.v.

utilized the concerns of the day as a setting for his religious message. The result, a sermon on Revelation 14:7, was expanded and published as *A Treatise of the Fear of God*; it contained a particularly scathing attack on hypocrites. The posthumous work *Israel's Hope Encouraged* probably belongs to this period too, for it refers to the time after the disclosure of the Popish Plot as one when people feared their throats would be cut and their children slaughtered.[71] The time was therefore propitious to ponder the lot of the wicked. Already basking in the success of *The Pilgrim's Progress*, Bunyan set about to describe '*the Life and Death of the Ungodly, and of their travel from this world to Hell*'.[72] The result was *The Life and Death of Mr. Badman* (1680), a work that must be placed in the historical context of the Popish Plot and the recriminations and concerns which it sparked. Those circumstances were clearly in Bunyan's mind as he wrote: 'England *shakes and totters already, by reason of the burden that Mr. Badman and his Friends have wickedly laid upon it*'.[73]

As Bunyan moved into the 1680s his evangelical, pastoral interests remained strong and are manifested in such publications as *The Greatness of the Soul* (1682), *A Holy Life* (1683), and *A Discourse upon the Pharisee and the Publicane* (1685). A successful author, he confronted not only readers who clamoured for more allegorical works but imitators anxious to exploit his popularity. Out of these circumstances came the second part of *The Pilgrim's Progress* (1684), with its reflections on Nonconformist life and principles. Echoes of Bunyan's earlier controversies with traditional Baptists such as Danvers, Paul, and Denne are evident. As Roger Sharrock has suggested, the characters of Fearing and Feeble-mind represented persons of tender conscience for whom the open-membership churches were particularly appealing.[74]

Bunyan's trips to London in this period rekindled his old flame for doctrinal controversy. He published his final work in this genre, *Questions About the Nature and Perpetuity of the Seventh-Day-Sabbath*, in 1685. The principal object of his attack was Francis Bampfield, whose congregation of Seventh-Day Baptists shared Pinners' Hall, Broad Street, with the Congregationalist church of Richard Wavel. Bunyan had preached to Wavel's flock in 1682, and the expanded version of

71. Offor, i, p. 585.
72. Bunyan, *The Life and Death of Mr. Badman*, ed. James F. Forrest and Roger Sharrock (Oxford, 1988), p. 1.
73. Ibid., p. 2.
74. Sharrock, *JB*, p. 141.

that sermon had been published as *The Greatness of the Soul*. Although Bampfield himself went to prison in February 1682, his congregation continued to meet and survived his death two years later. Bunyan found sabbatarian views sufficiently objectionable to attack them in his tract. His tone, however, was moderate, befitting his desire that sabbatarian Baptists not 'take it ill at my hand that I thus freely speak my mind'.[75]

London Nonconformists were likewise the occasion of Bunyan's foray into the seventeenth-century disputes concerning the role of women in religious affairs. Some precedent existed in Baptist circles for women to meet separately for spiritual exercises. The ladies of Thomas Lamb's General Baptist church had done so as early as the 1640s, and in 1645 they convened for lectures on Tuesday afternoons at Bell Alley, Coleman Street. One of those who spoke to them was the infamous sectary Mrs. Attaway, a member of Thomas Lamb's General Baptist congregation in London. In the early 1680s a 'Mr. K.' (possibly Benjamin Keach, William Kiffin, Daniel King, or Hanserd Knollys) supported the right of women to meet together for prayer.[76] When they learned of Bunyan's opposition to this practice and pressed him for his reasons, he responded with *A Case of Conscience Resolved* (1683). Such meetings, he argued, contravened biblical principles, were unnecessary because there were enough men to convene and direct worship, and were blemishes on the church because they manifested female 'unruliness'. Women must 'keep their places'.[77] The second part of *The Pilgrim's Progress*, which followed a year later, does not indicate that Bunyan retreated from the traditional role of male superiority, and should not be interpreted as an attempt by Bunyan to place women on a plane equal to that of men.

The most striking change that marks this period of Bunyan's life concerns his political outlook. The bitter struggle to exclude the duke of York from the line of succession, the campaign to remodel the corporations, the renewal of persecution, and the execution in 1681 of Stephen College, a supporter of the earl of Shaftesbury,[78] boded ill

---

75. *MW*, iv, p. 389. See Greaves, *SAR*, chap. 7.

76. For all these people, including Mrs. Attaway, see *BDBR*, s.vv. See also Dorothy Ludlow, 'Shaking Patriarchy's Foundations: Sectarian Women in England, 1641–1700', in *Triumph Over Silence: Women in Protestant History*, ed. Richard L. Greaves (Westport, Conn., 1986), chap. 3; N. H. Keeble, ' "Here is her Glory, even to be under Him": The Feminine in the Thought and Work of John Bunyan', in Laurence, pp. 131–47.

77. *MW*, iv, pp. 328–29. For a fuller explanation of this work see *MW*, iv, pp. xxxvii–xliv.

78. *BDBR*, s.v.

for the Nonconformists. Against this background Bunyan returned to matters of state in *The Holy War* (1682), a technically sophisticated but not altogether satisfying allegory. The relative obliquity of the allegory was a necessity ordained by the trying political conditions, while the multiple levels of meaning provided Bunyan with an opportunity to address levels of need ranging from the concerns of the individual soul to the endangered Dissenting community. As king of Mansoul, Diabolus clearly was a reminder of Charles II, even as such new burgesses and aldermen as Mr. Atheism and Mr. False Peace were caricatures of the Tory-Anglicans who ruled the land. In contrast, Bunyan's expectations of good governors were reflected in his account of Emanuel's work after he had gained control of Mansoul. Despite the persecution of the early 1680s, Bunyan did not include a call to arms in *The Holy War*. Instead, in the critical supplement to the allegory, *Seasonable Counsel: or, Advice to Sufferers* (1684) — a work regularly overlooked by students of Bunyan — he made it clear that in times of persecution the saints could do no more than patiently suffer and pray to God for deliverance from evil rulers. In this tract Bunyan expressed one of his profoundest insights: the necessity for Christians to suffer *actively* for righteousness by *willingly* embracing affliction.

The posthumous work *Of Antichrist, and His Ruine* almost certainly dates from this period, for it espouses the doctrine of Christian suffering enunciated in *Seasonable Counsel* and deals with some of the same political issues found in *The Holy War*. Although Bunyan implicitly but forcefully denounced Charles II in the allegory, in *Of Antichrist* he cautiously expressed loyalty to the king and attributed a special apocalyptic function to monarchs in general. When the Antichrist was overthrown, it would be at the hand of earthly sovereigns divinely ordained for that task. Before this could transpire, Bunyan contended, the church must undergo much severer persecution, even to the point that few visible churches will be left in the world.[79] Thus the conviction that massive suffering was imminent for the Nonconformists heavily influenced Bunyan's outlook in the early 1680s. Yet as a minister he not only warned of impending persecution but encouraged the godly to remain steadfast in their convictions. Perhaps the quieter tone of the second part of *The Pilgrim's Progress* was in part an attempt to calm Dissenters in the face of suffering: 'Be ye watchful, and cast away Fear; be sober, and hope to the End'.[80]

79. Offor, ii, pp. 61, 66, 74, 88. See chap. 5, infra, for a full discussion of Bunyan's views on church-state relations. For views of the Antichrist by Bunyan's contemporaries, see Christopher Hill, *Antichrist in Seventeenth-Century England* (London, 1971).

80. *PP*, p. 306.

The last phase of Bunyan's career commenced in the summer of 1686 when James II adopted a policy of cooperation with Nonconformists as part of his scheme to provide offices and other opportunities to Catholics. In addition to issuing a Declaration of Indulgence in April 1687, the king determined to remodel the corporations and commissions of the peace, thereby making way for Nonconformists and Catholics and thus undoing the Tory-Anglican dominance Charles had imposed. The story that Bunyan was offered 'a Place of Publick Trust'[81] cannot be corroborated, but he certainly did not oppose some cooperation with the king, for at least six members of his church accepted positions in the remodelled Bedford Corporation in the spring of 1688.[82] Bunyan's position vis-a-vis James is consistent with the views expressed in *Of Antichrist, and His Ruine* about the role of sovereigns in toppling Satan. Bunyan's unfinished commentary on Genesis, on which he was probably at work in these last years, did not espouse tyrannicide but called on the saints to 'stand their ground', pray for their rulers, and accept persecution as a divine means to purge the church.[83] But Bunyan must have been chary of the general drift of James' policies, for the commentary unmistakably opposes absolute monarchy.[84]

Bunyan's final years were extremely busy because of his preaching and writing. The strongly evangelical emphasis that commenced in earnest in 1675–76 continued without abatement to the end. The publications of these years — such as *Good News for the Vilest of Men* (1688), *The Work of Jesus Christ as an Advocate* (1688), *The Water of Life* (1688), and *The Acceptable Sacrifice* (1689) — are of a piece with *The Strait Gate* and *Come, & Welcome*. Nor did Bunyan the pastor forget the needs of children, for whom he wrote his emblem collection, *A Book for Boys and Girls* (1686). This work, suggests Graham Midgley, 'shows Bunyan at his best and most adventurous as a poet, and expresses more completely the many sides of his personality'.[85] Bunyan probably compiled it over a period of years and it thus reflects the changing circumstances of his later life.

Bunyan's relations with other Nonconformists in his final years were peaceful. His popularity in London remained high and undoubtedly contributed to the demand for his printed sermons. He preached the posthumously published *Desire of the Righteous Granted* in 1685

81. 'Continuation', p. 163.
82. *MW*, xi, pp. xvi–xviii.
83. Offor, ii, p. 456.
84. Ibid., ii, pp. 497–98; Tindall, p. 266.
85. *MW*, vi, p. lvii.

or 1686 to the open-membership congregation of Stephen More in Southwark, and delivered his *Last Sermon* in John Gammon's church in Boar's Head Yard, off Petticoat Lane. *Good News*, an invitation to the most immoral persons to convert, may also have been preached in London. Bunyan never retreated from his conviction that baptism must not be a necessary condition of church membership, but in these last years his tone was more conciliatory, perhaps because he was more mature or possibly because he had come to recognize the greater dangers that stemmed from Catholicism and the drift toward an arbitrary monarchy. In his poetic work *A Discourse of the Building, Nature, Excellency and Government of the House of God* (1688) he insisted on a reasonable degree of toleration within the church:

> For those that have *private* opinions too
> We must *make* room, or shall the Church undo;
> Provided they be *such* as don't impair
> Faith, Holiness, nor with good Conscience jarr.[86]

The sacraments have their symbolic value, but strife abounds when

> . . . *Moles* are *Mountains* made, or fault is found,
> With every *little, trivial, petty* thing.[87]

The only requirement for fellowship with the church was 'a *Certificate*, To shew thou seest thy self most desolate'.[88]

Here was the core of the Christian life — the experiential basis of faith, without which religious profession was barren and lifeless. For Bunyan this experience of living faith was possible only through the agency of the Holy Spirit. The conviction of the Spirit's inner work — in preaching and in prayer — had initially persuaded him to choose the path of Nonconformity, and the same conviction sustained him throughout his ministry. Although the various periods in Bunyan's career must be distinguished if we are to understand his development and the proper historical context of his works, his belief in the inner working of the Spirit and its implications for the Christian pilgrimage provided a unifying theme for his life as a Nonconformist.

86. *MW*, vi, p. 311.
87. *MW*, vi, p. 310.
88. *MW*, vi, p. 281.

4

The Organizational Response of Nonconformity to Repression and Indulgence: The Case of Bedford

In the 1670s Bunyan and his Nonconformist colleagues implemented an organizational plan developed during the imprisonment years prior to 1672. The purpose of the plan was to provide a network of preachers and teachers in the local villages throughout northern Bedfordshire and contiguous areas that would be strong enough to withstand further persecution. Implementation of the plan brought Bunyan into closer contact with Nonconformists to the south and east, as far away as London. Ironically Bunyan and his colleagues formulated the plan while they were imprisoned together at Bedford for their Nonconformity. Their success vividly illustrates the failure of the Stuart government to suppress religious dissent.

The prison years are poignantly described by a leading Restoration Quaker, George Whitehead, in words applicable to Bunyan: 'There was but little Respite from *Persecution* in *twelve Years* Time, from the Year *1660* unto *1672*, in which was the last War at Sea between the *English* and *Dutch*; so that one Judgment and Calamity followed another, *Plague, Fire, and War*, unto great Depopulation, and Devastation, shewing God's heavy Displeasure against *Persecution* and *Cruelty*'.[1] To some extent Bunyan was shielded from the turmoil of these years, despite his general loss of freedom. Yet his preaching forays from his cell, which his gaoler sometimes permitted (mostly after 1668), and the comings and goings of local Nonconformists imprisoned for shorter periods of time, kept him abreast of current events. The fact that he used these years to write a number of works, including *The Pilgrim's Progress*, is well known.[2] What is largely unrecognized is that these years

1. *The Christian Progress of That Ancient Servant and Minister of Jesus Christ, George Whitehead* (London, 1725), p. 346.
2. Tindall (p. 132) attributes the absence of publication between 1666 and 1672 to 'the profound silence in which Bunyan contemplated the approach of the millennium from 1666 to 1682'. The silence is better attributed to Bunyan's preaching forays and organizational work in these years.

— especially from 1666 to 1672 — were ones in which Bunyan worked out Nonconformist strategy with those who were imprisoned with him in the county gaol.

One of these men was John Wright of Blunham, a village between Bedford and Gamlingay, Cambridgeshire and the centre of an illegal Nonconformist group. Wright, a saddler, along with a grocer and three labourers, appeared before justices of the peace at Bedford on 15 January 1666 for having attended an unlawful conventicle in Wright's house. The defendants refused to pay their fines and were committed to the Bedford county gaol for ten days. Obviously unrepentant, the same five stood before justices of the peace on 30 April 1666 after again frequenting a conventicle. Wright and the others once more refused to pay their fines and went to prison for twenty days.[3] On both occasions Wright would have been in contact with the incarcerated Bunyan.

Despite the threat of such penalties the Blunham Nonconformists continued to meet, with predictable results. On 25 June 1666 another conventicle gathered, after which the justices of the peace committed Wright and five others to the county gaol at Bedford without bail; once again they joined Bunyan. Wright's name appears on a list of prisoners at the bar in the ensuing summer assizes. Also on that roster are the names of Bunyan and William Man, whose house at Stagsden, west of Bedford, would figure in Bunyan's plans in 1672. The list additionally includes William Wheeler of Cranfield, southeast of Newport Pagnell, who had met with Bunyan, John Burton, John Donne of Pertenhall (north of Bedford, near Kimbolton), and John Gibbs of Newport Pagnell[4] in 1658 'for the continuing of unity and preventing of differences among the congregations'.[5]

When Burton later became ill, the Bedford church asked for the assistance of Wheeler, Donne, Gibbs, and William Breeden, a tradesman of Newport Pagnell, in preaching and administering the Lord's supper. Later the same year Wheeler, Donne, and Gibbs met with the Bedford congregation to consider a successor to Burton. Wheeler was selected, but declined to serve.[6] Two years later the Bedford church invited Wheeler, Donne, Gibbs, and Francis Holcroft of Cambridge to preach to the congregation periodically.[7] Wheeler's subsequent incarceration in the county gaol would have kept Bunyan

3. Wigfield, pp. 167–69.
4. Ibid., pp. 170–71.
5. *Minutes*, p. 31.
6. Ibid., pp. 35, 36.
7. Ibid., p. 38.

apprised of Nonconformist activity in the region to the southwest of Bedford.

A list of prisoners in the county gaol around 1666 includes not only Bunyan's name but also the those of other Nonconformists with whom Bunyan would work in the 1670s. One of these was John Donne, who ministered to a congregation at Keysoe, north of Bedford, following (and possibly a few years before) his ejection from Pertenhall.[8] The names of Thomas and Simon Haynes also appear; the latter would be licensed in 1672 to preach at Bendhurst (Bolnhurst, south of Keysoe?).[9] The gaol lists for 1668 include the names of Bunyan and Simon Haynes for misdemeanours, and Donne and Thomas Haynes 'for transportacion'. The calendar for 12 March 1669 notes that Donne and Thomas Haynes were 'convicted upon the late statute for conventicles, and ordered banishment'.[10] Thomas Cooper and Samuel Fenne were also in the county gaol in 1669, having received sentences of six months for teaching at a conventicle.[11]

By the time the 1669 calendar was formulated, the 1664 Conventicle Act (16 Car. II, c. 4) had lapsed.[12] Gilbert Sheldon, archbishop of Canterbury, who followed a hard line toward Protestant Dissenters and Catholics, had ordered an inquiry in 1665 to determine the whereabouts of Nonconformist clergy, and now in 1669 ordered another to obtain information about Nonconformist meetings. Parliament had been in recess since 9 May 1668 and did not reassemble until 19 October 1669. At that time the House of Commons was primarily concerned with its privileges and displayed an inclination to investigate financial administration and consider impeachment. Consequently Charles II prorogued Parliament on 11 December before a new act governing conventicles could be framed. Not until 1670 did Parliament pass 'An Act to Prevent and Suppress Seditious Conventicles' (22 Car. II, c. 1), which repeated the main provisions of the 1664 Act but stiffened the penalties. A preacher faced a fine of £20 for a first offence and £40 for subsequent offences, and his congregation could be forced to pay if he could not. Allowing a conventicle to meet on one's premises could bring a fine of £20, whereas simple attendance entailed a fine of 5s. for the first offence and 10s. for subsequent infractions. In all cases, inability to pay meant

8. DWL Rix MSS 38.111, fols. 23, 25; *CR*, s.v.
9. DWL Turner MSS 89.18, Bedfordshire, fol. 31.
10. Wigfield, pp. 171–72.
11. Turner, i, p. 63.
12. See *CSPD 1668–1669*, pp. 256–57.

assessing the congregation. The act was especially infamous because it rewarded informers.

The Bedford congregation soon felt the impact of this law, the implementation of which brought more key men into close contact with Bunyan in the county gaol. On 15 May 1670 the Bedford church gathered at the home of the haberdasher John Fenne, where the shoemaker Nehemiah Coxe delivered the sermon. When informers reported the conventicle, William Foster, justice of the peace, issued a warrant for the arrest of the offenders. Nearly thirty people were apprehended at Fenne's house and fined. Coxe went to prison for criticizing the Church of England, 'then occasioned by the discourse of Mr. Foster'. When the conventiclers assembled again on Sunday, the fines were doubled. Several of those who were punished would play an important role in Bunyan's plans in 1672. They are the heelmaker Thomas Cooper (fined 40s.), the blacksmith Edward Isaac (fined 40s.), John Fenne (fined £5), Josiah Ruffhead (fined £3), and the haberdasher Samuel Fenne (fined £5).[13] The latter had been accused the previous year of 'intending to incite and move rebellion and sedition in this realm of England' after asserting that the king 'is not Governour of the Church of England'.[14]

Thus by the time of his release in 1672, Bunyan had numbered among his fellow prisoners at least nine men who would play significant roles in Nonconformist activities in the 1670s. They were John Wright, William Man, William Wheeler, John Donne, Simon Haynes, Nehemiah Coxe, Thomas Cooper, Samuel Fenne, and John Fenne (who was in prison with Bunyan in 1672).

Temporary relief from persecution came when Charles issued his Declaration of Indulgence on 15 March 1672. This prompted the Quaker George Whitehead to write to the king, seeking the release of imprisoned Friends. With two fellow Quakers he appeared before Charles and his council to state their case. Charles acquiesced, and a warrant was issued for the release of the Quakers in the Reading gaol. The sheriffs then received orders to provide the government with a list of all incarcerated Friends. The lord keeper submitted his report to the Council on 8 May, and an order was issued promising pardon to all Friends imprisoned for offences committed solely against the king.[15] Some 480 Quakers obtained pardons. According to Whitehead, solicitors for other Dissenters contacted him for advice on how their

13. *A True and Impartial Narrative of Some Illegal and Arbitrary Proceedings . . . in or near the Town of Bedford* (1670), pp. 3, 6–9.
14. Cited in Wigfield, p. 179.
15. Frank Bate, *The Declaration of Indulgence, 1672* (London, 1908), p. 100.

clients 'might be discharged with ours, and have their Names in the same Instrument; . . . I advised them to Petition the King, (with the Names of the Prisoners in it) for his Warrant, to have them inserted in the same Patent with the Quakers, which accordingly they did petition for, and obtain'.[16]

Conservatives were dismayed at the result. Sir John Reresby, normally a supporter of court interests, observed that the Declaration

> caused great uneasiness, not only in the houses of parliament . . . but throughout the whole kingdom; and was the most violent blow that had been given to the church of England from the day of the restoration. All sectaries now publicly repaired to their meetings and conventicles; nor could all the laws afterwards, and the most rigorous execution of them, ever suppress these separatists, or bring them to due conformity.[17]

John Evelyn remarked that as a result of the Declaration 'Papists and swarms of Sectaries [are] now boldly shewing themselves in their publiq meetings'. Evelyn insisted that he personally preferred 'some relaxations . . . discreetly limited, but to let go the reines in this manner, and then to imagine they could take them up againe as easily, was a false politiq and greatly destructive'.[18]

The royal pardon granted in September 1672 included Bunyan's name, and he quickly assumed a position of leadership among Evelyn's swarming sectaries. Evidence of that leadership as well as the organizational planning that occurred in the Bedford gaol is reflected in the May 1672 application for licences to preach and places to meet. The application is in the handwriting of either Bunyan or Thomas Taylor, a London tobacco merchant who served as an agent for many Nonconformists.[19] The names of Bunyan's fellow prisoners are on the application: John Wright, John Donne, William Man, Nehemiah Coxe, Thomas Cooper, John Fenne, and Samuel Fenne. George Farr is not, nor are Thomas Haynes and Samuel Haynes, though the latter was licensed to preach at Bendhurst (Bolnhurst?). A careful scrutiny of the names on the Bunyan-Taylor application reveals the general outline of the Nonconformist circle in which Bunyan was closely involved in the years after 1672.

16. Whitehead, *The Christian Progress*, pp. 350–59.

17. Sir John Reresby, *Memoirs & Travels*, ed. Albert Ivatt (London, 1904), p. 150.

18. *Diary of John Evelyn*, ed. William Bray (London, 1906), ii, p. 276 (entry for 12 March 1672).

19. Reproduced in Brown, between pp. 216–17.

The names on the application represent five churches — Keysoe, Cranfield, Bedford, Stevington, and Newport Pagnell — and their associated meetings in surrounding villages. Heading the list is John Donne, who applied to teach at his house and that of George Fowler in Keysoe. This was not part of the scattered Bedford congregation but a separate church, founded in 1652.[20] The episcopal returns of 1669 indicate the presence of approximately a hundred Independents and Quakers at Keysoe, being persons of allegedly 'meanest Quality'. Six men appear as heads and teachers of the Congregationalists, including the dyer George Fowler, at whose house the conventicle met, the dairyman Nathaniel Alcock, and a husbandman from Bolnhurst.[21] The entry in the returns for the latter village (south of Keysoe) refers to Donne, the ejected rector of Pertenhall: 'upon the Kings returne, he was apprehended teaching att a Conventicle by William Foster Esquire a Justice of peace . . . [and] committed to the goale att Bedford, where he should still remaine[; he has] . . . received his tryall upon the Statut for Banishment of Conventiclers, & [stands] Convicted thereof[.] He usually preaches at his house in Keysoe'.[22] Donne obtained his release from the Bedford gaol in 1672. His colleague on the 1672 application, George Fowler, had received the authority to preach from the Keysoe church seven years after its founding in 1652. The Keysoe church book records that on 30 March 1659 'Brother Fowler shall have the approbation of this Society to speak the word as occasion shall be offered, provided that this extend nott to a totall setting him apart to the work of the Ministery'.[23]

The activities of the Keysoe church are further reflected in the application of Nathaniel Alcock to teach at Ford End. The church book has this entry for 26 April 1659: 'Itt was agreed uppon that brother Nathaniel Alcock should have liberty to exercise that guift that God hath given him to speak the Word of God as he may have occasion'.[24] Alcock's inclusion with Fowler and others as a leader of the Keysoe Congregationalists in 1669 has already been noted.

Two names near the end of the application reflect the activity of the Keysoe church in the area around the Huntingdonshire border. Fowler sought a licence to teach at Upthorpe, and another member of

20. For its history see H. G. Tibbutt, *Keysoe Brook End and Keysoe Row Baptist Churches* (Keysoe, 1959).

21. Turner, i, p. 66.

22. Ibid., i, p. 65.

23. H. G. Tibbutt, ed., *Some Early Nonconformist Church Books* (Publications of the Bedfordshire Historical Record Society, vol. 51, 1972), p. 20; Tibbutt, *Keysoe Brook End*, pp. 8–9.

24. Tibbutt, *Nonconformist Church Books*, p. 20.

the Keysoe congregation applied to teach at Wonditch in the parish of Kimbolton.[25]

The second church represented on the application was that at Cranfield. Thomas Kent requested a licence to teach at Cranfield, southwest of Bedford, and William Jarvis applied to preach at Ridgmont (near Woburn) and Cranfield. The 1669 episcopal returns record the presence of about twenty Independents at Cranfield under the leadership of John Gibbs and the weaver William Jarvis of Ridgmont.[26] Kent was later associated with Gibbs at Newport Pagnell; the two were co-signers of a letter to the Bedford church in 1695 .regarding the temporary communion of a Newport Pagnell member with the Bedford congregation.[27] The Cranfield church, like that in Keysoe, was separate from the Bedford congregation.

In 1672 the church at Bedford requested more licences than any of the other four churches on the Bunyan-Taylor application. Bunyan himself applied for a licence to preach at Josiah Ruffhead's barn in Bedford. Edward Isaac, who like Ruffhead had been fined for attending a conventicle in 1670, sought a licence to teach at Goldington, east of Bedford. Isaac, a blacksmith, had only been a member in the Bedford church since October 1668 and was later called to the ministry at the same church meeting (on 21 December 1671) that appointed Bunyan pastor.[28] Gilbert Ashley, at whose house Isaac was to preach, was a man of local importance who could issue copper tokens in his own name, and who married Elizabeth, Bunyan's second daughter, in 1677.[29]

Thomas Cooper, the heelmaker, had joined the Bedford church in 1661.[30] Cooper, Thomas Honylove, John Fenne, and Samuel Fenne appear in the 1669 returns as the teachers of the approximately thirty 'Anabaptists' of the 'Meanest sort' in the parish of Bedford St. Paul's, 'the said Samuel Fenne & Thomas Cooper being lately apprehended teaching at a Conventicle by a warrant from William Foster, Esquire, one of His Majestys justices of the peace, & by him & John Gardner, Esquire, one other Justice of the peace, committed to a Goal for 6 months where they now remaine'.[31] The Bedford church had called Cooper to the ministry at the same time as Isaac in December 1671;

25. Ibid.
26. Turner, i, p. 68; ii, p. 857.
27. *Minutes*, p. 104.
28. Ibid., pp. 39, 72.
29. Brown, p. 394.
30. *Minutes*, p. 37.
31. Turner, i, p. 63. The term 'Anabaptist' is used in the 1669 returns in an abusive rather than a literal sense.

Cooper subsequently applied for a licence to teach at Oakley, northwest of Bedford.[32] His name was followed on the application by that of John Sewster, who was to teach at Kempston, southwest of Bedford. The selection of Sewster is curious, for as recently as January 1670 the church had delegated Bunyan and William Man to 'reason with Mr. Sewster about his desire of breaking bread with this congregation, without sitting downe as a member with us'.[33]

Another Bedford member, the yeoman John Whiteman, applied to teach at Cardington, southeast of Bedford; Cardington was an active Nonconformist town where the Presbyterians were strong. The 1669 returns report the presence of some fifty 'Anabaptists', of whom the leaders were Samuel Fenne, Sewster, and four men shortly to be introduced — John Waite of Toft, Cambridgeshire; Oliver Scott; Luke Aspin (Astwood?); and Edward Dent of Gamlingay, Cambridgeshire.[34] All of these men appear on the application to teach elsewhere. Whiteman, who was to preach here, had joined the Bedford church in 1657.[35] The church had appointed him, Bunyan, John Burton, and two others to meet with Donne, Wheeler, and Gibbs in 1658 to discuss unity among the respective congregations. Late in 1660 the church made him part of a team to admonish members who had been remiss in attending services, and in 1661 it asked him and a colleague to visit members living at Cardington.[36] When Wheeler declined the Bedford pastorate because his own congregation did not want to relinquish him, the Bedford group chose Whiteman and Samuel Fenne 'for their pastors and elders, to minister the word and ordinances of Jesus Christ to them'.[37] Whiteman continued his occupation as a yeoman after this selection; he died in 1672. Applications were also made for houses in Cardington and Cotton End (south of Cardington), the latter for the home of the noted London minister and friend of Bunyan, George Cokayne.[38]

Another of Bunyan's fellow prisoners, John Fenne, applied for a licence. The haberdasher had been in gaol with Bunyan in 1672, and, with Bunyan, Donne, Thomas Haynes, and Simon Haynes petitioned the crown for release on 8 May 1672. John Fenne had played an active role in the Bedford church from its early days and appears frequently

    32. *Minutes*, p. 72.
    33. Ibid., p. 42.
    34. Turner, i, p. 64.
    35. *Minutes*, p. 27.
    36. Ibid., pp. 31, 36, 38.
    37. Ibid., pp. 38–39.
    38. Turner, ii, p. 855; DWL Turner MSS 89.18, Bedfordshire, fols. 26–28. For Cokayne see *BDBR*, s.v.

in the church records as a signatory of letters. He became a deacon on 21 December 1671.[39] The 1672 application indicated that he would teach at the house of William Man (who had also been imprisoned with Bunyan) at Stagsden, west of Bedford. Fenne's house, however, also received a licence some five months after Ruffhead's barn had been licensed for Bunyan. Fenne's Bedford house was to accommodate the overflow from Ruffhead's barn,[40] thus underscoring the effectiveness of Bunyan's work and lending substance to the charges of Reresby and Evelyn regarding the effects of the Declaration of Indulgence.

Samuel Fenne, John's brother, applied for a licence to preach at Haynes, southeast of Bedford. A well-known Nonconformist in the Bedford area, he had joined the church in 1656, had become a co-pastor with Whiteman in 1663, and had appeared in the 1669 returns as one of the leaders at Bedford. He spent time in prison with Bunyan and served as co-pastor with him from 1671 until his own death in 1681.[41] Fenne had probably provided the organizational leadership to hold the widespread Bedford congregation together in the years between 1660 and 1672.

Another fellow prisoner of Bunyan's, Nehemiah Coxe, appears on the application in connection with Maulden, south of Bedford. Coxe's role at Bedford was brief and stormy. He had joined the church in May 1669 and a year later was preaching when the informers reported his conventicle to William Foster. Coxe's outspokenness got him thrown into prison on that occasion. The Bedford church called him to the work of the ministry in December 1671; he played an active role in the church until 1674, when he confessed to having created divisions in the congregation.[42] He reappears in 1676 when the Petty France church in London ordained him.[43] When Bunyan visited London in the years after 1676 he may have discussed the progress of Nonconformity with Coxe and been introduced to more London clergy through him.

Yet another Bedford member, Edward Dent, applied to teach at Edworth, a village southeast of Bedford and Biggleswade. No one was assigned to Biggleswade, nor were any members admitted from that town between 1670 and 1678 according to the Bedford church book. Yet a licence was issued for a house in Biggleswade, and this place could have been supplied from Edworth or even Cardington. Dent had become a member of the Bedford church in December 1669.[44] The

39. *Minutes*, pp. 71–72.
40. DWL Turner MSS 89.18, Bedfordshire, fols. 23, 23a–e.
41. *Minutes*, pp. 23, 38–39, 86.
42. Ibid., pp. 40, 72–73, 75–77.
43. W. T. Whitley, *The Baptists of London, 1612–1928* [London, 1928], p. 105.
44. DWL Turner MSS 89.18, Bedfordshire, fol. 41.

1669 returns indicate that he was active as a leader at both Cardington and Gamlingay, where he lived. The Bedford congregation called him to the ministry in December 1671, but he subsequently appears in the church records as a disciplinary case because of financial problems. The church withdrew communion from him in 1677 but forgave him in March of the following year. His name does not reappear in the church book until 1690.[45]

John Wright, a saddler and another of Bunyan's prison colleagues, applied to teach at Blunham, midway between Bedford and Gamlingay, where meetings of the Bedford church were sometimes held. Yet in the years between 1670 and 1678 people joined the Bedford church from twenty-six towns and villages in the area, though Blunham was not one of them. According to the 1669 returns Wright's congregation numbered about fifty 'Anabaptists'.[46] Apparently, therefore, major omissions exist in the Bedford records.

The 1672 application also indicates that the Bedford church was active at Gamlingay, where Luke Astwood sought a licence to teach. The 1669 returns indicate the presence of about forty Nonconformists in this village under the leadership of Oliver Scott, malster; Edward Dent, brickmaker; Samuel Smith, schoolmaster; and Luke Astwood, oatmealmaker.[47] Astwood joined the Bedford church at about the same time (December 1669) as Scott and Dent, indicating a major expansion eastward during this period. The Bedford congregation simultaneously called the three men to the ministry in December 1671.[48]

The yeoman John Waite applied to teach at Toft in Cambridgeshire. Francis Holcroft's gathered church in Cambridge had ejected him, and his acceptance into the Bedford church disrupted friendly relations between the two congregations. Waite was worshipping with the Bedford flock no later than 1670, but he did not become a member until July 1672. The church made him an elder in September of the same year.[49] With William Whitbread and William Man, the church delegated him 'to go to the meeting of the messengers of the adjacent congregations which was appointed at Stadgeden the 29th of this instant [October 1672]'.[50] An indication of Waite's activity at Toft appears in the 1669 returns. At his barn, '50 or 60, but many of them from other places', gathered for worship; of these there were 'more women then men'. The leaders were reportedly Waite; Oliver Scott of

45. *Minutes*, pp. 43, 72, 83, 91; Turner, i, pp. 37, 64.
46. Turner, i, p. 66.
47. Ibid., p. 37.
48. *Minutes*, pp. 43, 72.
49. Ibid., pp. 47–49, 68, 73, 75.
50. Ibid., p. 75.

Gamlingay, who is now listed as a weaver rather than a malster; and John Crooke, 'a Wandring Teacher'.[51]

Oliver Scott, the last member of the Bedford church to appear on the application, sought a licence to preach at Ashwell, Hertfordshire, southeast of Edworth. Scott's activities at Gamlingay and Toft, as reported in the 1669 returns, have been noted, as have his admission to the Bedford church in December 1669 and his call to the ministry by that congregation two years later.[52] The church book indicates that he played an active role in the congregation's affairs in the ensuing years.

Stevington is the fourth church on the Bunyan-Taylor application. Stephen Hawthorne applied to teach at Turvey, a village on the eastern bank of the Ouse. In 1673 Hawthorne became the pastor at nearby Stevington, in which capacity he appears in the Bedford church book as a co-signer of a letter of dismissal to Bedford in 1692. Daniel Negus also signed that letter as a deacon in the Stevington church.[53] He appears on the 1672 application as a teacher at Pavenham.

The 1669 returns report about fifty 'Anabaptists' at Stevington and another forty at Pavenham. The lacemaker John Reade and the yeoman Stephen Hawthorne of Turvey were the leaders at Stevington; the head at Pavenham was Thomas Lovell.[54] Reade died in April 1672, and the application requests a licence for John Allen to teach at the home of Reade's widow in Stevington. Allen's father, also John Allen, had been ejected as curate of Yarmouth, Norfolk, around 1661, and had died of the plague in 1665. The younger Allen also applied for a licence to teach at Radwell, north of Pavenham, but this was denied. Radwell was not included on the Bunyan-Taylor list, and the Bedford church book does not record the admission of any members from this village (though it does from Pavenham) in the years from 1670 to 1678. (Bedford had, of course, been drawing members from Radwell, to which it sent a visitor to deal with local members in 1658.)[57] Allen baptized two men at Stevington in 1674, and in November 1679 the Stevington church appointed him and Daniel Negus 'to teach publickly'.[58] Negus and Allen appear on the Stevington church roll in 1673. According to the Stevington records,

51. Turner, i, p. 37.
52. *Minutes*, pp. 43, 72.
53. Tibbutt, *Nonconformist Church Books*, p. 23; *Minutes*, p. 97.
54. Turner, i, pp. 64–65.
55. *CR*, s.v.
56. DWL Turner MSS 89.18, Bedfordshire, fols. 17–18.
57. *Minutes*, p. 30.
58. Tibbutt, *Nonconformist Church Books*, pp. 28, 30.

Negus was, in 1673, 'by the church chosen and appointed to provide for them bread and wine etc, and to receive that which is theirs, in the stead of brother John Reade who died . . . the fourteenth of the second month, 1672'.[59] The church records subsequently indicate that Negus 'reasumed the office of a deacon' in 1678,[60] possibly indicating that he, like Bunyan, had been in prison in the mid-1670s.

The Stevington church book has few entries for the years 1674 to 1678. Negus and Allen worked closely with Bunyan's congregation for a period before September 1680, when an entry in the Stevington minutes concludes that 'Brother Allen and Brother Negus should leave preaching at Kempston as servants to the Church at Bedford, and that if they would leave it to us, we would endeavour to supply the meeting with preachers'.[61] This entry illustrates how the major churches shared preachers to serve their satellite meetings.

Relations between Stevington and Bedford had been close for several decades. The Stevington church dates from 1655, a year before one of its members received permission to 'breake bread' with the Bedford group 'as the Lord shall give opportunity'.[62] The Bedford church dispatched visitors to its members at Stevington and Oakley as well as Radwell in 1658.[63] In 1669 it sent a letter to the churches at Stevington, Keysoe, and Newport Pagnell regarding disciplinary action against two it its members.[64] By 1673 both Stevington and Bedford appear to have had members at Oakley, Pavenham, and possibly Radwell. Like Bedford, Stevington drew its members from nearby towns and villages, including, in 1673, Milton Ernest, (Upper or Lower) Dean, Felmersham, Turvey, Chellington, and Clapham in Bedfordshire, and Wollaston (on the Bedfordshire border), Brafield on the Green, Hackleton, Horton, and Bozeat in Northamptonshire.[65]

The Northamptonshire aspects of Stevington's work are also reflected in the 1672 list. The Stevington church sought licences for members to teach at Wollaston and at Brafield on the Green, southeast of Northampton. Despite these efforts, a regular Congregationalist church was not established at Wollaston until the late eighteenth century, though Nonconformists preached at Wellingborough, four miles away.[66] Wollaston Nonconformists must have been attracted

   59. Ibid., p. 26.
   60. Ibid., p. 29.
   61. Ibid., pp. 7–8.
   62. *Minutes*, p. 23.
   63. Ibid., p. 30.
   64. Ibid., pp. 64–65.
   65. Tibbutt, *Nonconformist Church Books*, p. 5.
   66. Thomas Coleman, *Memorials of the Independent Churches in Northamptonshire* (1853), pp. 344–45.

to Wellingborough as well as Stevington. Bunyan probably learned of developments in Northamptonshire from one of his publishers, Nathaniel Ponder, who applied for and received a large number of licences for his county in 1672. He may have been connected with the Congregationalist church at Rothwell, northwest of Kettering, where John Ponder was one of the first deacons. Susannah Ponder's house at Rothwell was licensed, and the church's second minister, John Browning (licensed in 1672), married Susannah after the death of his first wife.[67]

The final church on the 1672 application was that at Newport Pagnell, Buckinghamshire. John Gibbs applied to preach at Newport Pagnell, as did another member at Olney. Connections between Newport Pagnell, Olney, and Bedford were close. The 1669 returns for Olney record the presence of 'about 200 [Nonconformists] but [they] Decrease', under the leadership of John Gibbs, William Breeden, and James Rogers, lacebuyers, and John or Samuel Fenne.[68] The Newport Pagnell congregation reportedly consisted of Gibbs' followers, in 'number, uncertain, [and in] qualitie, inferior tradesmen and mechanick people'.[69]

Gibbs was the son of the Bedford cooper, Samuel Gibbs (1647-1684). After receiving his B.A. degree from Sidney Sussex College, Cambridge, the younger Gibbs became vicar of Newport Pagnell. He was probably the J.G. who wrote the preface to Bunyan's early tract, *A Few Sighs from Hell* (1658).[70] His meeting in 1658 with Bunyan, Burton, and Whiteman of Bedford, John Donne of Pertenhall, and William Wheeler of Cranfield to improve relations between these churches has already been mentioned. In March 1660 the Bedford church asked Gibbs, Wheeler, Donne, and Breeden to conduct services while Burton was ill.[71] Gibbs, Wheeler, and Donne met with the Bedford church later the same year to find a successor for Burton. Gibbs was ejected from his Newport living between 24 August 1659 and 16 January 1661 'for refusing the Lord's Supper to the whole Parish'.[72] After his ejection he began preaching in a local barn, where the church met for thirty years, with 'a way of escape for the preacher being made through

67. *CR*, s.v.; Turner, iii, pp. 407ff; F. Ives Cater, *Northamptonshire Nonconformity 250 Years Ago* (Northampton, 1912), pp. 26–27.

68. Turner, i, p. 83.

69. Cited in Frederick W. Bull, 'History of the Independent Church, Newport Pagnell', *Transactions of the Congregational Historical Society* 4 (1909–10): 262.

70. *MW*, i, p. 398.

71. *Minutes*, pp. 31, 35.

72. Cited in Bull, 'History of the Independent Church', p. 260.

the wall at the rear . . . in case the meetings for worship should be interrupted' by government agents.[73]

About 1662 Gibbs founded a mixed church of Congregationalists and Baptists at Olney. In 1662 he, Donne, Wheeler, and Holcroft received invitations to preach periodically at Bedford.[74] Like Bunyan, Gibbs appears to have travelled frequently in the course of his ministerial duties. The 1669 returns indicate that he preached to about twenty Congregationalists at Cranfield and to some fifty or sixty 'meane people' at Newton Blossomville (east of Olney and southwest of Turvey), who were 'such as say they value not His Majesties Clemency a pin'.[75] What Gibbs taught is something of an enigma. He has been depicted as a Catabaptist, namely 'one who holds that baptism should be administered only to converts from Judaism or heathenism, and not to children of Christian parents'.[76] His views on baptism have also been compared to Bunyan's. In view of his close connections with Bunyan, the latter position is probably correct. The terms 'Catabaptist' and 'Anabaptist' were, of course, used primarily as abusive epithets rather than as precise theological terms in this period.[77] In 1672 Gibbs acquired a licence to preach in Newport as a Presbyterian, but he also obtained a licence to preach at Astwood, midway between Bedford and Newport Pagnell, as a Congregationalist. He continued his close relations with Bunyan into the 1680s despite the renewal of persecution in 1682. In 1684, for example, the magistrates fined forty people at Olney for not worshipping according to Anglican rites. To escape such persecution Nonconformists of the area met at Northey Farm, located where Bedfordshire, Buckinghamshire, and Northamptonshire meet. Here Bunyan and Gibbs preached, knowing that if the constables of one county approached they could flee into another.[78]

The 1672 application thus reveals a great deal about Nonconformist activity in Bedfordshire and the surrounding areas. It also provides a good outline of the Nonconformist circles in which Bunyan moved in the 1670s and 1680s. It may additionally indicate more in the way of

73. R. G. Martin, *The Chapel, 1660–1960: The Story of the Congregational Church, Newport Pagnell, Bucks.* (Newport Pagnell, 1961), p. 4.

74. *Minutes*, p. 38.

75. Turner, i, pp. 68, 84.

76. W. Williams, *Concerning the Ministers Ejected in 1662 in North Bucks and North Oxon, and the Conventicles Held Therein in 1669 and 1672* (Aylesbury, 1912), p. 12.

77. Maurice F. Hewett, 'John Gibbs, 1627–1699', *Baptist Quarterly* 3 (1926–27): 320–21.

78. *CR*, s.v.; Bull, 'John Gibbs', *Transactions of the Congregational Historical Society* 10 (1927–29): 81–87; [J.J. Garner], *History of the Congregational Church at Olney* (Olney, Buckinghamshire, 1929), pp. 3–4.

mutual cooperation among key churches of this region than merely 'Bishop' Bunyan's leadership. The 1672 application lists twenty-seven men in twenty-six towns and villages in six counties. These numbers reflect five principal churches: Bedford, Stevington, Keysoe, Newport Pagnell, and Cranfield. Bedford sought approval for teachers for no less than twelve of its satellite meetings: Blunham, Goldington, Oakley, Kempston, Cardington, Stagsden, Haynes, Maulden, Edworth, Gamlingay, Toft, and Ashwell. Stevington applied for licences for four of its satellite meetings: Turvey, Pavenham, Wollaston, and Brafield on the Green. The gathered church at Keysoe requested licences for its branches at Upthorpe, Wonditch, and Ford End. Cranfield sought a licence for its affiliate at Ridgmont, and Newport Pagnell for its branch at Olney. Leading members of at least two of these five key churches — Bedford and Keysoe — had been incarcerated with Bunyan. The leaders of two others — Gibbs of Newport Pagnell and Wheeler of Cranfield — were significantly involved with the Bedford church during Bunyan's imprisonment. Close relations, involving intercommunion, had been established with the fifth church — Stevington — as early as 1656.[79]

What, then, does the 1672 Bunyan-Taylor application reveal? It is evidence of the cooperation of five churches, worked out during years of persecution, to ensure that, when circumstances permitted, organization would be improved and an ample supply of preachers and teachers provided. The case of Bedford is best documented. In 1669 four of the Bedford men on the 1672 application — Coxe, Dent, Astwood, and Scott — joined the church. One — Isaac — had been admitted the preceding year, and another — Waite — though attending by 1670, had to delay until 1672 because of dismissal difficulties with Holcroft's congregation in Cambridge. Even more striking are the figures of admission to the ministry at Bedford in 1671. Bunyan and Samuel Fenne were obviously deep in organizational plans. When Bunyan joined Fenne as co-pastor, Cooper, Isaac, John Fenne, Coxe, Astwood, Dent, and Scott (all of whom are on the 1672 application) were 'solemnely approve[d] . . . and called to the worke of the ministery'.[80] Because of his dismissal problem, Waite could not be admitted to the ministry until the next year. Clearly men such as Bunyan, Samuel Fenne, Donne, Allen, and Gibbs were determined to see that potential government repression in the future did not unduly disrupt Nonconformist activities in this area through loss of leadership.

79. *Minutes*, p. 23.
80. Ibid., p. 72.

The basis for this organizational concept likely lies in the earlier use of visitors to reach church members in the scattered communities. Again Bedford best illustrates this. In March 1658 the church had appointed visitors for Bedford, Elstow, Kempston, Houghton Conquest, Wilshamstead, Cardington, Oakley, Stevington, and Radwell, all in Bedfordshire. The church assigned visitors to the same places, excluding Stevington and Radwell, in May of the same year.[81] In 1661 the congregation determined that 'the severall members of the Church be all visited betwixt this and the next Church meeting, and that the members intrusted with that worke and duty be all present at the next meeting, and give an account of their performance therein'. The places to be visited were Bedford, Cardington, Kempston, Oakley, Wilshamstead, Houghton Conquest, Haynes, Elstow and 'Fensom' (Felmersham?). The visitors 'may as they shall see occasion from what they heare or observe, deale severally with them that they visit, and desire their generall appeareance, if it may be, at the next church meeting'.[82] Effective guidance of (or control over) the members of a far-flung gathered church could be enhanced if, instead of occasional visitors, it appointed teachers for specific localities. Another benefit was the opportunity for more consistent worship on the part of members in outlying areas. Bunyan, Samuel Fenne, Donne, and other Nonconformist prisoners must have weighed these considerations, as well as the availability of sufficient preachers and teachers, in the late 1660s and early 1670s. The Nonconformists in this area improved their organization considerably in 1672 over what it had been in earlier years. This development had a two-fold impact on Bunyan in the years from 1672 to his death in 1688. First, it provided the framework in which he conducted the bulk of his ministerial work. Secondly, it provided him with a group of supporting teachers who carried on pastoral work while he was preaching outside the area or when he was again imprisoned in 1676-77.

The list of members received into the Bedford church between 1670 and 1678 indicates the extent of Bunyan's activities in the 1670s. The congregation drew its members almost entirely from the area to the south and east of Bedford. Pavenham, to the northwest, is an exception. The members admitted in these years range from Eynesbury, Huntingdonshire, to the northeast, near St. Neots; to Madingley and Toft, both near Cambridge; to Morden in Cambridgeshire, Ashwell in Hertfordshire, and Edworth and Southill in Bedfordshire, to the southeast; and to Clophill and Maulden, Bedfordshire,

81. Ibid., p. 30.
82. Ibid., p. 38.

to the south. Lidlington appears, but this is more likely Litlington, Cambridgeshire, because of the location of the church meeting on that occasion. Members also came from such places as Cockayne Hatley in Bedfordshire and possibly from East Hatley or Hatley St. George in Cambridgeshire; and from Potton, Edworth, Haynes, Northill, and Ravensden in Bedfordshire.

The 1672 application confirms that the major thrust of the Bedford church in the 1670s was to the south and east. The Keysoe church covered the area north of Bedford, while the Stevington congregation handled the northwest. The west and southwest were the province of the Newport Pagnell-Olney church, and Cranfield ministered to the area further to the southwest. As a consequence Bunyan, Samuel Fenne, and their Bedford colleagues concentrated on the area to the south and east of Bedford.

The repressive policies of Archbishop Gilbert Sheldon and his Tory-Anglican supporters only served to provoke imprisoned Nonconformists to respond with a more effective organizational plan that strengthened the roots of the movement at the local level. The toleration that finally came on a permanent basis in 1689 was in part an implicit recognition that this organizational response had been successful.

5

Bunyan and Nonconformity in the Midlands
and East Anglia

Before Charles II issued his Declaration of Indulgence on 15 March 1672,[1] Bunyan and fellow Nonconformists from the Bedfordshire area had developed an organizational plan designed to provide an ample supply of preachers and teachers for the dissenting churches at Bedford, Stevington, Keysoe, Cranfield, and Newport Pagnell. The latter four towns ring Bedford to the north and west, leaving a natural sphere for Bunyan's activities to the south and east. With few exceptions, this region, extending to London, occupied his attention on those occasions when he left the northern Bedfordshire area in the course of his ministerial work.

One of these exceptions occurred on 6 October 1672, his first Sunday as a free man, when he preached at Leicester, licensed locally as 'a congregationall person'. The records of the borough of Leicester indicate that he 'shewed his licence to Mr. Maior, Mr. Overing, Mr. Freeman, and Mr. Browne being there present the vi[th] day of October 1672 being Sunday'.[2] Nonconformists obtained licences for only four houses in Leicester in October 1672. Of these, three were Presbyterian, and the fourth was for the house of Nicholas Kestian. Kestian had been ejected from his position as rector at Gumley, near Market Harborough, Leicestershire in 1662, and was preaching at nearby Great Bowden in 1669. He had a licence to minister as a Presbyterian at the house of R. Kestian in Great Bowden in 1672, and apparently as a Congregationalist at his own home in Leicester. Bunyan may have preached at the latter house.[3]

Baptists were also active in Leicester. The 1669 Episcopal Returns list five Baptist teachers in this city, namely William Mugg, William Inge,

---

1. *Documentary Annals of the Reformed Church of England*, ed. Edward Cardwell (Oxford, 1844), ii, pp. 333–37.
2. Cited in Brown, p. 235.
3. *CR*, s.v.

William Wells, William Christian, and Richard Farmer (who also taught at Kilby, Arnesby, and Kibworth).[4] Another Baptist leader in Leicester was the apothecary Richard Coleman, who had served on the Common Council from 1642 to 1654 before becoming a Particular Baptist. After the Restoration Coleman was elected as an alderman, but was briefly imprisoned in 1667 for Nonconformity. When Bunyan visited Leicester Coleman was rich and influential, and 'had been evangelizing as far afield as Watford [Welford, near Naseby?], which he had supplied since 1655, and which he continued to serve till his death about the end of the century'.[5] On 9 December 1672, after Bunyan's visit to Leicester, Baptists applied for a licence to meet at Coleman's house. Given the date of the application Bunyan probably did not preach here, though Coleman's influence might have made it possible.[6]

The enigma of Bunyan's relation with Leicester Nonconformists remains. No evidence indicates that he knew Kestian or Coleman prior to October 1672. The suggestion that Bunyan may have served under Major Ellis with the garrison of Newport Pagnell in their defence of Leicester in May 1645 against Prince Rupert is unlikely because Bunyan was mustered in Major Charles Bolton's company on 27 May 1645.[7] Even if Bunyan was at Leicester in 1645, he would have had to develop ties there in subsequent years, but we have no evidence of this. More likely, a leading Leicester Nonconformist, such as Kestian or Coleman, met Bunyan in the course of their travels between Leicester and London, or in the City. Whatever the case, Bunyan apparently never returned to Leicester after this visit.

The area to the south and east provided a fruitful sphere for Bunyan's work, as membership records in the Bedford church book indicate. Of the sixty-nine licences issued in 1672 for Bedfordshire, sixty were designated Congregational and two Independent, whereas only six were Presbyterian and one was Baptist.[8] As Bunyan ministered in this area he came into contact with other gathered churches in Cambridgeshire, southern Bedfordshire, Hertfordshire, Essex, and Suffolk.

One of these was the gathered church of Francis Holcroft in Cambridge. Holcroft, a native of West Ham, had been ejected in 1662 as the Independent vicar of Bassingbourn, Cambridgeshire,

---

4. Turner, ii, pp. 767, 769.

5. Anon., 'Early Leicester Baptists', *Baptist Quarterly* 1 (April 1922): 76.

6. Turner, i, p. 70; ii, p. 769; 'Early Leicester Baptists', pp. 74–77; Douglas Ashby, *Friar Lane: The Story of Three Hundred Years* (1951), pp. 16–18.

7. 'Early Leicester Baptists', p. 75; Roger Sharrock, in *GA*, p. 133, note to § 13.

8. DWL Turner MSS 89.18, Bedfordshire, fols. 1–2.

and as a fellow of Clare College, Cambridge. He subsequently organized a gathered church in Cambridgeshire with the assistance of Joseph Oddy, a former fellow of Trinity College, Cambridge; Samuel Corbyn, a former conduct of Trinity; and the yeoman John Waite, who later joined the Bedford church. Joseph Williamson obtained information about their activities from informers. The collection of such data was not undertaken consistently, and was dropped by the end of 1663. Nevertheless Williamson did learn that Holcroft 'lyes at Widdow Haukes att Barly in Harfordshire', that he 'hath meetings of 300 at a time', and that he also 'meets with many hundreds at Cambridge'.[9] His assistant, Oddy, reportedly lived at Meldreth, three miles northeast of Royston, where 'convencions of many hundreds both Independents & Baptists' gathered. Oddy and another of Holcroft's assistants, Thomas Lock, took turns riding around Hertfordshire, Cambridgeshire, and Bedfordshire 'to gather concorse of people to their meetings'.[10] Lock specifically called in 'Harfordshire, Cambridgeshire at Hitchkin [Hitchin] & Pauls Wallden [southeast of Stevenage], and at Bedford, at Shefford, & Romney'.[11]

Holcroft's sphere of activity centred at Cambridge but extended to southern Huntingdonshire in the north and the northern half of Hertfordshire in the south.[12] He was often incarcerated in Cambridge Castle between 1663 and 1685, though, like Bunyan, he periodically made brief forays from prison to preach. His position was undoubtedly ameliorated by his friendship, dating back to his undergraduate days at Clare College, with John Tillotson.[13] The episcopal returns of 1669 place Holcroft at Cambridge, Oakington, Histon, Over, Willingham, Haddenham (all to the northwest and northeast of Cambridge), and Stow cum Quy, to the east. Like Bunyan, Holcroft had ties with Leicestershire, for the 1669 returns indicate that he preached at Hucklescoate. In 1672 he applied for licences at Cambridge, Meldreth (to the southwest), and Willingham (to the northwest).[14] The absence of licences for other places does not necessarily mean a decline in Nonconformity, for Holcroft's work was especially pronounced in the

---

9. Turner, 'Williamson's Spy Book', *Transactions of the Congregational Historical Society* 5 (1912): 250. For Holcroft, Corbyn, and Oddy see *BDBR*, s.vv.

10. Turner, 'Williamson's Spy Book', p. 245.

11. Ibid., p. 252.

12. Ibid., p. 302.

13. *DNB*, s.v.; *BDBR*, s.v.; Geoffrey F. Nuttall, *Visible Saints: The Congregational Way 1640–1660* (Oxford, 1957), pp. 28–29.

14. Turner, iii, pp. 296–97.

villages of the upper Rhee valley, including not only Meldreth but also nearby Shepreth, Fowlmere, Thriplow, Barrington, and Orwell.[15]

Oddy generally handled the northern Cambridgeshire areas for Holcroft. Nathaniel Bradshaw, rector of Willingham, had prepared the way. When Bradshaw departed in 1667, Oddy left Meldreth to take his place. Samuel Corbyn assisted Oddy at Willingham, and James Day at Oakington. Other Nonconformist meetings gathered at Histon, Cottenham, Landbeach, and Waterbeach.[16]

A more precise indication of Holcroft's activities is provided in the Rawlinson Manuscripts in the Bodleian Library, which contain 'The number of the names of the disciples in the church of Jesus Christ in Cambridge-shire on the 26 of the second Month 1675'. The list is divided into geographical regions.

	Geographical Area	Men	Women
1.	Cambridge, Trumpington, Chesterton, Histon	26	83
2. *N.W.*	Willingham, Over, Houghton (Hunts.)	21	48
3. *N.*	Histon, Cottenham	8	22
4. *N.*	I. of Ely, Somersham, Needingworth (Hunts.)	31	41
5. *N.E.*	Stow cum Quy, Burwell, Snaiwell	8	19
6. *Essex*	Audley End, Elmdon, Debden, Thaxted	15	8
7. *S.*	Ickleton, Chishill, Barley (Herts.)	8	14
8.	Barrington, Orwell, Thriplow, Croydon	34	65
9. *S.W.*	Bassingbourn, Meldreth	27	63

Later in the list, Meldreth ('Mildred') occurs again, with the names of eight women and nine men. The names of one man and one woman also appear in the list under the additional heading of Meldreth and Foxton ('Meld: and Moxten'). Near the end of the list are the names of 'the Saints gathered by our Lord Jesus out of this his Garden to the Heavenly Countrey; with those who dy'd after they made their Confessions before they were added to the Church'. One of these names is that of Samuel Corbyn, minister. The list concludes with the name of a woman from Eversden and a man from Toft. The preponderance of women in Holcroft's congregation parallels that of various other gathered churches, including those at

15. Margaret Spufford, 'The Dissenting Churches in Cambridgeshire from 1660 to 1700', *Proceedings of the Cambridge Antiquarian Society* 61 (1968): 75.
16. Ibid., p. 77.

Bedford, Broadmead Bristol, Fenstanton, and Norwich.[17] Essentially, therefore, the activities of Holcroft, Oddy, and their colleagues in Cambridgeshire paralleled the work of Bunyan, John Donne, and others in Bedfordshire.

Like Bunyan, Holcroft and Oddy engaged in controversy with the Quakers, particularly Samuel Cater (1627-1711), a carpenter from Littleport, near Ely. Cater had been a Baptist, serving as an elder in the Littleport Baptist church (which was associated with Henry Denne, one of Bunyan's friends) by 1655. After James Parnell converted Cater to Quaker tenets, the Baptists excommunicated Cater and his brother Ezekiel in May 1655.[18] Holcroft attacked the Quakers in 1664 in his *Six Sheets Against Friends*, which provoked a reply from the Cambridgeshire Quaker John Aynsloe entitled *A Besome of Truth, to Sweep away the Refuge of Lies* (1664).[19] Not until April 1676 did Holcroft, Oddy, and Cater tangle. In a public dispute at Thriplow, south of Cambridge, Holcroft allegedly argued that 'to affirm that every one is enlightened with the Light of Christ, is Cursed Idolatry'. He accused the Friends of denying 'the Man Christ Jesus, who is now at the Right Hand of his Father in the Highest Heaven' and the doctrine of original sin.[20] Objecting to Cater's account of the debate, Holcroft and Oddy retorted in the *Apostacy of the People Called Quakers* (1676). The inevitable counter-response was Cater's *The Innocent Cleared and the Guilty Made Manifest* (1676), in which he, John Webb, and Jacob Barker offered to dispute again. One of Cater's remarks in this tract possibly referred to Bunyan's early writings against Edward Burrough: 'And to prove us Deceivers, he [Holcroft] tells us of some of his Brethren, he calls Ministers, have

---

17. Bodleian Rawlinson MSS D. 1480, fols. 123–26. Spufford has compared this list of members with the 1674 Hearth Tax. The evidence suggests that Nonconformists in Willingham were essentially from the class of smaller yeomen, not the poor or the rich. At Orwell, on the other hand, Nonconformity spread throughout the social strata, with no relationship between religious views and material prosperity. Orwell was smaller than Willingham and was situated on the clay uplands. Willingham, however, was a pastoral village on the edge of the fens. 'The Social Status of Some Seventeenth-Century Rural Dissenters', *Popular Belief and Practice, Studies in Church History*, viii (Cambridge, 1972), pp. 203–11. For statistics on sex distribution in the sects, see Richard T. Vann, *The Social Development of English Quakerism, 1655–1755* (Cambridge, Mass., 1969), p. 82. Vann's research does not reveal female preponderance among the Friends.

18. Joseph J. Green, 'Biography of Samuel Cater of Littleport in the Isle of Ely' (1914), BL Typescript 10855.g.15., fols. 6–16; *BDBR*, s.v.

19. Joseph Smith, *Bibliotheca Anti-Quakeriana* (London, 1873), p. 233.

20. [Cater], *A Relation of Some of the Most Material Matters That Passed in a Publick Dispute at Thriploe . . . the 15th Day of the 2d Month 1676* [1676], pp. 3, 6.

writ Books against us, which Books have been already answer'd by us, and their dark Works detected'.[21] Cater attacked Thomas Hicks' *A Dialogue Between a Christian and a Quaker* (1673), 'which in Truth and Reality was no such matter, but [Hicks] himself stated what Question he pleased, and answered them how he would'.[22]

With such strikingly parallel interests in the work of the gathered churches and the repudiation of the Quakers, and being neighbouring preachers, as it were, a close relationship between Bunyan and Holcroft was likely. As early as 1662 the Bedford church had invited Holcroft, John Donne of Keysoe, William Wheeler of Cranfield, and John Gibbs of Newport Pagnell to conduct its services.[23] The controversy surrounding John Waite of Toft ultimately ruined these friendly relations. At Toft, in the barn of Daniel Angiers, Bunyan had once preached to the people who organized the Nonconformist church there. By 1669 Waite was a leader of this church. After Holcroft's ejection, Waite, Oddy, Corbyn, and Bard served as elders to minister at Great Eversden. All four men subsequently went to prison, but Waite escaped while Bard left the church. Admonished to return to the congregation, they refused; hence 'the church proceeded against them for theire not ansoerin their call and some other crims that was against them, and they was coot of[f] from the church but some was dissatisfied'.[24]

Waite began associating with the Bedford church, which wrote to Holcroft's congregation on his behalf in 1670.[25] Bedford noted that Waite had been 'cast out' by Cambridge and desired the reasons for this action, especially in view of the past amity between the two churches. In the absence of such reasons, the Bedford congregation indicated that it would continue to have communion with Waite. The reply from Cambridge, which was read at a meeting of the Bedford church in November 1670, accused Waite of being a railer and blasphemer who

21. Cater, *The Innocent Cleared and the Guilty Made Manifest* (1676), p. 9.

22. Ibid., p. 13. Hicks was also attacked by George Whitehead in *The Dipper Plung'd* [1673?] and *The Quakers Plainnes Detecting Fallacy* (1674), by William Penn in *Reason against Railing* (1673) and *The Counterfeit Christian Detected* (1674), and by William Loddington in *The Christian a Quaker* (1674). For Hicks see *BDBR*, s.v. For a broader perspective of Quaker interests in these years, see M. G. F. Bitterman, 'The Early Quaker Literature of Defense', *Church History* 42 (June 1973): 203–28, especially pp. 225–27, where the Quaker concern with prophecy and victory over their enemies is discussed.

23. *Minutes*, p. 38.

24. Cited in Spufford, 'The Dissenting Churches', p. 87.

25. *Minutes*, p. 47.

caused strife and contention in the Cambridge congregation. Holcroft's people were affronted that the Bedford flock would hold communion with such a person.[26] The Bedford church drafted a reply in the same meeting, contending that the charges against Waite were too general and accusing Holcroft of 'attempting to stirre up a jealousye in our members against the faithfulnes of our teachers'.[27] The Cambridge church refused to respond, but Holcroft let it be known that no more letters from Bedford would be read in his congregation. For its part the Bedford church admitted Waite to membership in July 1672, made him an elder two months later, and assigned him to teach at Toft.[28]

The breach between the two churches remained unhealed during Bunyan's lifetime. It also had an impact on Nonconformity at Hitchin, Hertfordshire.[29] Nonconformists were meeting there in the late 1660s, sometimes gathering for services in Wainwood dell, near Preston.[30] Earlier Henry Denne had been one of fifteen 'Orthodox Divines' appointed by Parliament in 1642 to lecture at St. Mary's, Hitchin, but he resigned in 1644 after adopting Baptist convictions. Hitchin Nonconformists disagreed among themselves on baptism, which led to division in the congregation. Holcroft and Waite preached at Hitchin on various occasions,[31] as did the Baptist Thomas Hayward of Kensworth, Hertfordshire. In 1669 the Hitchin group became embroiled in the Waite controversy. They sought advice from two leading Congregationalist divines, John Owen and George Griffith, who had received an account of the incident from Holcroft's messengers. Owen and Griffith judged that Holcroft's people had erred and should receive Waite and Beare into fellowship again. 'Nor do we therefore know any rule of the gospel that will be infringed by your [Hitchin's] continuing to honour Mr. Waite for his work's sake'. The London divines in turn condemned members of Holcroft's church who were travelling throughout Cambridgeshire to denounce Waite, especially since Owen and Griffith had already communicated their

26. Ibid., pp. 48–49, 52–53.

27. Ibid., pp. 54–56.

28. Ibid., pp. 67, 68, 73, 75.

29. When Wilson was dismissed to Hitchin (where Waite had preached) in 1677, a group of Hitchin members 'sought their dismission to Holcroft's church on doctrinal grounds, and later formed a true Independent church in Hitchin'. Spufford, 'The Dissenting Churches', p. 88.

30. Edward Foster, *Brief Outline of the Tilehouse Street Church, Hitchin, with a Few Anecdotes of the Foster Family* (Hitchin, 1856), p. 5.

31. G. E. Evans, *Come Wind, Come Weather: Chronicles of Tilehouse Street Baptist Church, 1669–1969* (London, 1969), pp. 4, 10.

judgment in writing to Holcroft's church. The letter reflects internal dissension and separation at Hitchin: 'As touching those five of your number that dissent and separate themselves from you[r] body, our present advice is that you would be much in prayer for them, carry it in all love, with tenderness towards them'. Owen and Griffith signed the letter 'in the name and by the appointment of several Elders of churches walking in and about London'.[32]

Affection for Waite as well as the varying views of the Hitchin people on baptism must have prompted them to turn to Bedford for leadership. At a meeting on 25 April 1673 the Bedford church considered a request from Hitchin for the services of Nehemiah Coxe, Bunyan's former fellow prisoner. Either the church's refusal to give up Coxe prompted divisive words on his part, or such words persuaded the congregation at Bedford to reject Hitchin's request. In any case, when the Bedford church met at Cotton End on 7 May 1674, Coxe confessed to his wrong doing and Hitchin asked for the services of John Wilson. This meeting took no action on the Hitchin request.[33] Not until 29 March 1677 did Bedford acquiesce.[34] Wilson's induction as the new pastor occurred on 20 April 1678, with representatives from Bedford and London in attendance. Samuel Fenne represented Bedford, but Bunyan was not present. From London came Anthony Palmer, preacher at Pinners' Hall (1669-79); Thomas Kelsey, a surety for Bunyan in 1677 and almost certainly a member of George Cockayne's Independent church in Red Cross Street; and John James.

The month before Wilson's induction, John Donne's Keysoe congregation acted on a matter involving Hitchin. The Keysoe church was willing 'that iff that sentence agst Eliz. Pall be reversed [the offence is not recorded] and Hitchin congregation receive her it will be noe offence to any off us'.[35] The good will of Keysoe must have been welcome, for throughout the 1670s and 1680s Wilson and his flock had difficult times. Wilson was arrested in 1681 (the year the church drew up a covenant) and imprisoned in the Hertford gaol for seven years. The congregation met in a variety of places, including Wainwood dell near Preston, the village green and Widow Heath's cottage at Preston, and John Harper's house at Maydencroft. According to an oral tradition, Bunyan preached in Harper's tithe barn. The Foster brothers (John, Edward, Matthew, Michael, Joseph, and Richard) of

32. *The Correspondence of John Owen (1616–1683): With an Account of His Life and Work*, ed. Peter Toon (London, 1970), pp. 146–48.

33. *Minutes*, pp. 75–77.

34. Ibid., pp. 82–83.

35. DWL Rix MSS 38.111, fol. 31.

that village, who were members of the Hitchin congregation, reportedly aided Wilson while he was imprisoned and allowed Nonconformist clergy to take refuge in their house.[36] John Foster owned a copy of the 1691 edition of Bunyan's popular sermon, *Come, & Welcome, to Jesus Christ*.[37]

The Kensworth Baptist church, whose minister, Thomas Hayward, had preached at Hitchin before Wilson's time, apparently had connections with the Bedford congregation. By July 1675 Hayward's flock numbered 390, with members in Hertfordshire and Bedfordshire. They lived in such places as Preston, St. Albans, Hemel Hempstead, Harpenden, Welwyn, Hitchin, Baldock (near Ashwell, in Bedford's sphere of influence), and Pirton, near the Bedfordshire border.[38] In effect, the Bedford, Cambridge, and Kensworth gathered churches formed a triangle with roughly discernible borders of demarcation. Sending Wilson to Hitchin very nearly created an outpost in a neighbouring congregation's jurisdiction.

If tradition is correct, Bunyan may have antagonized Hayward and his Kensworth congregation when, about 1675, he preached to a group of Luton Nonconformists who had broken away from the Kensworth church. They allegedly met in secret at Dallow Farm to hear Bunyan preach. The farm was not far from Hunsdon House, later called Preston Castle, where the six Foster brothers of the Hitchin church lived.[39] If the tradition that Bunyan preached at Coleman Green in the parish of Sandridge, northeast of St. Albans, is valid, this too would have brought him into Hayward's sphere, for Kensworth members came from Sandridge, St. Albans, Wheathampstead, Welwyn, and Harpenden.

Bunyan also reportedly preached at Bocking, Essex, to the east of Hitchin and Kensworth. The leading Restoration Nonconformist in this area was Samuel Bantoft, who had graduated B.A. (1642) and M.A. (1645) from Jesus College, Cambridge, and had been a fellow there from 1644 to 1650. Bantoft served as vicar of Stebbing, west of Braintree, from 1654 until his ejection in 1662, and subsequently obtained a licence in September 1672 to preach in Braintree as a

36. William Urwick, *Nonconformity in Herts.* (1884), pp. 641, 645, 648–49. Cf. Evans, *Come Wind*, pp. 6–7; H. C. Jenkins, *The Back Street Meeting House: An Account of the Early Days of Independency in Hitchin* (1970), p. 40.

37. Brown, p. 234 n.

38. Urwick, *Nonconformity in Herts.*, pp. 212–13, 217.

39. Brown, pp. 233–34.

Presbyterian.[40] During Charles II's reign a Baptist church also met in this town in Back Lane before moving to Sandford Pond Lane. Tradition has it that Bunyan preached in Bocking, staying with the English and Tabor families.[41] If so, Braintree Nonconformists presumably heard him preach. Bunyan's church sent a letter of dismission to Braintree Nonconformists in 1676 in response to a request for the transfer of Samuel Hensman. The reply indicates either that the letter of request had outlined the tenets of the Braintree church or that knowledge of these beliefs had been acquired in some other way, such as a visit from Bunyan. The letter from Bedford praises the open communion principles of the Braintree church: 'you are not ridged in your principles, but are for communyan with saints by saints'.[42] This would not have been Bantoft's church if he was correctly depicted in 1672 as a Presbyterian, though such designations were sometimes incorrect. Bantoft has been claimed as the founder of the Congregational church at Braintree, and is included in Surman's Index of Congregational Biography.[43] Without further evidence it is impossible to determine whether the Bedford letter went to Bantoft's church or the Baptist congregation.

Another tradition records that Bunyan preached in the house of the Burkitts at Sudbury, Suffolk.[44] The Nonconformist situation in this area does not exclude such a possibility. The Independent movement throughout Suffolk remained reasonably strong after 1662, in part because thirteen of the twenty Congregational ministers continued to work in Suffolk after their ejection.[45] A letter of Edward Reynolds, bishop of Norwich, dated 6 July 1670, notes that the parish church of All Saints, Sudbury, having no minister, 'is made use of by Non-Conformists and Un-Licensed Preachers'.[46] Reynolds stopped this practice, but the Declaration of Indulgence injected new life into

---

40. *CR*, s.v.; *BDBR*, s.v.; DWL Surman's *Index of Congregational Biography (Ministerial), c. 1640–1956*, s.v.; T. W. Davids, *Annals of Evangelical Nonconformity in the County of Essex* (1863), p. 475; Harold Smith, *The Ecclesiastical History of Essex Under the Long Parliament and Commonwealth* (Colchester, [1932]), pp. 361–62.

41. G. Doris Witard, *The History of Braintree Baptist Church, Essex* (1955), pp. 19–20.

42. *Minutes*, p. 82.

43. Frederick West, *A Sketch of the History of Nonconformity in the Neighbourhood of Braintree and Bocking* [1891], p. 12; DWL Surman's *Index*, s.v.

44. Ashley J. Klaiber, *The Story of the Suffolk Baptists* [1931], p. 39.

45. R. Tudor Jones, *Congregationalism in England, 1662–1962* (London, 1962), p. 73.

46. Cited in John Browne, *History of Congregationalism . . . in Norfolk and Suffolk* (1877), p. 444.

Sudbury Nonconformity in 1672. Samuel Blower received a licence as a Congregational minister to teach at a barn in Sudbury.[47] A licence for a Presbyterian meeting was also granted for a local house.[48] Blower became the minister at Castle Hill, Northampton, around 1674 or 1675,[49] and was succeeded at Sudbury by the Congregationalist Samuel Petto, who remained there until his death in 1711. Some light on Petto's activities in Sudbury is shed by allegations made in 1684 against the mayor, John Catesby, who had reportedly allowed Petto to live in the vicarage at All Saints' during the preceding decade.[50] The mayor also purportedly favoured Baptists, Congregationalists, Presbyterians, and Quakers, whose conventicles were attended by strangers as well as local residents.[51] Bunyan probably took advantage of this favourable atmosphere. He of course knew John Owen, who wrote a preface to Petto's *The Difference Between the Old and New Covenant Stated* (1674). Petto was also acquainted with Holcroft and Oddy, for the three were present in 1674 at Bury St. Edmunds for the ordination of Thomas Milway. Petto had commented in 1658 that many Congregational churches in Suffolk included members who entertained doubts about paedobaptism,[52] and thus he would have found kinship with Bunyan on this issue.

The thrust of Bunyan's activities to the southeast culminated in London. His contacts there with such men as Owen, Griffith, Palmer, George Cokayne, Richard Wavel, and Matthew Meade are discussed in Chapter 9.

Because Bedford's sister churches at Stevington, Keysoe, Cranfield, and Newport Pagnell handled the territory to the north and west of Bedford, Bunyan could concentrate his activities to the southeast. Beyond the northern Bedfordshire region, many persons, ranging from the fringes of Cambridgeshire to Suffolk, Essex, Hertfordshire, and London, must have heard the former tinker preach what he felt, what he 'smartingly did feel'.[53]

47. Turner, ii, p. 920; *BDBR*, s.v.
48. Turner, ii, p. 909.
49. DWL Surman's *Index*, s.v.
50. *CR*, s.v.; *BDBR*, s.v.
51. Klaiber, *Suffolk Baptists*, p. 39.
52. Nuttall, *Visible Saints*, pp. 96, 119.
53. *GA*, § 276 (p. 85).

6

The Spirit and the Sword: Bunyan and the Stuart State

'Oh I was as if I was on the Ladder, with the Rope about my neck', Bunyan mused about his early months in the cold cell of a Bedford gaol, comforted only by the thought that his last words on the scaffold might convert another sinner.[1] He was now face to face with the resurrected Stuart state, the earlier demise of which he had probably pondered very little. His military service had been confined to a county garrison at Newport Pagnell rather than the New Model Army, which bore the brunt of the fighting against the royalist forces. Only in the heady days of religious enthusiasm following his conversion did he begin to consider political issues, and then it was almost certainly through the eyes of the Fifth Monarchists, such as John Child, a fellow member of the Bedford gathered church.[2]

Not until 1660 did Bunyan have to confront a government openly hostile to his religious principles, Charles' promise of liberty to tender consciences notwithstanding. Uncertain of their future, the Bedford congregation set apart 12 December as a day of special prayer for the churches and the nation in order that God 'would direct our governors in their meeting together'.[3] Bunyan himself was scheduled to preach a month earlier, on 12 November, to a conventicle at Lower Samsell, though a warrant had already been issued for his arrest. 'Had I been minded to play the coward, I could have escaped' he recalled, but instead he rejected a friend's plea to flee. In a spirit reminiscent of William Strode's defiance when Charles I schemed to arrest leading members of Parliament, Bunyan proclaimed: 'I will not stir. . . . Our cause is good'.[4] He was, in fact, resolved to ascertain what

1. *GA*, § 335; cf. § 333.
2. See chap. 8, infra.
3. *Minutes*, p. 36.
4. 'A Relation of the Imprisonment of Mr. John Bunyan', ad cal. *GA*, p. 105. For Strode see *BDBR*, s.v.

the magistrates could say or do to him, inasmuch as he was convinced that he had done no wrong. Already, perhaps, John Foxe's *Acts and Monuments* was having an impact on him, for he was willing to suffer in God's cause in the expectation of a future reward. A sense of bravado and a determination not to provide a poor example to weaker saints were operative as well: 'I had shewed myself hearty and couragious in my preaching, and had . . . made it my business to encourage others; therefore . . . if I should now run, and make an escape, it will be of a very ill savour in the country'.[5] In short, fidelity to the Gospel outweighed obedience to the state.

But what, precisely, was Bunyan's attitude toward the Stuart government? The answer to this question has been the subject of sharp disagreement among Bunyan specialists. On the one hand, Bunyan's prominent Evangelical disciple and nineteenth-century editor, George Offor, was convinced that in his political views Bunyan was 'a thorough loyalist' and a proponent of 'high monarchial principles'.[6] At the other extreme, William York Tindall has asserted that 'Bunyan cherished a deep and natural hatred of both king and government, like any normal Baptist of the time'.[7] Bunyan proclaimed his loyalty to the monarchy and disavowed sedition, but such statements, Tindall insisted, were required by both expediency and conformity to Baptist practice. Although Particular and General Baptist confessions of faith typically contained articles professing obedience to magistrates, Tindall has pointed to the treasonous activities of such Bunyan acquaintances as Vavasor Powell, Hanserd Knollys, Henry Jessey, and Henry Danvers.[8] To mask his own seditious sentiments, according to Tindall, Bunyan used the oblique techniques of allegory and Biblical exegesis. Such 'indirection relieved his feelings, communicated his ideas to the saints, and hid them from all but the closest scrutiny of the authorities'.[9] Despite the practice of this 'politic duplicity', Tindall argues, Bunyan was telling the truth when he professed his innocence of sedition, for in his mind those who were loyal to God's commands could not simultaneously be guilty of treason.[10]

---

5. 'A Relation', p. 106. The Welsh Independent Vavasor Powell similarly rejected advice to flee after being summoned before the Privy Council. Anon., *The Life and Death of Mr. Vavasor Powell* (London, 1671), p. 131. For Powell see *BDBR*, s.v.

6. Offor, i, p. 732 n.

7. Tindall, p. 137.

8. Ibid., p. 136. For all these men see *BDBR*, s.vv.

9. Tindall, p. 139.

10. Ibid., p. 142.

Most writers have avoided the extremes presented by Offor and Tindall, preferring to skirt the issue of Bunyan's attitude toward the magistrate. John Brown, in a biography that verges on making Bunyan heroic, contented himself with the observation that Bunyan 'was a law-abiding subject, and held it to be his duty to behave himself under the King's government as became a man and a Christian, and if only opportunity were given him he would willingly manifest his loyalty to his prince by word and deed'.[11] Brown provides no hint of sedition or hostility toward monarchy on Bunyan's part, even when he discusses the critical posthumous works, *Of Antichrist, and His Ruine* and *An Exposition of the First Ten Chapters of Genesis*.[12] The leading modern authority on Bunyan, Roger Sharrock, remarked only that he 'remained a staunch and consistent supporter of civil obedience'.[13]

Bunyan's conscious decision to disobey statutory law by addressing a conventicle in November 1660 and consequent imprisonment resulted in a temporary fear of the gallows but no remorse for his defiance. On the contrary, incarceration reinforced his resolve to stand firm for his right to preach. To Justice Francis Wingate's offer to release him if sureties would guarantee his silence, Bunyan retorted: 'I should not leave speaking the word of God' or do anything to 'dishonour my God, and wound my conscience'.[14] For this recalcitrance, some two months after his arrest Sir John Keeling sentenced him to three more months in prison and threatened perpetual banishment if he remained obdurate. Under the law, should Bunyan be found in the realm without a royal licence subsequent to being exiled, he faced the gallows.[15]

In the months that followed, Bunyan commenced the legal studies that are reflected in such later works as *The Advocateship of Jesus Christ*. When Paul Cobb, a well-meaning clerk sent by the justices of the peace, visited him in prison in a futile attempt to persuade him to capitulate, Bunyan lectured him on jurisprudence: 'I conceive that that law by which I am in prison at this time, doth not reach or condemn, either me, or the meetings which I do frequent: That law was made against those, that being designed to do evil in their meetings, make

---

11. Brown, p. 146.
12. Cf. the similar silence of Monica Furlong, *Puritan's Progress: A Study of John Bunyan* (London, 1975).
13. Sharrock, in *GA*, p. 161.
14. 'Relation', pp. 107, 109.
15. Ibid., p. 118.

the exercise of religion their pretence to cover their wickedness'.[16]

The act in question, 35 Elizabeth I, c. 1, he insisted, did not ban private meetings solely for the purpose of worship. Nor would he accept Cobb's attempt to refute that argument by associating it with the recent abortive rising of Thomas Venner and his Fifth Monarchist disciples. Bunyan's apparent earlier attraction to the Fifth Monarchists notwithstanding, he joined most religious radicals in prudently disavowing the insurrection. Moreover, he pointedly underscored his loyalty to the state: 'I look upon it as my duty to behave myself under the King's government, both as becomes a man and a Christian; and if an occasion was offered me, I should willingly manifest my loyalty to my Prince, both by word and deed'.[17] But such a profession of loyalty did not bear the same meaning for Bunyan as it did for Cobb and his associates. To Bunyan, loyalty to the prince was predicated on prior fidelity to God's precepts, which included the exercise of such divinely bestowed gifts as preaching.[18]

In defending his position, Bunyan cited three authorities: Scripture, statute, and John Wyclif (as quoted in the *Acts and Monuments*). Willingly, he embraced the Pauline doctrine of obedience to the higher powers as divinely ordained (Rom. 13:1–7), but he was also quick to point out that Jesus and Paul had suffered at the hands of magistrates even while accepting this 'ordinance'. The crucial key was in distinguishing the two forms of obedience: 'The one to do that which I in my conscience do believe that I am bound to do, actively; and where I cannot obey actively, there I am willing to lie down and to suffer what they shall do unto me'.[19] Here, then, is a clear affirmation

---

16. Ibid., pp. 119–20. A letter from Cobb to Roger Kenyon, dated 10 December 1670, has apparently not been noticed by Bunyan scholars: 'One Benyon was indicted upon the Statute of 35 Elizabeth, for being at a Conventicle. He was in prison, and was brought into Court and the indictment read to him; and because he refused to plead to it, the Court ordered me to record his confession, and he hath lain in prison upon that conviction, ever since Christmas Sessions, 12 Chas. II. And my Lord Chief Justice Keelinge was then upon the Bench, and gave the rule, and had the like, a year ago, against others. Benyon hath petitioned all the Judges of Assize, as they came [on] the Circuit, but could never be released. And truly, I think it but reasonable that if any one do appear, and afterwards will not plead, but that you should take judgment by *nihil dicit*, or confession'. *Historical Manuscripts Commission* 35, *Fourteenth Report*, Appendix, Part IV, p. 86. This is definitive proof that Bunyan was not released and rearrested in 1666.

17. 'Relation', p. 120.

18. Ibid., p. 122.

19. Ibid., pp. 124–25.

of the classic doctrine of passive resistance, as espoused, for example, by Martin Luther.[20]

Bunyan used statute too in his defence. Displaying a remarkable degree of sophistication in a person of his modest educational background, he distinguished between the letter of the law and the intent of its makers. 'I would not entertain so much uncharitableness of that parliament in the 35th of *Elizabeth*, or of the Queen herself, as to think they did by that law intend the oppressing of any of God's ordinances, or the interrupting [of] any in the way of God.'[21] The statute itself, he pointed out, concerned only those who used religion to cloak incendiary designs. By way of substantiation, he deftly quoted the crucial clause of the Elizabethan act, which singled out meetings held 'under colour or pretence of religion'.[22]

Finally, Bunyan turned to Wyclif for support. Although there is no evidence that he had ever read Wyclif's writings or subsequent Lollard literature, he knew Wyclif's story from Foxe's account. To Cobb's plea that he forbear preaching at least for the immediate future, Bunyan responded: '*Wickliffe* saith, that he which leaveth off preaching and hearing of the word of God for fear of excommunication of men, he is already excommunicated of God, and shall in the day of judgment be counted a traitor to Christ'.[23]

During the exchange with Cobb, Bunyan offered a revealing insight into his views about the critical issue of the nature of government. As Christopher Hill has pointed out, the influence of the radical tradition was greater on Bunyan than was his impact on it, and one might therefore expect to find him espousing republican ideology.[24] After all, many soldiers who fought on the parliamentary side in the civil war, as Richard Baxter observed, were persuaded 'sometimes for State Democracy'.[25] The Presbyterian Robert Baillie generalized —

20. Bunyan did not accept the view of active resistance previously espoused by such British Protestants as John Ponet, John Knox, Christopher Goodman, and John Milton. See Richard L. Greaves, *Theology and Revolution in the Scottish Reformation: Studies in the Thought of John Knox* (Grand Rapids, Mich., 1980), chap. 7.

21. 'Relation', p. 121.

22. Ibid. See *The Statutes of the Realm* (London, 1819), vol. iv, pt. 2, pp. 841–43. The actual words of the statute are 'under colour or pretence of any exercise of Religion'. The statute was clearly intended 'for the preventinge and avoydinge of suche great inconvenyence and perills as might happen and growe by the wicked and daungerous practises of seditious sectaries and disloyall persons'. Bunyan's understanding of the statute was correct.

23. 'Relation', p. 122.

24. Christopher Hill, *The World Turned Upside Down: Radical Ideas During the English Revolution* (New York, 1973), p. 328.

25. *Rel. Bax.*, bk. 1, pt. 1, § 77 (p. 53).

inaccurately — that sectaries sought the liberty to overthrow all kings and parliaments, and in their place to 'set up . . . the whole multitude, in the Throne of absolute Soveraignty'.[26] The more extreme radicals did, in fact, oppose monarchy as the tool of the priests and the rich.[27] A pronounced anti-monarchical bent existed in the Fifth Monarchy tradition, as the saints called for action to topple sovereigns preparatory to the rule of the godly. John Tillinghast boldly proclaimed that 'the overthrowing [of] the Thrones of the kings, is to be performed by the Saints', in whose hands both civilian and military power must reside.[28] Such was the ideological environment in which Bunyan began to formulate his concept of government.

Rather than embracing republican tenets, Bunyan steered an indifferent course. To Cobb he said: 'I did look upon myself as bound in conscience to walk according to all righteous laws, *and that whether there was a King or no*'.[29] In other words, the precise form of government was of no immediate consequence to Bunyan, though he would later criticize absolute monarchy. His basic indifference reflects the influence of certain strains of the radical tradition, though clearly not the republicans, Levellers, or Diggers. Like Baxter, Bunyan was convinced that all forms of governing power originated with God, and he would probably have embraced Baxter's thesis that God did not prescribe a single polity.[30] 'The reason why God did not Universally by his Law tye all the World to One forme of Government', Baxter asserted, 'is because the difference of persons, times, places, neighbours, &c. may make one forme best to one people, and at one time, and place, that is worst to another.'[31] Whereas Bunyan was presumably content to let

26. Robert Baillie, epistle to *Anabaptism, the True Fountaine of Independency, Antinomy, Brownisme, Familisme* (London, 1647).

27. Cf., e.g., anon., *Light Shining in Buckingham-shire* (n.p., 1648), reprinted in *The Works of Gerrard Winstanley*, ed. George H. Sabine (New York, 1965), p. 615. In a far more radical vein than Bunyan would accept, another anonymous radical asserted that 'God gave the office of a King in his wrath, and . . . Kings and Priests are Jewish ceremonies'. *Tyranipocrit, Discovered with His Wiles, Wherewith He Vanquisheth* (Rotterdam, 1649), p. 3.

28. John Tillinghast, *Mr. John Tillinghasts Eight Last Sermons* (London, 1655), p. 68. For a summary of Fifth Monarchist political views, see B. S. Capp, *The Fifth Monarchy Men: A Study in Seventeenth-Century Millenarianism* (London, 1972), pp. 50–55, 151–52.

29. 'Relation', p. 124 (my italics).

30. Richard Baxter, *A Holy Commonwealth, or Political Aphorisms, Opening the True Principles of Government* (London, 1659), pp. 121, 127. In 1667 John Owen pleaded that 'we have no form of government, *civil or ecclesiastical*, to impose on the nation'. *The Works of John Owen*, ed. William H. Goold, 16 vols. (London, 1850–53), xiii, p. 549.

31. Baxter, *Holy Commonwealth*, p. 78.

the matter rest at this point, Baxter argued stringently that monarchy is the best form of polity because it corresponds the closest to nature.[32] The leading Arminian Independent, John Goodwin, was another who postulated that monarchy, aristocracy, and democracy were all divinely bestowed, 'not any of them determinately, or with exclusion of the rest'.[33]

Despite their theological differences, a statement made by George Fox to Charles II might just as well have come from Bunyan: 'We, for our selves, desire no greater Liberty, either in things Religious, or in things Civil . . . than we desire all others might enjoy: And if such a Government as this be set up, then if he that is Chief in taking care and seeing that Justice may be done to all without respect of persons, if he be called a King, a Judge, a Protector, or General, we shall not be against either or any of the Names'.[34] Though Bunyan did not embrace any single form of government, from the outset he insisted that a Christian must submit to duly-constituted authority, bearing 'patiently the penalty of the law' if in conscience he or she could not obey the dictates of the state.[35]

During his early years in the Bedford county gaol, Bunyan set aside strictly political questions in order to concentrate on the subjects of prayer and Christian suffering. In his apology for extempore prayer, *I will Pray with the Spirit* (*c.* 1662), Bunyan lashed out not at the king or his magistrates but at those doctors of the established church who imposed the Book of Common Prayer, a human invention 'neither commanded nor commended of God'.[36] With obvious personal bitterness, he protested that one who lived peaceably could nevertheless be condemned as seditious simply for refusing, in good conscience, to accept a form of worship that had not been divinely mandated. Silencing ministers and threatening offenders with the gallows or exile was, he claimed, blatantly antichristian persecution.[37]

Having established the context of righteous suffering in his prayer tract, Bunyan reinforced this theme in his *Prison Meditations* (1663). Gaol became a school of Christ in which the elect prepared to die, victims of an ungodly regime.[38]

32. Ibid., pp. 94–95.

33. John Goodwin, *Anti-Cavalierisme, or, Truth Pleading as Well the Necessity, as the Lawfulness of This Present War* (London, [1642]), p. 7.

34. George Fox, *A Collection of the Several Books and Writings*, 2nd ed. (London, 1665), p. 118.

35. 'Relation', p. 124.

36. *MW*, ii, p. 283.

37. *MW*, ii, pp. 283–85.

38. *MW*, vi, p. 45.

> *Just* thus it is, we suffer here
>   For him a little pain,
> Who, when he doth again appear
>   Will with him let us reign.[39]

Those who quailed before such suffering were exhorted to render the ultimate sacrifice:

> . . . make the *Tree* your stage
>   For Christ *that* King potent.[40]

Bunyan was, in fact, less concerned with Charles II and his secular officials than with those propertied Puritans who had made their peace with the Restoration state.

> When we did walk at liberty,
>   We were deceiv'd by them,
> Who we from hence do clearly see
>   Are vile deceitful Men.
> These Politicians that profest
>   For base and worldly ends,
> Do now appear to us at best
>   But Machivilian Friends.[41]

Hypocrisy had a worse sting than persecution. Betrayal was particularly odious to those such as Bunyan who were embittered by the sudden collapse of the Good Old Cause.

Between 1663 and 1665 Bunyan turned increasingly to millenarian themes, reflecting his apparent earlier attraction to the Fifth Monarchists. The promise that suffering saints would eventually reign with King Jesus was expanded in *One Thing is Needful* (1665) to include an apocalyptic vision of the Last Judgment, replete with a Christ who

> . . . comes with Head as white as Snow;
> With Eyes like flames of fire;
> In Justice clad from top to toe,
> Most glorious in attire.[42]

Those who persecute the saints have cells reserved for them in the great 'Prison with its locks and bars,/Of Gods lasting decree'.[43]

39. *MW*, vi, p. 49.
40. *MW*, vi, p. 50.
41. *MW*, vi, p. 47.
42. *MW*, vi, p. 72.
43. *MW*, vi, p. 93.

Having denied the saints liberty to worship in accord with the dictates of their consciences, the condemned must suffer where

> ... Conscience is the slaughter-shop,
> There hangs the Ax, and Knife,
> 'Tis there the worm makes all things hot.[44]

Although Bunyan clearly had his tormentors in mind when he penned this exercise in apocalyptic vengeance, he wisely refrained from making this explicit.

The millenarian themes are equally in evidence in *The Holy City*, a companion work to *One Thing Is Needful*, published the same year and certainly intended to be read in tandem. This time, however, the tone is quieter, the role of governors more explicit and positive. Bunyan is careful to assure traditional rulers that the holy city, the Gospel church, is not a revolutionary institution posing a threat to their sovereignty. 'The Governours of this World', he wrote, 'need not at all to fear a disturbance from her, or a diminishing of ought they have'. Because the church's interests are not material, '*She will not meddle with their Fields, nor Vineyards, neither will she drink of the water of their Wells*'. Those who charge the church with treason lie, for it is not, nor has it ever been, 'a Rebellious City, and destructive to Kings, and a Diminisher of their Revenues'.[45]

Tindall's contention that Bunyan despised kings is roundly refuted in the pages of *The Holy City*. On the contrary, monarchs are accorded a clear measure of respect: 'The people of the Nations they are but like to single-pence and half-pence, but their Kings like Gold Angels and Twenty-shilling-pieces'.[46] Yet his own knowledge of Charles I and Charles II, coupled with the influence of a radical tradition that depicted kings as the root of tyranny,[47] led him to the provocative conclusion that most rulers were enamoured with 'Mistres *Babylon*, the Mother of Harlots, the Mistres of Witchcrafts, and Abominations of the Earth'. They not only fornicate with her but defend her from 'the Gunshot that the Saints continually will be making at her by the

44. *MW*, vi, p. 94.
45. *MW*, iii, p. 96. For Bunyan's millenarianism, see J. Sears McGee's introduction to *MW*, vol. iii, pp. xxxii–liv; Aileen Macleod Sinton [Ross], 'Millenarianism in the Works of John Bunyan' (Ph.D. diss., University of Alberta, 1986).
46. *MW*, iii, p. 166.
47. Cf. *Light Shining in Buckingham-shire*, p. 613.

force of the Word and Spirit of God'.[48] Bunyan, however, resisted the conclusion that monarchs should be toppled as aiders and abettors of supreme evil. It was simply a matter, he said, that kings were the last to come to Christ, the first being the poor. But their coming was a certainty: 'The Kings must come to *Jerusalem*'.[49]

Victory over temporal sovereigns, however assured, would be a tumultuous business. Although rulers must eventually succumb to grace, this would only happen after an unsuccessful war with the Lamb. Just as Darius, Cyrus, and Artaxerxes assisted Ezra and Nehemiah in reconstructing Jerusalem, so would some monarchs help build the holy city, but 'the great conquest of the Kings will be by the beauty and glory of this City, when she is builded'.[50] Rulers who ultimately refuse to accept the church 'must take what followeth',[51] a harsh fate vividly depicted in *One Thing Is Needful*.

Perhaps the most striking fact about *The Holy City* is Bunyan's refusal to attribute final responsibility for the church's persecution to temporal sovereigns. Instead he laid it at the foot of the Antichrist, the '*Mistres of Iniquity*', who used witchcraft to beguile rulers into vexing the saints.[52] As his own incarceration stretched from months into years, Bunyan sought a deeper meaning for this suffering. The answer lay in the form of an earthly purgatory in which saints were readied for entry into God's presence: 'The Church in the fire of Persecution is like *Esther* in the perfuming Chamber, but making fit for the presence of the King', or like gold 'on which the fire of Persecution and Temptation hath done its full and compleat work'.[53] Through the overarching work of providence, then, rulers who persecuted the church were, in Bunyan's mind, agents of the divine plan, more to be pitied than hated, but never to be violently resisted.

Bunyan's prison writings are straightforward in presenting a doctrine of passive resistance, and no evidence indicates that they were intended as a mask to conceal covert support for insurrection. Between August 1661 and March 1662, Bunyan used the occasional liberty given to him by his gaoler to travel to London. He may have gone solely to procure spiritual guidance from such friends as George Cokayne, John Owen, George Griffith, and Anthony Palmer, or he may have obtained legal advice. His enemies were convinced that he went to the City to 'plot

48. *MW*, iii, p. 167.
49. *MW*, iii, pp. 166–67.
50. *MW*, iii, pp. 166–67.
51. *MW*, iii, p. 97.
52. *MW*, iii, p. 169.
53. *MW*, iii, pp. 139–40.

and raise division, and make insurrection', but Bunyan denied the charge.[54] Cokayne and his associate, Nathaniel Holmes, both avowed millenarians, were preaching to illegal conventicles in this period, and Cokayne was suspected of writing seditious tracts. Palmer, a recent convert to the Fifth Monarchists, was regarded in government circles as one of the 'violent projecting men'. In 1661 he was preaching against the Restoration court, and late the following year the state suspected him of participating in Ensign Thomas Tong's plot to assassinate the king and the dukes of York and Albemarle, seize Windsor Castle, and reinstitute the republic.[55] We have no proof that Bunyan knew of such activities.

In the years that followed, Bunyan's imprisonment must have become stricter. His name is not recorded in the Bedford church book between October 1661 and November 1668, but in the latter year the expiration of the 1664 Conventicle Act led to an increase of Nonconformist activity.[56] As a direct consequence, fears of new plots began to spread. From York, a customs collector warned Joseph Williamson in October 1669 that unlawful meetings of Dissenters looked suspiciously like those which had preceded the recent rebellion,[57] while from Coventry another of Williamson's correspondents expressed concern the following month about the growth of conventicles.[58] In May, Williamson had been warned by Daniel Fleming, writing from Westmorland, that the Presbyterians were 'now designing some mischeif'. 'Faction', he cautioned, 'will strike (notwithstanding all their fair and gilded pretences) at the crowne as well as at the miter'.[59] Although there was far more smoke than fire, the concerns were genuine enough. The Bedford church to which Bunyan belonged was caught up in these suspicions, particularly after brother Humphrey Merrill 'began in an obscure way to charge the Church with rebellion'. In an appearance before the quarter sessions no later than September 1669, Merrill recanted the profession of faith he had made to the Bedford church, but he went further by testifying 'that they had their hands in the blood of the king: that they were disobedient to government, and that they were not a church'.[60] These were probably

54. 'Relation', p. 130.
55. *BDBR*, s.vv. Cokayne, Holmes, Palmer, and Tong; Greaves, *DUFE*, pp. 112–29.
56. For the persecution of Bedfordshire Nonconformists in this period, see Wigfield, pp. 167–72.
57. PRO SP 29/266/30.
58. PRO SP 29/267/89.
59. PRO SP 29/260/23.
60. *Minutes*, pp. 41–42.

the emotional reactions of an embittered member or the inventions of a timid soul afraid of the justices before whom he stood. It can hardly be more than coincidence that in the first year of Bunyan's renewed attendance at church meetings, the congregation was accused of treasonable activity. The same year Bunyan's colleague, Samuel Fenne, was blamed for 'intending to incite and move rebellion and sedition in this realm of England', but apparently only because he denied the royal governorship of the Church of England.[61] As we have seen, these were also the years in which Bunyan and the Nonconformists who were imprisoned with him worked out the strategy by which they established a network of preachers in Bedfordshire and the surrounding counties that enabled the Nonconformists to survive later attempts to suppress them.

Released at last in 1672, Bunyan became embroiled almost immediately in a controversy involving one of his favorite themes, church membership and communion. In his initial contribution, *A Confession of My Faith* (1672), which sparked the dispute, he was at pains to insist that nothing in his principles savoured of rebellion or heresy, or was in any way grounds for spending a dozen years in prison, threatened by perpetual exile or hanging. He intended the *Confession* as a vindication of his innocence, and for that reason he reiterated his doctrine of passive disobedience: *'Neither can I in, or by the superstitious inventions of this world, consent that my Soul should be governed, in any of my approaches to God, because commanded to the contrary, and commended for so refusing'*. On this point he would not relent, though professing himself *'at all times a peaceable, and an obedient Subject'*.[62]

Most contemporary sectarian confessions of faith included an article on magistracy, which provided Bunyan with an obvious reason to incorporate such a statement in his confession. A typical article is found in the 1656 Confession of the Western Association of Baptists, one of the leaders of which was Thomas Collier:

> That the ministry of civil justice (being for the praise of them that do well, and punishment of evildoers) is an ordinance of God, and that it is the duty of the saints to be subject thereunto not only for fear, but

61. Wigfield, p. 179. Suspicion that the congregation was engaged in treasonable activity may have been a factor in its persecution in May 1670. See the account in *A True and Impartial Narrative of Some Illegal and Arbitrary Proceedings . . . in and near the Town of Bedford* (n.p., 1670).

62. *MW*, iv, p. 136.

for conscience sake . . . and that for such, prayers and supplications are to be made by the saints.[63]

In a similar fashion Bunyan postulated that magistracy is a divine ordinance, adding that it is a judgment of God to be without magistrates. After quoting Romans 13:2-6, he returned to the theme of passive resistance: 'Many are the mercyes we receive, by a well qualified Magistrate, and if any shall at any time be otherwise inclined, *let us shew our christianity in a patient suffering for well doing, what it shall please God to inflict by them*'.[64]

An illustration of how Bunyan intended this doctrine to be practised appeared in another work published the same year, *A Defence of the Doctrine of Justification by Faith*, a refutation of Edward Fowler's *The Design of Christianity* (1671). Bunyan had no use for the Latitudinarian Fowler, rector of Northill, Bedfordshire, whom he mercilessly castigated as one who could, 'as to Religion, turn and twist like an Eel on the Angle; or rather like the Weather-cock that stands on the Steeple'. Because Fowler had turned his back on the Puritan principles he had espoused in the 1650s, Bunyan found it appropriate to lecture him that obedience to the state does not extend to the point of denying the fundamentals of the faith. The implicit lesson was sufficiently manifest: the turncoat rector should have stood his ground, rejected the demands of the Stuart state to conform, and suffered alongside Bunyan and his confederates.[65]

In the decade that ensued, not even a temporary return to prison in 1676-77 prompted Bunyan to deal with the issue of obedience to the state.[66] Only when Charles II dismissed three successive Parliaments in the epic struggle to exclude the duke of York from the line of succession did Bunyan choose to speak out once more on matters of state. This time he did so through the medium of a complex

63. *Baptist Confessions of Faith*, ed. William L. Lumpkin (Chicago, 1959), p. 215. Cf. the comparable statements in other confessions, pp. 169, 194, 283–84, 331. Owen's view was similar: '*Magistracy we own as the ordinance of God*, and his majesty as the person set over us by his providence in the chief and royal administration thereof. In submission unto him, we profess it our duty to regulate our obedience by the laws and customs over which he presides in the government of these nations'. *Works of Owen*, xiii, p. 548; cf. p. 578. For Collier see *BDBR*, s.v.

64. *MW*, iv, p. 153. Cf. Fox, *A Collection*, p. 120. In contrast, John Goodwin asserted that violent action against the civil authorities was justified when their commands ran counter to the maxims of God. *Anti-Cavalierisme*, pp. 9–10.

65. *MW*, iv, p. 102.

66. Richard L. Greaves, 'The Last Imprisonment of John Bunyan', *Northamptonshire and Bedfordshire Life* 5 (June 1975), 17.

allegory with multiple levels of meaning. Critics who fault Bunyan for undertaking such a technically difficult and ambitious work ought to consider the need for such obliquity. Thanks to *The Pilgrim's Progress*, Bunyan was now an acclaimed author, with his first allegory reaching its eighth edition in the year *The Holy War* (1682) was published. The device of multiple allegory afforded him the opportunity to address several needs at once, ranging from the soul's struggle with evil to the contemporary political crises that boded ill for Nonconformists. The king and his agents had launched their scheme to remodel the corporations, thereby ensuring domination by men whose principles were staunchly Tory and Anglican. In August 1681 the state's decision to hang and quarter Stephen College for his intemperate advocacy of exclusion made him a Whig martyr. His declaration of innocence deliberately evoked memories of the Marian martyrs: 'I earnestly pray mine may be the last Protestant blood that murdering Church of Rome may shed in Christendom and that my death may be a far greater blow to their bloody cause than I could have been by my life'.[67] In these perilous times for the Nonconformists, Bunyan felt it was incumbent to address the major issues.

The political message of *The Holy War* was barely concealed. When Diabolus seized control of the town of Mansoul, he became not mayor but king — a pointed reference to Charles II. If that allusion slipped by, no reader could escape the obvious parallel when Diabolus remodelled the corporation, replacing Lord Understanding, the lord mayor, with Lord Lustings, and Mr. Conscience, the recorder, with Forget-good. Among the new burgesses and aldermen were caricatures of those Tory-Anglicans who were assuming office around the country — Mr. Atheism, Mr. Whoring, Mr. False Peace, and Mr. Haughty. Command of the castles was placed in the hands of new governors, Spite-God, Love-no-light, and Love-flesh.[68] As a former gaolhouse lawyer, Bunyan could not resist having Diabolus 'make havock of all remains of the Laws and Statutes of *Shaddai*, that could be found in the Town of *Mansoul*'. He 'spoiled the old Law Books'.[69] Not only did Diabolus treat Gospel ministers with hostility, but he permitted the town to be filled with atheistic pamphlets as well as obscene ballads and romances. In short, Diabolus was a 'rebellious Tyrant'.[70]

The radical nature of *The Holy War* stems from this attack on the government of Charles II, not from a revolutionary social vision.

67. *CSPD 1680–81*, pp. 416–17.
68. *HW*, pp. 17, 25–26.
69. *HW*, pp. 24, 26.
70. *HW*, pp. 28 (quoted), 30, 40.

Christopher Hill correctly calls attention to the large number of Diabolonian lords and gentlemen in the allegory,[71] but a comparable contingent of aristocrats was in Emanuel's service. In striking contrast to Gerrard Winstanley, who regarded Jesus as 'the greatest, first, and truest Leveller that ever was spoke of in the world', Bunyan made Christ the greatest peer in the kingdom.[72]

Bunyan was not content merely to deplore the ills of Charles' rule in the 1680s, but went on to provide a vision of the godly sovereign. When Emanuel regained control of Mansoul, he imposed 'new Laws, new Officers, new motives, and new ways'. The Diabolonians went to prison (Bunyan's touch of poetic justice), while Lord Understanding and Mr. Knowledge received positions of responsibility. In addition to providing Mansoul with ample ministers of the Gospel, Emanuel bestowed a new and just charter.[73]

During the brighter days of the 1670s, Bunyan depicted the life of the saints as a pilgrimage, but the Popish Plot, the exclusion controversy, Stephen College's execution, and the renewed repression of Nonconformists called for tougher imagery. Thus, *The Holy War* was conceived. Although he remained out of prison, Bunyan returned once more to the theme of persecution and suffering. Because of sin, he said in *A Holy Life* (1683), God had given the saints 'over to the hand of the Enemy' and delivered them 'to the tormentors'.[74] Still, Bunyan resisted a call to arms. Instead he wrote at length about Christian suffering at the hands of the state in a poignant treatise entitled *Seasonable Counsel: or, Advice to Sufferers* (1684).

Setting aside the theme of conflict, Bunyan took up his pen to write once more of passive disobedience. Christians, he acknowledged, are all monarchs, but he was quick to qualify this democratic theme by insisting that each had dominion only over himself or herself. The saints' duty is to mind their own business, attend to their callings, and let the magistrates fulfil their responsibilities. If the rulers are wicked, Christians can do no more than cry to God for deliverance, for all other attempts to secure relief are impermissible. 'Let not talk against Governours, against Powers, against Men in Authority be admitted. ... *Meddle not with those that are given to change*'. The believer must fear God, honour the monarch, and render appropriate

71. Hill, *The World Turned Upside Down*, p. 329.

72. Winstanley, *Works*, p. 386; *HW*, p. 67. The lack of a radical social perspective in *The Holy War* is also underscored by the absence of women in the narrative.

73. *HW*, pp. 85 (quoted), 119–32, 137, 145.

74. *MW*, ix, p. 265.

duty to the magistrates, which entails obeying them and thanking God for their rule.[75]

The positive nature of Christian suffering is critical to the entire discourse. Simply to endure persecution is not enough, for the saint must *actively* suffer for righteousness by willingly accepting affliction instead of sinful action. Rather than rebel, Christians must 'sit still and be quiet, and reverence the ordinance of God: I mean affliction'.[76] Suffering thus becomes an aspect of Christian worship. 'Let us learn like Christians to kiss the Rod, and love it.' Persecution is both providentially determined and a just consequence of sin. 'The rod is fore-determined, because the sin of Gods people is foreseen. . . . Let us not look upon our troubles as if they came from, and were managed only by Hell.'[77] This point is crucial, for it prohibits active rebellion against agents of persecution, the tools of God in the providential administration of suffering for the cleansing and edification of the elect. Only in this context can Bunyan, after more than a dozen years in prison, proclaim that he has 'oft-times stood amazed both at the *mercy* of God, and the *favour* of the Prince towards us; and can give thanks to God for both: and do make it my Prayer to God for the King, and that God will help me with meekness and patience to bear what ever shall befall me for my professed subjection to Christ, by men'.[78]

A deeper understanding of the role of sovereigns and magistrates in the divine scheme reinforced the positive affirmation of suffering. According to Bunyan, God has not only ordained the powers that be, but now orders them as well. They serve as his rod or staff for the ultimate benefit of his people. As his ministers, one of their functions is to execute his wrath on those who commit evil, but they are also his agents even when they persecute the saints. Eventually — and ironically — the elect will be avenged when the persecutors, though divine agents, are punished, but that task is reserved solely to God. In the meantime, Bunyan was convinced that God always kept the rage of the persecutors within the bounds he determined. Every magistrate could therefore be said to render some good to Christians, even if it was only to exercise a purging function.[79] Acceptance of the doctrine of providence was basic to Bunyan's argument: 'Let us take heed of admitting the least thought in our minds of evil, against God, the King, or them that are under him in imploy, because, the cup, the

75. *MW*, x, pp. 33–35, 38–39, 98–100.
76. *MW*, x, pp. 37, 41–43.
77. *MW*, x, pp. 35, 72–73, 96–97.
78. *MW*, x, p. 35.
79. *MW*, x, pp. 33–35, 69–72, 96–97, 100–102.

King, all men, and things are in the hand of God'. Tyrannicide is flatly unacceptable. Bunyan pointed to the story of Abishai in 1 Samuel 26:7-8 as an illustration of a good man who, because of an erroneous conscience, contemplated assassinating a king. One who cannot obey a ruler because of scruples of conscience has no option but to suffer meekly and patiently.[80]

Early in this discourse on Christian suffering, Bunyan went out of his way to signal his quiescent intentions to the masters of the Stuart state.

> I speak not these things, as knowing any that are disaffected to the Government: (for I love to be alone, if not with godly men, in things that are convenient.) But because I appear thus in publick, and know not into whose hands these lines may come, therefore thus I write. I speak it also to shew my Loyalty to the King, and my love to my fellow Subjects: and my desire that all Christians should walk in ways of peace and truth.[81]

In 1684 Bunyan was still in contact with Cokayne, who had been fined for illegal preaching in 1682 and 1683; Palmer had died in 1679 and Owen in 1683. The government fined Griffith for illegal preaching in 1684, two years after a member of his congregation had admitted knowing Richard Goodenough, a suspected Rye House plotter. Another of Bunyan's London associates, the Congregationalist minister Richard Wavel, was frequently arrested in 1683 and 1684, and one of Bunyan's regular printers, Francis Smith, continued to experience legal difficulties in this period.[82] No wonder, then, that Bunyan felt he might be under observation and suspected of complicity in seditious plotting. However, no evidence connects Bunyan with active resistance to the Stuart regime.

The works Bunyan published in the period between 1685 and his death in 1688 contain only scattered references to the themes of magistracy, obedience, and suffering. In his *Discourse upon the Pharisee and the Publicane*, which deals essentially with justification and prayer, Bunyan reiterated his theme that God would avenge the elect against unjust magistrates, judges, and tyrants.[83] He restated the companion

80. *MW*, x, pp. 32, 36 (quoted), 39–40. In the Geneva Bible the note to 1 Samuel 26:9 is careful to explain that the restriction against killing a monarch applies only to a 'private cause: for Jehu slew two Kings at Gods appointment'. Bunyan chose to ignore this.

81. *MW*, x, p. 40.

82. *BDBR*, s.vv. Cokayne, Goodenough, Wavel, and Smith.

83. *MW*, x, p. 113.

notion of suffering in the poetic lines of *A Discourse of the . . . House of God* (1688):

> A Christian for *Religion* must not fight,
> But put up *wrongs*, though he be in the *right*.[84]

The same year Bunyan returned in *Solomon's Temple Spiritualized* to his essentially positive view of kingship. As in *The Holy City*, he thought monarchs would some day be highly impressed with the glory of the church.[85]

Some of Bunyan's most important statements on the state and the role of Christian obedience appear in his posthumous publications, particularly *Of Antichrist, and His Ruine* and *An Exposition of the First Ten Chapters of Genesis*. According to most commentators, he probably composed the posthumous works in the period between 1666 and 1672 or between 1682 and 1688. The former was a period of apparently little literary activity, unless, as is highly likely, Bunyan used this time to write the first part of *The Pilgrim's Progress*. The bitterness of prison life would help to explain the explosively apocalyptic imagery in *Of Antichrist, and His Ruine*, and the obvious political overtones of this work and the commentary on Genesis would account for his reluctance to see them through the press. The commentary, moreover, lay unfinished, perhaps because he was working on it at the time of his release. Yet nothing in the other posthumous works would account for a lengthy delay in publication, and it therefore seems almost certain that all of these works date from the 1680s. But were the critical millenarian tract and the Genesis commentary written in the last years of Charles II's reign, against a background of remodelling and the imposition of Anglican domination, or do they date from James II's reign, with its heightened fear of Popery under a Catholic monarch, but also with two Declarations of Indulgence and an overt attempt to woo the support of Dissenters and offer them positions of authority? Unquestionably, the first part of this period was one of intensified radical activity that included the abortive Rye House plotting and the futile uprisings of Argyll and Monmouth.

The prefatory epistle to *Of Antichrist* contains a profession of loyalty to the king as well as a warning to Christians not to blame temporal authorities, especially monarchs, for the affliction of the church. They 'seldom trouble churches of their own inclinations'.[86] The root cause

---

84. *MW*, vi, p. 302.
85. *MW*, vii, p. 33.
86. Offor, ii, p. 45.

of such vexation, Bunyan averred, was sin. As so often in his writings, he turned to Scripture to substantiate his case. Although the Persian kings had hindered the Jews from building their temple, the Jews treated them tenderly and lovingly, submitting their bodies and goods, enduring affliction, serving them faithfully, and preserving their lives from the hands of assassins. If Persian decrees contravened divine law, the Jews remained loyal to God, 'yet with that tenderness to the king, his crown and dignity, that they could at all times appeal to the righteous God about it'.[87]

Bunyan gave monarchs a distinctive apocalyptic function. The Antichrist could be toppled only by the aid of kings, with the preachers slaying his soul and the sovereigns his body. This role, Bunyan explained, is divinely allotted to monarchs because of the gross abuse inflicted on them by the Antichrist. In undertaking this task, God will strip the rulers of all compassion in order to achieve total destruction. However, certain kings (including Charles II?) are sufficiently bewitched by the Antichrist to stand by him, and thus by divine judgment must be 'left in the dark'. Providentially, other rulers will be enticed away from the Antichrist by God in order that 'he might train them up by the light of the gospel, so that they might be expert, like men of war, to scale her walls, when the king of kings shall give out the commandment to them to do so'.[88] With this return to the imagery of *The Holy War*, Bunyan provided a militancy that is lacking in the quiescent *Seasonable Counsel*, written after *Of Antichrist*. The violent images extend to the destruction of the Antichrist by sword-wielding kings who serve as divine agents to punish evil. The justice of such scourging is appropriate because the Antichrist has 'turned the sword of the magistrate against those that keep God's law' and has made that sword 'the ruin of the good and virtuous, and a protection to the vile and base'.[89]

Deliverance from the Antichrist, Bunyan avowed, is certain but not yet at hand. Before he can be overthrown, 'there will be such ruins brought upon the spirit of Christianity, and the true Christian church state, before the Antichrist is destroyed, that there will for a time scarce be found a Christian spirit, or a true visible living church of Christ in the world'.[90] From the depths of desolation God will call on monarchs and other temporal rulers to deliver the elect from the grasp of the

87. Ibid., ii, p. 73.
88. Ibid., ii, pp. 61 (quoted), 74. In *Of Antichrist* Bunyan refers to the Antichrist as both masculine and feminine.
89. Ibid., ii, pp. 72, 77 (quoted).
90. Ibid., ii, p. 66.

Antichrist. Obviously reflecting the concerns of the Nonconformists with whom he came into contact in the early 1680s, Bunyan repeatedly urged the saints patiently to await the time when the kings would commence their work of deliverance. The task will begin in God's time, and if this does not occur as rapidly as Christians hope, they must, Bunyan exhorted, seek the fault in themselves. 'Know that thou also hast thy cold and chill frames of heart, and sittest still when thou shouldest be up and doing'. Displaying sympathy for rulers, Bunyan reminded his readers that they were responsible for the government of entire kingdoms and additionally were hampered by the presence of flattering Sanballats and Tobiases.[91]

Toward monarchs, then, the saints must be patient and understanding. 'Let the king have verily a place in your hearts, and with heart and mouth give God thanks for him; he is a better saviour of us than we may be aware of, and may have delivered us from more deaths than we can tell how to think'.[92] Perhaps Bunyan was contemplating how favourably Charles II compared to Mary I and Philip II, or perhaps even to Louis XIV. Bunyan insisted that every saint has a responsibility to pray for the king to have a long life, wisdom, an awareness of any conspiracies against him, and the ability to drive evil persons away.[93]

Reflecting on the discourse *Of Antichrist*, Tindall concluded rather skeptically that Bunyan's 'fulsome exculpation' of temporal rulers owed more to prevailing political conditions than to pity or love.[94] After the striking condemnation of Charles II in *The Holy War*, it is indeed difficult to find Bunyan looking upon monarchs positively. Yet *Of Antichrist, and His Ruine* was composed between *The Holy War* and *Seasonable Counsel* (1684), which marks the maturation of Bunyan's doctrine of Christian suffering and a concomitant turning away from the militant imagery of confrontation. Bunyan can thus affirm that 'I do confess myself one of the old-fashion[ed] professors, that covet "to fear God, and honour the king" '.[95]

An Exposition of the First Ten Chapters of Genesis sets such a different tone that Tindall has referred to it as an 'exercise in veiled sedition' and, less provocatively, 'a prophetical allegory of seventeenth-century politics'. Although this characterization has some merit, Tindall incorrectly argues that Bunyan refers unequivocally to kings as tyrants and does not try to conceal the notion of open warfare between saints

91. Ibid., ii, pp. 62, 73, 74 (quoted).
92. Ibid., ii, p. 74; cf. p. 62.
93. Ibid., ii, p. 74.
94. Tindall, p. 135.
95. Offor, ii, p. 74.

and rulers.[96] The crucial passages deal with the accounts of Cain and Nimrod.

To Bunyan, Cain was a destroyer, a curse, a disciple of the devil, and 'a figure of all such as make false and strange delusions'. In contrast to Abel and his descendants, who were destined to be victims of persecution, Cain's posterity became rulers and lords who 'tyranically afflict[ed] and persecute[d]'.[97] When Cain murdered his brother, he was attempting to extirpate all true religion. With apocalyptic overtones, Bunyan even wrote of the great conflict between the armies of the Lamb and of Cain. Here, then, was the perfect occasion for Bunyan to espouse a theory of tyrannicide, but he went no further than to allow the godly to call for divine vengeance on their persecutors. Indeed, he virtually brushed aside tyrants as nuisances: 'Tyrants matter nothing, . . . nor how much they destroy'.[98] Rather than overthrowing them, the Christian must hope for their salvation, bless them while they curse, and pray for them while they persecute. Admittedly, said Bunyan, Satan uses tyrants to threaten and molest the church, but in the face of laws contrary to Christian principles the saints must 'stand their ground, and not . . . shrink like Saul, till God shall send others to take part with them'. Tyrannical persecution serves a useful function by purging the church of carnal predilections.[99]

Like the Seeker William Erbery, Bunyan regarded Nimrod as the instigator of absolute monarchy. Perhaps in company with some of the Baptists, he even viewed Nimrod as a symbol of Charles II, though he may have been thinking of Louis XIV or James II.[100] The Biblical image of Nimrod as a hunter dovetailed nicely with Bunyan's depiction of Nimrod and others of his ilk as persecutors, for 'the life, the blood, the extirpation of the contrary party, is the end of their course of hunting'. Thus Bunyan reminded his audience that subsequent persecutors in Scripture were compared to Nimrod.[101] This interpretation was common enough, being found, for example, in the annotations to the Geneva Bible, which make Nimrod 'a cruel oppressor & tyrant' (Genesis 10:8). 'His tyrannie came into a proverbe

96. Tindall, pp. 134, 141.

97. Offor, ii, pp. 442, 445. The Quakers too saw Cain as the symbol of a persecutor. Tindall, p. 266.

98. Offor, ii, pp. 445, 446 (quoted), 447, 456.

99. Ibid., ii, pp. 437, 445, 456 (quoted), 473.

100. Tindall, p. 266; Offor, ii, p. 497. For Erbery see *BDBR*, s.v.

101. Offor, ii, p. 497. Cf. Edmund Ludlow, *A Voyce from the Watch Tower, Part Five: 1660–1662*, ed. A. B. Worden, Camden Society, 4th Series, vol. 21 (London, 1978), p. 11.

as hated bothe of God and man: for he passed not to commit crueltie even in Gods presence' (Genesis 10:9).

Bunyan took pains to make Nimrod the creator of an iniquitous state religion, reminding Nonconformists of the established church in their own country. In the Biblical account, those who did not accede to Nimrod's religion faced persecution. 'That sin therefore which the other world was drowned for was again revived by this cursed man, even to lord it over the sons of God, and to enforce idolatry and superstition upon them.'[102] First Nimrod and then his followers ostentatiously exalted themselves by utilizing the state church to reinforce their political supremacy. On this point the radical influence on Bunyan is unmistakable: his thesis evokes the old Leveller and Digger assertion that the established clergy are a crucial prop of the monarchy.[103] In sharp contrast to the Levellers and Diggers, however, Bunyan had no interest in pulling up monarchy root and branch.

Despite his basic indifference to constitutional polity, Bunyan sharply criticized absolute monarchy. 'First the tyranny began at Babel itself, where the usurper was seen to sit in his glory'.[104] But Nimrod, the usurper, was, for Bunyan, the founder of absolute monarchy, leaving the inescapable conclusion that absolute kings are tyrants. Nimrod was particularly insidious, in Bunyan's estimation, because he provided an example for inferior rulers to impose their own 'pretended' religion rather than the simplicity of the Gospel. 'Hence note, that what cities, that is, churches soever have been builded by persons that have come from Romish Babel, those builders and cities are to be suspected for such as had their founder and foundation from Babel itself'.[105] Bunyan's direct link between absolute monarchy and Catholicism suggests that the immediate object of his attack in this commentary was James II or Louis XIV, not Charles II, who professed the Roman faith only on his deathbed. If Nimrod is in fact James II, the composition of this work probably followed *Of Antichrist, and His*

102. Offor, ii, p. 497.
103. Offor, ii, p. 498; Winstanley, *Works*, p. 372; *Light Shining in Buckingham-shire*, p. 615.
104. Offor, ii, p. 498. Bunyan appears reluctant to admit openly, as did the Presbyterian Thomas Hall, that tyrants are ordained by God. 'If Tyrants', said Hall, 'were not ordained by God, we must exclude his providence from the greatest part of the world'. According to Hall, tyrants are used by God to punish ungrateful and rebellious people, much as Bunyan said. Implicitly, Bunyan would have to accept God's role in ordaining tyrants. Like Bunyan, Hall repudiates anti-tyrannical risings and calls for obedience as far as a Christian can go in good conscience. Hall, *The Beauty of Magistracy* (London, 1660), pp. 43–44, 46.
105. Offor, ii, p. 498.

Ruine, which had been written prior to the early spring of 1683.[106] Bunyan probably began the commentary in the period from about 1686 to 1688, with his death accounting for its incompletion.

The commentary on Genesis is neither hostile to monarchy per se nor a call to violent action as a means of deposing tyrants. Instead the political thrust of the commentary is directed at absolute monarchs (tyrants) and state churches which persecute those who reject their tenets. With respect to the futility of forcing the ungodly and the godly alike into one ecclesiastical institution, Bunyan mused: 'What laws have been made, what blood hath been shed, what cruelty hath been used, and what flatteries and lies invented, and all to make these two waters and people one?'[107] Bunyan does not hesitate to castigate persecutors, even those who carry on this work in the guise of a reason of state, but nowhere does he call on the saints to rise up and overthrow them.[108]

Several other posthumous works return to themes that appeared in Bunyan's earlier publications. One of the most interesting reflects the dismay manifested in *The Holy War* when Diabolus trampled the statutes of Shaddai. On one level this was a sign of the reprobate's disrespect for divine maxims, but on another it was an attack on the Magna Carta. Bunyan was sarcastic in his criticism of those who had no respect for the common law, regardless of their social status: 'The old laws, which are the Magna Charta, the sole basis of the government of a kingdom, may not be cast away for the pet that is taken by every little gentleman against them'.[109] This contrasts sharply with the view of extreme radicals, such as the Leveller Richard Overton, who referred disdainfully to the Magna Carta as 'a beggerly thing, containing many markes of intollerable bondage'.[110]

Bunyan also expressed respect for the law — and ultimately the

106. See chap. 10, infra.

107. Offor, ii, p. 420. Advocates of a stringently imposed religious uniformity argued in precisely the opposite manner that religious diversity would lead to armed conflict: 'Different Opinions and Practices in matters of Religion ... do naturally improve into contentious *Disputes*; and those Disputes, if not restrain'd, break out into Civil Wars'. Anon., *A Seasonable Discourse Against Comprehension* (London, 1676), p. 10. To this argument, an anonymous Nonconformist, possibly John Humfrey, retorted in 1675 that the Dissenters were obedient to civil authority, though their ultimate loyalty was to God. As Bunyan himself argued, this position, according to the Nonconformist, entailed no 'disloyal or Rebellious Principles'. *The Peaceable Design* ([London], 1675), sig. A4r.

108. Offor, ii, p. 489.

109. Offor, i, p. 600.

110. [Richard Overton], *A Remonstrance of Many Thousand Citizens* ([London?], 1646), p. 15. See *BDBR*, s.v.

monarch — in *Paul's Departure and Crown*. At the head of every statute, Bunyan observed, was the phrase, 'Be it enacted by the King's most excellent Majesty', the intent of which was to make the law respected and glorious. Bunyan understood, too, the general popularity of the monarchy among the masses, for 'we see . . . what power and place the precepts of kings do take in the hearts of their subjects, every one loving and reverencing the statute, because there is the name of the king'. Because of such respect, rebellion was a word that made the world tremble.[111] These are odd statements indeed if Bunyan was the inciter to sedition that Tindall makes him out to be.

Bunyan nevertheless cautioned against placing excessive trust in princes, citing Psalm 118:8-9 and Psalm 146:3. The Stuarts, he hinted, had betrayed such trust in the recent past. In *Israel's Hope Encouraged*, he remarked ruefully that since the discovery of the Popish Plot, 'our days indeed have been days of trouble, . . . for then we began to fear cutting of throats, of being burned in our beds, and of seeing our children dashed in pieces before our eyes'. The proper course of action, he asserted, would have been to trust in God, but instead the people put their faith in Charles II, Parliament, London, good mayors and sheriffs, and anti-papal statutes. From the perspective of the reign of the Catholic James II, Bunyan regarded this trust as misplaced.[112] Yet he refused to call for a political revolution, reminding his readers in *The Saints' Knowledge of Christ's Love* that monarchs had their power from God and exercised it within his restraints. God retains 'the bridle . . . in his own hand, and he giveth reins or check, even as it pleaseth him'. This was always done, Bunyan assured his readers, for the well-being of the elect.[113]

In one of his last works, *The House of the Forest of Lebanon* (1692), Bunyan took the opportunity to refute those who continued to cling to the old Fifth Monarchy idea about instituting the kingdom of God by force.[114] It was '*extravagant*', he insisted, to think of such a kingdom in temporal terms, or that it might be inaugurated by physical weapons. 'I confess my self an alien to these notions, and believe and profess

---

111. Offor, i, p. 732.
112. Offor, i, p. 585.
113. Offor, ii, p. 21.
114. Bunyan's opposition to the more revolutionary Fifth Monarchists was based fundamentally on their use of violent means, not on their threat to magistracy and monarchical polity. In contrast, Thomas Hall condemned the Fifth Monarchists for seeking 'a parity and equality amongst all Christians . . . [with] no Superiours, nor Inferiours, but all fellow-creatures well met'. *The Beauty of Magistracy*, p. 18.

the quite contrary, and look for the coming of Christ to Judgment personally, and 'twixt this and that, for his coming in Spirit, and in the power of his Word to destroy Antichrist, to inform Kings, and so to give quietness to his Church on Earth; which shall assuredly be accomplished, when the reign of the *Beast* . . . is out'.[115]

As for the church, its role in these chiliastic events was not one to alarm the state. A hint of *The Holy War*'s militancy remains, for the church is portrayed as 'God's Tower, or Battery, by which he beateth down Antichrist', but the weapons are only spiritual — the Word of God, whose destructive power is restricted to Satan, sin, and lovers of evil.[116] Perhaps more significantly, Bunyan insisted that this spiritual war is not offensive but defensive. To temporal authorities, the church poses no threat, for the saints 'know their places, and are of a peaceable deportment'.[117] The church has no mission to destroy monarchs, subvert kingdoms, or cause desolation. Christ 'designs the hurt of none: His Kingdom is not of this world, nor doth he covet temporal matters; Let but his wife his Church alone, to enjoy her purchased priviledges [which are concerns of the soul], and all shall be well'. If, however, the saints are afflicted by persecution, those responsible will ultimately be slain by the sword of the Spirit, a threat Bunyan reinforced by quoting Revelation 11:5. Yet the church itself, Bunyan contended, engaged in no sedition.[118]

Throughout his career, excepting only his youthful period of military service (which predated his conversion), Bunyan stood constant in his advocacy of passive disobedience to state decrees that contravened divine precepts. In his judgment he was no more guilty of sedition than were Jesus and Paul, Jeremiah and Daniel.[119] He came closest to treasonable assertions in *The Holy War*, with its striking parallels between Diabolus and Charles II, but nowhere in his writings did he call for Nonconformists to take up arms against a tyrannical Stuart sovereign. Neither is there any evidence to indicate that Bunyan plotted insurrection, the accusations of his enemies notwithstanding. Bunyan was no political revolutionary. Only if his recurring references to persecuting rulers and their ultimate judgment at the hands of God were misinterpreted as a call to rebellion could his views be seditious in their effect. A spirit of militancy was indeed present in works such as

115. *MW*, vii, pp. 172–73.

116. *MW*, vii, p. 167.

117. *MW*, vii, pp. 149–53, 172 (quoted).

118. *MW*, vii, pp. 128–29, 153 (quoted). The note to Rev. 11:5 in the Geneva Bible likewise explains that the killing is 'by Gods worde'.

119. Offor, ii, pp. 19, 465; *MW*, vii, pp. 212–13.

The Holy War and *Of Antichrist, and His Ruine*, but this was a militancy of the spirit, not the sword. Compared to *Seasonable Counsel*, such works reflect the inherent tension embodied in the very concept of passive resistance. While the exhortations to suffer patiently in *Seasonable Counsel* exemplify passivity, so the more militant works encourage the saints to resist the forces of evil, albeit always in the context of a spiritual struggle.

Two things stopped Bunyan from advocating violent action. One was his conviction that temporal authorities always acted as divine agents, no matter how cruelly they persecuted the saints. Tyrannicide was therefore impossible because it was tantamount to an act against God. The other restraining factor was the positive way in which Bunyan conceived of suffering. It was not merely something to be endured but virtually an act of worship, calling for the active participation of the believer through willing acceptance. In the confrontation with the Stuart state, victory was only possible for those who could find 'Joy, under the cross',[120] the spiritual experience of suffering for the right cause in the right way. 'Wherefore, my brethren, my Friends, my enemies, and all men', Bunyan concluded, 'what Religion, Profession, or Opinion soever you hold; Fear God, honour the King, and do that duty to both, which is required of you by the Word and Law of Christ: and then . . . you shall not suffer by the Power for evil-doing'.[121] In the end, the sword would bow to the Spirit.

120. *MW*, x, p. 101.
121. *MW*, x, p. 104.

7

Bunyan and the Changing Face of Popery, 1665–1684

Throughout most of Bunyan's career anti-Catholicism was not a dominant theme in his writings, and the same was probably true of his sermons. To a large degree this was because of the fact that in the aftermath of his conversion he was preoccupied with a substantive dispute against the Quakers — a quarrel that reflected the intense struggle for identity and recruits that was waged among the groups at the sectarian end of the religious continuum. In the 1670s Bunyan's primary opponents were strict Baptists opposed to his open-membership, open-communion principles. As a controversialist, then, Bunyan did not direct his attention to contemporary Catholic authors, nor did the Bedford church have difficulty with members converting to Catholicism. At the personal level, Catholics apparently played little if any role in Bunyan's life. However, anti-Catholicism had been a fundamental part of the Protestant tradition in England since Tudor times, and in Puritan and Nonconformist circles such feelings were often very intense. At two points in Bunyan's career — in the mid-1660s and again in the early 1680s — he launched broad attacks against Catholicism. This essay is especially concerned with the latter period.

In his earliest works Bunyan displayed little interest in Catholics apart from some passing references to persecution that reflected his reading in John Foxe's *Acts and Monuments*.[1] When, in the context of the Restoration, he wrote in defence of extempore prayer against efforts to reimpose the Book of Common Prayer, he made a point of accusing those, including popes and bishops, of 'cursed presumption' who required aspects of worship not ordained by God. He even made an intemperate comparison of English prelates to the Marian bishop, Edmund Bonner (*c.* 1500-1569), 'that blood-red Persecutor'.[2] In the early years Bunyan

1. Cf. *MW*, i, pp. 63, 314, 358.
2. *MW*, ii, pp. 253, 283. Cf. *MW*, p. 314: 'How many souls hath *Bonner* to answer for think you? and several filthy blind Priests?'

primarily thought of Catholics in terms of persecution, an outlook shaped largely by Foxe and shared by other Nonconformists. From his cell in London's Newgate prison in 1663, for instance, the General Baptist John Griffith similarly referred to the 'blood that *Bonner* and the rest of those [Catholics] did spill' in Mary Tudor's reign.[3]

The views of Bunyan and Griffith reflected the fresh fears of Catholicism stirred by the re-establishment of the Episcopalian state church as well as the sweeping ejection of ministers who refused to conform between the Restoration and St. Bartholomew's Day 1662. In his farewell sermon the Congregationalist Samuel Slater cautioned his followers that 'Popish Idolatry' was 'the grossest Idolatry that ever was, because there is the fairest pretence of worshipping JESUS, and yet they turn him into an Idol' by venerating icons and 'breaden gods', an allusion to the detested doctrine of transubstantiation. More ominously, the Presbyterian Edmund Calamy the elder warned of an abundance of priests and Jesuits in England who could easily seduce a people prone 'to run headlong back again to the Garlick and Onions of *Egypt*'. Griffith apparently agreed, for he did not direct the brunt of the attack in his prison meditations against the Anglicans who gaoled him but the Catholics; he devoted a substantial section of his verse to

> . . . a brief Discovery
> Of *Romes* foul filthy stuff and trumpery.

The seriousness with which Nonconformists viewed the Catholic threat is nowhere more apparent than in Richard Baxter's *Fair-Warning*, which set forth no less than twenty-five reasons why Catholics must not be tolerated. In addition to the usual catalogue of alleged Roman errors, such as idolatry, blasphemy, and heresy, Baxter charged Catholicism with infidelity to the Bible, the destruction of civil government, and the seduction of people from 'the great Rule God hath given to live by and be saved'.[4]

Against this background and in the context of imprisonment and mounting fears for his own life, Bunyan first demonstrated substantive interest in Catholicism. This came in the millenarian treatise *The Holy City: or, the New Jerusalem*, first printed in 1665 and probably written in 1664–65. Throughout its pages Bunyan denounced the Roman

---

3. John Griffith, *Some Prison-Meditations and Experiences* (1663), p. 74.

4. Samuel Slater, in *The London-Ministers Legacy to Their Several Congregations*, 2nd ed. (1662), p. 60; Edmund Calamy, *Eli Trembling for Fear of the Ark* (Oxford, 1663), p. 12; Griffith, *Prison-Meditations*, p. 69; Richard Baxter, *Fair-Warning* (London, 1663), *passim* (quotation is from p. 1). For Slater and Calamy see *BDBR*, s.vv.

Antichrist, 'the *Lady of Kingdoms, the Well-favoured Harlot, the Mistres of Witchcrafts and the Abominations of the Earth*'. Despite — or perhaps because of — his personal plight, Bunyan defiantly proclaimed Rome's certain downfall and sarcastically derided its tottering, staggering dominion. Fears for his own execution could only have intensified his memories of earlier martyrs, yet he was optimistic that the holy city — the church — would escape from its captivity under the Antichrist, from 'spiritual *Sodom* and *Egypt*', the infamous era of apostacy. While Bunyan roundly castigated 'the Romish Beasts' for corrupting Apostolic doctrine with their 'dirt and filthiness', he held out hope for the restoration of its pristine purity.[5] In this work he treated Catholicism in a cosmic rather than a controversial context — its significance apocalyptic, its destruction certain, its evil beyond challenge. The pedigree of *The Holy City* extended back into the sixteenth century, but it was also unmistakably the product of the gloomy mid-1660s and deepening state repression.

In the late 1660s Nonconformist hopes for toleration grew, buoyed by the end of the Second Dutch War and thus of suspicion that Nonconformists were collaborators with the enemy, and by the imminent expiration of the 1664 Conventicle Act (1 March 1669, when Charles prorogued Parliament). While conservative Dissenters such as Baxter hoped for comprehension in the state church, others, led by Bunyan's friend John Owen, championed liberty of conscience for Protestants. In January 1668 Samuel Pepys noted in his diary that 'there is a great presumption that there will be a Toleration granted'. The Catholics had been widely blamed for the fire of London, but in general the late 1660s was a period in which anti-Catholic rhetoric cooled. In *The Cure of Church-Divisions*, written around 1668, Baxter sanctioned 'communion' with Catholics who were Christians, though he insisted that the '*Papal Catholick Church*' itself was not a true church but 'a pack of rebels' who had debased Christianity with a multitude of superstitions. He also warned against the papacy's efforts to unify the church, which, he charged, were historically at the root of the divisions in Christendom. Catholicism could not be ignored, but its threat seemed less foreboding. This was certainly Bunyan's view as he expressed it in the first part of *The Pilgrim's Progress*, composed about this time. Bunyan reduced Giant Pope, who at one time had tyrannically dispatched Christians to cruel deaths, to an insane, arthritic, nail-biting hulk who crouched in his cave and

5. *MW*, iii, pp. 72, 79–80, 103–104, 135, 140, 149.

watched pilgrims pass by. Bunyan's focus in this episode, of course, was on the English experience.[6]

Concern with Catholicism again began to mount in the mid-1670s as the prosecution of conventiclers intensified and Charles II's foreign policy increasingly tilted toward France. In 1675 the Presbyterian Nathaniel Vincent and other Dissenting clerics in the London area preached twenty-five sermons against Popery, 'one of the *greatest visible Enemies* that Christ has in the world', in a series of morning lectures at Southwark. One sermon was devoted to the proposition that the pope is the Antichrist, while others refuted the Catholic position on the authority of tradition and the papacy, transubstantiation and the Roman view of the sacraments, the use of images, and salvation by works as well as faith.[7] Bunyan had contacts in Southwark and may have heard some of these lectures.

Probably no book was more influential in inciting the outburst of anti-Catholic rhetoric in the late 1670s and early 1680s than Andrew Marvell's *Account of the Growth of Popery, and Arbitrary Government in England*, which appeared in 1677. This was an especially potent work because its principal concern was not with the traditional theological objections to Catholicism but with an alleged conspiracy to change England's traditional government into an absolute tyranny and its Protestantism into Popery. Marvell derided the latter as no religion in the proper sense but a compound of the most ridiculous and impious elements in Judaism, Islam, and paganism coupled with its own peculiar absurdities. The inflammatory language of the Whig pamphleteer Henry Care contributed to the outburst of anti-Catholic hysteria in 1678. The ordinary priest, he charged, was

> a Ghostly Factor to Retail out his Holiness's braided Wares; a kind of Spiritual *Kidnapper* for Souls: One might take him for a *Conjurer*; for he uses an *unknown* Tongue, transacts most of his Business in *Hugger-mugger*, comes in secretly, and crawls up and down in *Corners*

---

6. *The Diary of Samuel Pepys*, ed. Robert Latham and William Matthews, 9 vols. (Berkeley and Los Angeles, 1970–75), ix, p. 31; Baxter, *The Cure of Church-Divisions* (London, 1670), pp. 83–84, 276; Bunyan, *PP*, p. 65. In his *Defence of the Doctrine of Justification by Faith* (1672), Bunyan compared the views of the Latitudinarian Edward Fowler to those of the Jesuit Edmund Campion (1540–1581).

7. Nathaniel Vincent, et al., *The Morning-Exercise Against Popery* (London, 1675), passim (quotation is on sig. A3r). Cf. John Owen, *A Discourse Concerning the Holy Spirit* (London, 1674), pp. 213, 380; Owen is attacking Catholic ceremonies and confession. John Corbet offered a typical Nonconformist view of transubstantiation in depicting it as 'the giving of Divine Honour to a morsel of Bread; and therefore a most stupid, and stupendious kind of Idolatry' and 'Bread-worship'. *The Remains of the Reverend and Learned Mr. John Corbet* (London, 1684), pp. 191–92.

like a Serpent, and with a few *frightful words*, as *Heresie, Purgatory, Catholick Cause, Infallibility*, and the like, Transforms people as he lists, and *Jilts* them first of their *Wits*, and next of their *Money*: . . . the Plot is upon your *Purse*.

Care castigated the Jesuits as bellwethers of the Roman flock who were devoted to the promotion of rebellion, treason, and murder; whereas other Catholics sported the badge of superstition, that of the Jesuits was sedition and subtlety.[8]

As Jonathan Scott has argued, the Popish threat was not imaginary, particularly in view of the resurgent Catholicism on the continent and in Ireland. Protestant sufferings in France, the German states, and Piedmont sparked concern among English Protestants, who feared a similar fate, especially if Catholic powers mounted an invasion. Charles fed these fears by his alliance with France, and emotions ran exceedingly high following the revelation in late 1678 that he had accepted funds from Louis XIV in return for repeatedly proroguing Parliament. The allegations of Titus Oates and Israel Tong heightened tensions, which must be understood in a European context.[9] But however rational the original concerns about militant Catholicism were, the reaction to the stories of Oates and Tong amounted to hysteria.

The Popish Plot was both a product and an exacerbater of anti-Catholic hostility, which in turn fuelled Whig demands to exclude James, duke of York, from the succession. Writers such as Charles Blount effectively linked Popery and tyranny as they sketched an England ruled by the army and bled by arbitrary taxes. Events as disparate as the Great Fire of London and the 1678 Covenanter rebellion in Scotland were blamed on hapless Catholics. *The Weekly Pacquet of Advice from Rome* and the appended *Popish Courant* maintained a drumbeat of vitriolic criticism against Rome from their inception in 1679 until the summer of 1682. Directed primarily toward people who could not afford the time or money to peruse anti-Catholic tomes such as John Owen's *The Church of Rome No Safe Guide* (1679), or who lacked the requisite education to understand their theological arguments, the *Weekly Pacquet* and *Popish Courant* combined

8. Andrew Marvell, *An Account of the Growth of Popery, and Arbitrary Government in England* (Amsterdam, [1677]), pp. 3–4; [Henry Care], *The Character of a Turbulent, Pragmatical Jesuit and Factious Romish Priest* (London, 1678), pp. 2, 6.

9. Jonathan Scott, 'England's Troubles: Exhuming the Popish Plot', in *The Politics of Religion in Restoration England*, ed. Tim Harris, Paul Seaward, and Mark Goldie (Oxford, 1990), pp. 115–19.

satire, fiction, and invective with a smattering of history and a hefty
dose of Nonconformist ideology. Popery, sneered the inaugural issue,
'is generally so silly a Foppery, that it deserves none of our Passions
but *Scorn*, bating only their *Idolatries* and *Cruelties*, which rather require
our *Compassion* and *Detestation*'. Ensuing issues accused the pope of
supporting prostitution and ignorance, satirized the Society of Judas
(i.e. the Jesuits), and charged Catholics not only with the infamous
Popish Plot but with perpetrating a sham Presbyterian conspiracy.
'Though our Plots are continually detected and *defeated*, yet still
we must *Plot on afresh*, because 'tis our *Diabolical-Catholick Nature* to
be doing Mischief'. In short, Popery was not only idolatrous and
blasphemous but treasonable and even atheistic because it repudiated
true religion.[10]

Bunyan's reaction to the Popish Plot and the ensuing hysteria is aptly
summarized in a short passage in his posthumous work, *Israel's Hope
Encouraged*. After the plot's discovery, he reflected, 'we began to fear
cutting of throats, of being burned in our beds, and of seeing our
children dashed in pieces before our faces'. Bunyan, however, was
apparently referring to the general reaction of English Protestants
rather than to his own feelings, for nothing in his writings from this
period hints at such personal fears. He could not, of course, have
been ignorant of what was transpiring around him. On his trips to
London he would have seen not only the regular newspapers but
almost certainly the inflammatory *Weekly Pacquet*. Moreover, his friend
John Owen was at this point condemning Catholicism for its faulty
soteriology, its recourse to violence as a means of keeping people
from the true faith, and 'the Insupportable Yoke that this Guide puts
on Kings and *Soveraign Princes*, on pretence of its divine Right of an
universal Guidance of them and all their Subjects'. Owen may have
introduced Bunyan to his assistant, Robert Ferguson, who was then
castigating Catholics for their purported conspiracies against Charles,
the Protestant religion, and the English people.[11]

10. [Charles Blount], *An Appeal from the Country to the City* (London, 1679),
pp. 1–5, 9, 24–25; *The Weekly Pacquet of Advice from Rome*, 4 vols. (London, 1679–82),
i, pp. 2–3, 55–56, 64, 79, 104, 239; ii, sig. A2r; ii, pp. 80, 135, 223, 295, 359; iv,
pp. 161–62.

11. Offor, i, p. 585; John Owen, *The Church of Rome No Safe Guide* (London,
1679), pp. 42–46; Robert Ferguson, *A Letter to a Person of Honour, Concerning the Black
Box* ([London], 1680), p. 4. Referring to the perceived Catholic threat, Edward Harley
wrote in May 1679: 'I know not a security from that danger if wee doe not sincerely
take Christ to be our Lord and King'. Harley Papers, Portland Manuscripts, BL Loan
29/183, fol. 10r.

If Bunyan's published works are a reliable indicator of his preaching interests at this time, he had relatively little to say at first about the alleged Catholic danger. Like any good preacher, he utilized contemporary concerns to drive home his message. Those who followed his argument in *A Treatise of the Fear of God* must have been reminded of another kind of fear then current in the land. Bunyan's warning that those who tried to overthrow divine authority faced punishment at the Last Judgment may have been an allusion to Catholics, and the security precautions undertaken in London may have inspired his depiction of the heart as the principal fort of God which must be secured by fearing the divine. Contemporary readers would also have been reminded of Sir William Waller's search for suspicious Catholics by Bunyan's reference in *Mr. Badman* to a royal messenger in quest of traitors, or of an expected French invasion when Bunyan mentioned setting beacons aflame.[12] But this was virtually to ignore contemporary events in comparison, say, to John Owen, who warned in 1680 that 'we can have no other expectation from the Prevalency of . . . [the Catholic] Interest in this Nation, but utter Extirpation and Destruction'.[13]

The Whigs commonly hurled that charge in their vain attempt to prevent the duke of York's accession to the throne. The battle was especially intense in 1681, the year Bunyan composed *The Holy War*. Writers such as Elkanah Settle and John Phillips launched a direct attack on James, insisting that he would bring disaster as the sovereign. In a passage suggestive of one who had read the *Acts and Monuments*, Phillips recalled 'the Butcheries, Slaughters, Massacres, Devastations and Depopulations of Popish Rage'. From around the country came Whig-inspired petitions to members of Parliament asking for protection from Popery and tyranny. The Particular Baptist Benjamin Keach joined the fray, publishing *Sion in Distress* in part 'to promote the *Just Odium* of my *Native Countrey* against so *destructive* and *malignant* an *Enemy*', namely Catholicism. Keach denounced the church of Rome as a prostitute, its history filled with flaming faggots that had destroyed the innocent. He was adamant that this '*absurd* and *irreligious Tribe*' not be given authority in England. Although the relentless campaign of charged rhetoric failed to dislodge the duke of York, it enflamed Nonconformist emotions. On 17 November 1681 a crowd

---

12. *MW*, ix, pp. xix–xx, 19, 21; Offor, i, pp. 590, 593. For Waller see *BDBR*, s.v.

13. [John Owen], *An Account of the Grounds and Reasons on Which Protestant Dissenters Desire Their Liberty* [1680], p. 2.

of Londoners held a blatantly anti-Catholic procession that included
representations of Sir Edmund Godfrey; pilloried Irishmen; a 'Devils
Regiment' comprising monks, friars, and Jesuits; a papal herald; and
'the *He-whore* Mystical *Babylon*, the Pope himself in all his *Pontificalibus*'.
When the procession reached Smithfield, site of the Marian burnings,
the marchers consigned the papal effigy to the flames.[14]

The same year a Nonconformist possibly known to Bunyan prompted
Richard Janeway to publish William Dell's *The Increase of Popery in England*,
a work that Roger L'Estrange had seized as it was about to be printed in
1667. Dell had opened his pulpit at Yelden, Bedfordshire, to Bunyan in
1659, and may have entrusted a copy of the manuscript to him before
his own death at Westoning in 1669. The author of the postscript to
this work, who had presumably been its custodian, stated that he had
previously written that '*Antichrist* is now in his Old Age, and draws near
his End, yea is drawing his last breath', a view compatible with Bunyan's.
Yet he had also called for the banishment of all French and 'Outlandish'
men, and thus was probably not Bunyan. In any case, he shared the
pronounced hostility to Catholicism as a religion of blood diametrically
opposed to Christ.[15]

In this explosive atmosphere Bunyan wrote *The Holy War*, a sophisticated work with multiple levels of allegory, the most fundamental of
which dealt with the soteriological issue of the soul's justification and
sanctification. But the militant imagery cannot be divorced from the
contemporary historical context, and the allegory must be read against
a background of the Popish Plot and the exclusion controversy. Anti-
Catholicism is not immediately evident as the plot unfolds, yet as Roger
Sharrock and James Forrest have suggested, Mansoul's second lapse
may signify the decline of the primitive church's ideals in the face of the
papacy's rise. According to this interpretation, Emanuel's subsequent
rescue of the city would reflect the Protestant Reformation.[16] Because
the allegory operates at multiple levels, Bunyan may also have been
referring to the ebb and flow of Christianity in England. We know
he thought highly of the reforms introduced by Henry VIII and

14. [Elkanah Settle], *The Character of a Popish Successor* (London, 1681), pp. 2, 12;
[John Phillips], *The Character of a Popish Successor . . . Part the Second* (London, 1681),
p. 23; *Vox Patriae* (London, 1681); Benjamin Keach, *Sion in Distress*, 2nd ed. (London,
1681), sig. A3r; pp. 40–41' *Impartial Protestant Mercury*, no. 60 (15–18 Nov. 1681). For
Keach see *BDBR*, s.v.

15. Anon., postscript to William Dell, *The Increase of Popery in England* (London,
1681), pp. 3, 15, 17. For Dell see Eric C. Walker, *William Dell, Master Puritan*
(Cambridge, 1970).

16. *HW*, p. xxviii.

Edward VI, as well as those of Elizabeth I. The fact that the allegory concludes with an explicit indication that the struggle will continue fits the circumstances of the country during the exclusion controversy. *The Holy War* may therefore reflect both the cosmic struggle of the forces of Christ against those of the Antichrist or papacy, and the more immediate battle to preserve England for Protestantism.

This essay is not the place to attempt a reinterpretation of the allegory in its immediate historical context, but several hints are readily apparent. The popular preoccupation with conspiracies, especially from 1678 on, is reflected in the scheme of the Diabolonian lords to return control of Mansoul to Diabolus. The cabal was, of course, discovered by Mr. Prywell (Sir Edmund Godfrey?), who dutifully reported to the lord mayor. The town was thereafter notified by the tolling of 'the *Lecture-bell*', perhaps a reference to Nathaniel Vincent's morning-lectures against Popery in Southwark. That the alleged conspirators intended to massacre the inhabitants of Mansoul is evocative of charges made during the Popish Plot as well as of the 1641 massacre of Protestants in Ireland. Moreover, as Sharrock and Forrest have noted, the account of the Bloodmen, whose name was 'derived from the *malignity* of their nature, and from the fury that is in them to execute it upon the Town of *Mansoul*', refers both to the civil persecution of Dissenters by Charles' government and to the forces of the Antichrist in the last days. The interpretation is complicated by the fact that one of the officers of the Bloodmen is Captain Pope, whose fellow captains include an infamous succession that runs from Cain and Nimrod to Judas. Bunyan's explanation that 'all these spirits', including the tyrannical, 'are joined in one' under Captain Pope clearly underscores the anti-Catholic tone of the passage.[17]

The fact that the allegory operates imperfectly at various levels renders any *consistent* explanation apart from the soteriological virtually impossible, but does not negate Bunyan's efforts to encourage his readers to explore multiple interpretations, including those focusing on both the immediate historical context and the cosmic scale. Both of the latter are directly relevant to the intense anti-Catholicism of the period, and both should be studied in connection with the almost contemporaneous treatise, *Of Antichrist, and His Ruine*. Bunyan probably composed this work in mid- or late 1682, after *The Holy War* and *The Greatness of the Soul*, but before the discovery of the Rye House plotting and the composition of *A Holy Life*.[18]

17. *HW*, pp. 162, 181, 227–35.

18. W. R. Owens, 'The Date of Bunyan's Treaties *Of Antichrist*', *The Seventeenth Century* 1 (July 1986), 153–55; chap. 10, infra.

Work on *The Holy War* took Bunyan back to the millenarian interests he had pursued in *The Holy City*; hence the strongly apocalyptic discourse *Of Antichrist* was a natural accompaniment to the new allegory, which reflected those same millenarian concerns. *Of Antichrist* was also overtly anti-Catholic, an outlook probably reinforced by similar concerns among other Dissenters. John Owen, for instance, continued to hammer away at the Catholics in 1682, denouncing the Roman church as 'that *Idolatrous Antichristian State* which is foretold' in the Bible, and with which there can be no compromise. That theme was replete with political overtones for a nation faced with the prospect of a Catholic sovereign. Princes who defect to the papacy, Owen averred, place both themselves and their subjects in bondage. Owen's assistant, Robert Ferguson, simultaneously kept up his attacks on Catholicism, with particular reference to the threat posed by James' expected ascendancy.

> Yea, so pestilent and infectious a thing is *Popery*, that when once it hath insinuated it self into, and possest the minds of Princes, it not only infatuates them to depopulate their Kingdoms, by destroying and driving into banishment the best and most useful subjects of their dominions; but it so far *fascinates* them, as to make them forget their own protection and defence, as well as to abandon the safety and preservation of those of their people that agree with them in the same belief.

Catholicism, he argued, prompts them to persecute the very Protestants who would sacrifice their lives and estates to defend the realm. Ferguson insisted that if the Catholics governed England, the principles of their faith would obligate them to extirpate all Protestants.[19] Whether Bunyan met Ferguson through Owen can only be a matter of conjecture, but Owen and Ferguson certainly explored this issue, and Bunyan undoubtedly discussed it with Owen when he visited London.

Despite the common tendency to equate the pope with the Antichrist — an identification made, for example, in the *Weekly Pacquet* — Bunyan's Antichrist was the Devil. Yet the church of the Antichrist,

---

19. [John Owen], *A Brief and Impartial Account of the Nature of the Protestant Religion* (London, 1682), pp. 19, 31; [Robert Ferguson], *The Third Part of No Protestant Plot* (London, 1682), pp. 1, 3–4, 15. Cf. W.J., *A Letter from an Ignoramus to His Correspondent* (London, 1682), p. 2; J.O., *Comfort in Affliction* (London, 1682), pp. 10–13 (J.O. was not John Owen).

which 'reacheth as far as the beast with seven heads and ten horns hath dominion', possessed characteristics virtually synonymous with those Bunyan attributed to Rome, including spiritual prostitution, murders, thefts, blasphemy, and witchcraft. Bunyan's equation of the 'great Babylon' with 'the mother-church, as she calleth herself', left no doubt that the Roman church was at least the core of the Antichrist's body. Moreover, the assertion that the Antichrist claimed to be for Christ even while insisting that tradition as well as Scripture is authoritative identified him with Catholic ideology. Bunyan was clearly thinking of Catholic practice when he condemned flattering titles, false miracles, and the 'Popish edicts' and penal laws that enforced the religion of the Antichrist. He also denounced 'the abominable filthiness' of Antichristian worship and praised Henry VIII, Edward VI, and Elizabeth I for terminating it in England, thereby further reinforcing in his readers the identification of the Antichrist with Catholicism.[20]

Bunyan offered various reasons to explain why the Antichrist had to be destroyed, all of which contributed to making this treatise an anti-Catholic polemic. The Antichrist faced ruin in the first place for usurping divine power by requiring the worship of something other than God. The Antichrist also erred by seeking the headship of the church, including a pretence to infallibility and the imposition of 'unwritten verities, abominable traditions, blasphemous rites and ceremonies'. Moreover, the Antichrist blasphemed the Holy Spirit by claiming that the latter sanctioned unscriptural worship, by asserting the necessity of tradition, by establishing an unbiblical ecclesiastical polity, by claiming false miracles, and by the immorality of priests, friars, and Jesuits, the tail of the beast. He also accused the Antichrist of slaying saints, most recently in such places as France, Ireland, and Piedmont, and of plotting. 'Witness those plots, designs, conspiracies, and frequent attempts that are . . . continually on foot in the world for the commission of murders', a comment Bunyan's readers would immediately have associated with the alleged Popish Plot. The Antichrist also had to be destroyed because he had confounded divinely ordained government by using the magistrate's sword against the godly. He was also cited for covetousness inasmuch as everything religious in the Catholic church — including indulgences, preferments, and pardons — was allegedly for sale. Finally, the Antichrist would be ruined because he had opposed the establishment of Christ's

20. *Weekly Pacquet*, iii, p. 462; Offor, ii, pp. 46, 50–52, 55, 57.

kingdom in the world.[21] This was obviously a sweeping indictment of Catholicism.

For Bunyan, and very likely for his readers, there was no doubt about the justice or certainty of the Antichrist's fall; the more crucial questions involved the means and timing of his destruction. By late 1682 Ferguson, similarly convinced of the evils of Catholicism, was actively engaged in plans for a general insurrection aimed at preventing James' accession to the throne. The duke of Monmouth subsequently accused Owen, George Griffith, and Matthew Meade, all known to Bunyan, of knowing about this insurrection, raising the intriguing possibility that Bunyan himself may have learned something of the plans from his friends. In his treatise on the Antichrist he included a curious passage apparently directed toward his London colleagues. After noting that he was in favour of blessing his persecutors, he added that he had had 'more peace in the practice of these things, than all the world are aware of'. Such a claim was not unusual, and in fact reflected the Nonconformist ethic of suffering. But Bunyan then went on to say that 'I only drop this, because I would shew my brethren that I also am one of them; and to set them right that have wrong thoughts of me, as to so weighty matters as these'.[22] Could these 'wrong thoughts' have been an assumption that he supported an insurrection?

In his treatise on the Antichrist, Bunyan refused to embrace a doctrine of active resistance. 'The recovery of the light of the gospel from under Antichristian mists, and fogs of darkness' will be under-taken by Christ, 'not by might nor power, but by the spirit of his mouth, and the brightness of his coming'. God, Bunyan argued, would first slay the soul of the Antichrist and then his ordinances would 'moulder away'. Masses, prayers for the dead, icons, pilgrimages, unscriptural fasts, monks' vows, and 'the beastly single life of their priests' would disappear. The ruination of the Antichrist would, he predicted, be a gradual affair, with monarchs wielding the sword to destroy his body, the synagogue of Satan. The church would assist in this work of destruction, but only by its faith and prayers.[23]

21. Offor, ii, p. 74–79. Concern for the fate of Piedmont Protestants had been expressed in a sonnet of John Milton, 'On the Late Massacre in Piemont' (1655); it reflected the militant feeling stirred by Catholic persecution among many Protestants: 'Avenge, O Lord, thy slaughtered Saints'. *The Complete Poetical Works of John Milton* (Boston, 1899), p. 77.

22. Offor, ii, p. 74; chap. 10, infra.

23. Offor, ii, pp. 48–49, 55, 72. In contrast with Bunyan's position, compare Samuel Johnson's contention that 'Passive Obedience is Popery established by a Law, when ever the Prince shall please'. *Julian's Arts to Undermine and Extirpate Christianity* (London, 1689), p. vi; Johnson wrote this in 1683.

The time of the Antichrist's downfall, Bunyan indicated, is known only to God, and he was critical of previous authors who had attempted to pinpoint the date. Nevertheless Bunyan was convinced that the work of delivering the true church had already begun through the agency of temporal powers. Given the suffering of the saints in the 1680s, this presumably would have raised eyebrows among his readers; hence Bunyan likened recent persecution to the last icy winds of winter that heralded the coming of spring: 'let then the blasts at present, or to come, be what they will, Antichrist is assuredly drawing towards his downfall'. Certain signs presaged the Antichrist's fall, Bunyan suggested, the first of which alluded to the Popish Plot: 'when we . . . see that plots and conspiracies, that designs for utter ruin, are laid against God's church all the world over', and shelter for the saints no longer exists, then the demise of the Antichrist is at hand. The imminence of the Antichrist's ruin would also be evident when some monarchs and nations began to revolt against Antichristian dominion; but leadership was unmistakably vested in sovereigns, not their subjects. 'Antichrist shall not down, but by the hand of kings.' Moreover, the end was imminent when all but devils repudiated Babylon, the Antichristian or Catholic church. Then would come the slaying of the witnesses, a time in which believers would no longer testify against the Antichrist and a '*living* church' would cease to exist in the world, much to the joy of the Antichrist and his disciples.[24] Thus Bunyan expected the short-term triumph of Catholicism before its destruction at the hands of God and the chosen monarchs. This would help explain Bunyan's reluctance to support any effort to take up arms to alter the succession or the form of government, as some radicals advocated.

The prospect of a Catholic king and reports of the growing persecution of Huguenots in France kept memories of the martyrs vivid in Bunyan's mind.[25] But it was the discovery of the Rye House plotting — a planned general insurrection and a conspiracy to assassinate the royal brothers — in June 1683 that prompted Bunyan to devote an entire treatise to the ethic of godly suffering. References to the *Acts and Monuments* increased in *Seasonable Counsel*, and he provided a fresh reminder of how Catholics had purportedly cut the throats and smashed the heads of Protestant children in Ireland, France, and Piedmont. After insisting that suffering was a Christian duty, Bunyan offered his readers advice on how to suffer, even to the point of becoming martyrs. The Antichrist, he warned, was still alive, and

24. Offor, ii, pp. 58–69, 72, 74, 81–82.
25. Ibid., ii, p. 44; *MW*, ix, pp. 235, 309, 345.

the devil was not yet locked up in the bottomless pit, yet throughout this treatise there is little hint of anti-Catholic polemic. The persecutors of the saints were the professed Protestants of the Church of England, against whom Bunyan would counsel no rebellion. On the contrary, he attempted to distance himself from the accused Rye House plotters and to stress the importance of suffering for the Gospel. If he read the final speech of William Lord Russell, he would have agreed that Catholicism is 'an Idolatrous and Bloody Religion', but he adamantly refused to sanction armed resistance, even in self-defence.

Some commentators have suggested that the figure of Giant Maul in the second part of *The Pilgrim's Progress* represents the Catholic church, but this does not square with Bunyan's treatment of Catholicism in the works that immediately preceded part two of the allegory. Of all the dangers attributed to Catholicism, sophistry was hardly important. Moreover, Great-heart's slaying of Giant Maul contradicts Bunyan's conviction that in the last times Catholicism would be, for a time, virtually supreme.[26] Giant Pope had been a pathetic figure in the late 1660s, but this was no longer the case in 1684. Catholicism was not only a major international power but a cosmic force in the millenarian calculations that underlay *The Holy War* and were the dominant theme of *Antichrist*. That Bunyan retreated from his hard-hitting assault on Catholicism in the early 1680s must be attributed to the catastrophe that befell the Nonconformists as a result of the government's discovery of the abortive Rye House plotting. The accession of the Catholic James II in 1685 would clearly trouble Bunyan. Yet once James had adopted a policy of toleration for Nonconformists and conciliation with the Whigs, Bunyan did not object when members of his congregation cooperated with the government in the remodelled Bedford Corporation.[27] Divine providence, he was convinced, directed even the actions of Catholic rulers.

26. *PP*, pp. 244–45, 347–48.
27. *MW*, xi, pp. xv–xix.

8

Bunyan and the Fifth Monarchists

Bunyan authorities have not traditionally associated him with the radical millenarians known as the Fifth Monarchists.[1] Only William York Tindall, in an analysis of Bunyan's millenarian principles, suggested their affinity with the views of the Fifth Monarchy Men.[2] An overlooked passage in one of Bunyan's works, however, indicates that he was at one time an adherent of Fifth Monarchist ideology. The work in question, *The Advocateship of Jesus Christ* (more commonly known under the second-issue title, *The Work of Jesus Christ as an Advocate*), was published in May 1688, shortly before Bunyan's death.[3] Unlike several of his posthumous works, this book was not concerned with millenarian themes but with Christ's role as an attorney who pleads the cause of the elect before God the supreme judge. Nevertheless, near the end of this work Bunyan recalled that 'I did use to be much taken with one Sect of Christians, for that it was usually their way, when they made mention of the Name of *Jesus*, to call him, *The blessed King of Glory*'. Upon reflection — in a climate charged with tension as hostility to James II mounted — Bunyan calmly observed that 'Christians should do thus; 'twould do them good'.[4] He was not, of course, suggesting a revival of the Fifth

---

1. See, e.g., Brown,; Sharrock, *JB*; Monica Furlong, *Puritan's Progress* (London, 1975); Lynn Veach Sadler, *John Bunyan* (Boston, 1979); E. Beatrice Batson, *John Bunyan: Allegory and Imagination* (London, 1984). But also see Hill, *JB*, pp. 96–99. Hill had earlier noted Bunyan's radicalism; see *The World Turned Upside Down* (New York, 1973), pp. 328–31; *Some Intellectual Consequences of the English Revolution* (Madison, Wis., 1980), pp. 13–14, 47.

2. Tindall, chap. 6.

3. *The Term Catalogues, 1668–1709 A.D.*, ed. Edward Arber, 3 vols. (London, 1903–6), ii, pp. 222–23.

4. *MW*, xi, p. 194. This work was first issued in the same year under the title, *The Advocateship of Jesus Christ*. For the emphasis on Jesus as king see, e.g., John Rogers, *Jegar Sahadutha* (London, 1657). The manifesto of Thomas Venner's 1661 rising was entitled *A Door of Hope: or, a Call . . . unto the Standard of Our Lord, King Jesus.* Vavasor

Monarchy movement, but reminding his readers that their ultimate sovereign was Christ, not James II.

The passage is not important for its relevance to political conditions in 1688 but for its indication that Bunyan had once apparently been a disciple of the Fifth Monarchists, a fact not hitherto known. Unfortunately, he did not indicate at what point in his career he was attracted to this group, but it was either the period between his conversion in 1653 and his imprisonment seven years later, or the period from about the publication of *The Holy War* in 1682 to the collapse of the Fifth Monarchy movement in 1685.

Bunyan had ample opportunity to learn of Fifth Monarchy views in the 1650s. Members of the Bedford congregation of John Gifford, to which Bunyan belonged, were, with others in the county, excited about the prospects of godly rule when Oliver Cromwell summoned the Assembly of Saints (the so-called Barebones Parliament) in 1653. Their letter to Cromwell, professing to see the hand of providence in the fall of the Rump, included the signature of John Bunyan, though this may have been a yeoman of the same name.[5] With the Protectorate, however, came disillusionment, and hostility flared when Cromwell considered accepting the crown. On 14 April 1657 a group of Bedfordshire men signed a petition, *The Humble and Serious Testimony of Many Hundreds*, expressing their belief in 'the full destruction of Antichrists Kingdome', the advancement of the kingdom of Christ, and the wrongfulness of the assumption of monarchical rule by Cromwell. Whether Bunyan was a signatory of this millenarian petition is not known, but at least two of his friends — John Fenne and Richard Cooper — later admitting signing.[6] In the same year John Thurloe, who directed Cromwell's spy network, learned that the Bedford silkweaver John Child was a Fifth Monarchist agent.[7] It is of exceptional interest that Child and Bunyan were not only members of the same church at this time but active partners in the congregation's work. On 28 June 1657, for example, the church sent

Powell composed a hymn in 1654 'To Christ Our King', reprinted in Louise Fargo Brown, *The Political Activities of the Baptists and Fifth Monarchy Men in England During the Interregnum* (Washington, D.C., 1912), p. 51.

5. *Original Letters and Papers of State Addressed to Oliver Cromwell*, ed. John Nickolls (London, 1743), p. 92.

6. Brown, pp. 101–103; *A Collection of the State Papers of John Thurloe*, ed. Thomas Birch, 7 vols. (London, 1742), vi, pp. 228–30. There is no evidence that Fenne and Cooper were Fifth Monarchists.

7. *Thurloe State Papers*, vi, p. 187.

Bunyan, Child, and Fenne to visit a man at Stoughton, and the three men worked together on other occasions. In November 1656 Bunyan and Child participated in a dispute with Quakers.[8] The two men must have spent a good deal of time together discussing religious matters, and Child surely would have explained his Fifth Monarchist principles to Bunyan during this period.

The case for the presence of Fifth Monarchist sentiment in the Bedford congregation is further strengthened by the church's ties with Fifth Monarchy leaders in London. In 1657 the church agreed to set apart a week for special prayer as part of a national campaign instigated by Henry Jessey, a millenarian sectary closely associated with the Fifth Monarchists and a man whom Bunyan would come to admire greatly.[9] When Child expressed a desire to withdraw from the Bedford congregation in 1658, members hoped he could be dissuaded by Jessey, the Fifth Monarchist John Rogers, and John Simpson, who had only recently recanted his Fifth Monarchist views after a period of imprisonment.[10] Simpson's congregation, of course, was an approved place of transfer for Bedford members who moved to London. When John Gifford's successor, John Burton, became ill late in 1660, the church needed ministerial assistance and turned for advice to Simpson, Jessey, and George Cokayne, a known Fifth Monarchist in the early 1650s who was active again in the 1660s. Although much of his career was spent in London, Cokayne was a Bedfordshire man.[11]

The affinity between the Bedford church and these London ministers, three of whom were at some point Fifth Monarchists and the fourth a fellow traveller, strongly suggests the presence of Fifth Monarchist sentiment in the Bedford congregation. That Bunyan shared this apparent persuasion is a distinct possibility in view of his close relationship to the Fifth Monarchist agent, John Child. Further support for this view appears in Bunyan's earliest writings. His first two works — *Some Gospel-Truths Opened* (1656) and *A Vindication of Some Gospel-Truths Opened* (1657) — were anti-Quaker polemics, a reflection of the activities in which he had been engaged with Child. In the first of these, Bunyan's simple millenarianism is manifest in his prophecy of the imminent return of Christ 'in flaming fire' to

8. *Minutes*, pp. 29–30; *MW*, i, p. xxiv.

9. *Minutes*, p. 28. For Jessey see *BDBR*, s.v.

10. *Minutes*, p. 31; B. S. Capp, *The Fifth Monarchy Men: A Study in Seventeenth-Century English Millenarianism* (London, 1972), pp. 276–78. For Rogers and Simpson see *BDBR*; for Simpson see also Greaves, *SAR*, chap. 4.

11. *Minutes*, p. 34. For Cokayne see *BDBR*, s.v.

establish his kingdom and to 'purge out all things that offend' in it.[12] The eschatological tone was considerably less pronounced in *A Vindication*, but here Bunyan's attempt to refute Edward Burrough's critique of his first book dictated the content. Even so, Bunyan made an explicit reference to the millennium.[13] In *A Few Sighs From Hell* (1658), Bunyan's principal concern was an exposition of the story of Dives and Lazarus (Luke 16), yet even here he warned that a time was coming when the persecuted saints would triumph over their oppressors.[14] The context, however, was not millenarian but the traditional punishment of the evil in hell. Nor was his last work of the 1650s, *The Doctrine of the Law and Grace Unfolded* (1659), an exposition of covenant theology, concerned with millenarian themes.[15] Thus, if Bunyan was drawn to Fifth Monarchy views in the mid-1650s, by about 1658 his ardour had apparently cooled. This was not unusual: Cokayne, Simpson, and Child had similarly retreated from Fifth Monarchist convictions, though Cokayne and possibly Simpson later reaffirmed them.

The government was concerned about radical activity in the Bedford congregation and apparently had informers watching it. In April 1657 Robert Fitzhugh, the mayor of Bedford, interrogated persons suspected of plotting; one of them was John Eston, a founding member and elder of the church.[16] In November 1660 Bunyan himself was arrested for illegally preaching at a conventicle when the authorities feared the possibility of an insurrection.[17] A rebellion in fact occurred the following January when Thomas Venner and his supporters rose for King Jesus, bringing considerable disrepute on the Fifth Monarchist cause.[18] That April, Bunyan was visited in prison by Paul Cobb, a clerk sent by the justices of the peace. When Bunyan persisted in defending his right to hold private meetings for religious worship, Cobb referred to Venner's insurrection and the 'glorious pretences' of the rebels; 'Yet indeed they intended no less than the ruin of the kingdom and commonwealth'. Bunyan's response — commonly cited to demonstrate his antipathy to the Fifth Monarchists — abhorred the insurrection and affirmed his 'duty to behave myself under the King's government, both as becomes a man and a christian'. Moreover, he pointedly observed

    12. *MW*, ii, pp. 87, 89, 92.
    13. *MW*, i, pp. 173, 205. Child, Burton, and Richard Spencly wrote the epistle to this work; ibid., p. 121.
    14. *MW*, i, pp. 284–85.
    15. *MW*, ii, pp. 11–226.
    16. *Thurloe State Papers*, vi, pp. 228–30; *Minutes*, pp. 15, 17.
    17. 'A Relation of the Imprisonment of Mr. John Bunyan', ad cal. *GA*, p. 105.
    18. Capp, *The Fifth Monarchy Men*, pp. 199–200; Greaves, *DUFE*, pp. 50–57.

that 'it doth not follow, that because they did so, therefore all others [Fifth Monarchists or sectaries in general] will do so'.[19] This was a prudent response for a man in prison, and the disavowal of Venner was something Bunyan shared with numerous religious radicals.[20] Even in 1657 most Fifth Monarchists had refused to join Venner,[21] so that disavowing him can hardly be equated with a repudiation of the Fifth Monarchy movement.

In prison Bunyan steeled himself with the hope of Christ's imminent return to relieve his suffering saints. In 1661 Bunyan wrote of the time when Christ 'will come in Glory great . . ./ To give his Saints their long expected meat'.[22] By 1665 Bunyan had turned increasingly to millenarian themes as he looked ahead in his *Prison Meditations* to the time when King Jesus 'will with him let us reign'. With 'Christ *that* King potent' the saints would 'get the Victory'.[23] Apocalyptic imagery fills *One Thing Is Needful* (1665), with its vivid depiction of the Last Judgment.[24] This poetry was a natural accompaniment of one of Bunyan's major millenarian works, *The Holy City* (1665), an expanded version of a prison sermon on Revelation 21.

In *The Holy City* Bunyan frankly acknowledges the debate over such eschatological questions as the timing of Christ's return, the reality of an earthly millennium, and whether or not the heavenly city would possess 'outward glory'.[25] Of this, however, Bunyan was certain: The church would conquer and rule over its enemies. 'Now shall she . . . have a complete Conquest and Victory over all her Enemies; she shall reign over them; the Law shall go forth of her that rules them, and the Governours of all the World at that day shall be *Jerusalem*-Men'.[26] This is emphatically an earthly kingdom, to be established when, in the imagery of the Apocalypse, the last vial has been poured and the final trumpet has sounded. Bunyan explained the millennium as a thousand-year period devoted to building the heavenly city. At the outset of the millennium an angel, he asserted, will bind the devil in the bottomless pit, thereby delivering the saints from outward persecution and false doctrine, setting the stage for their anticipated reign.[27] The future bodes ill for most sovereigns, for 'they

19. 'Relation', p. 120.
20. See Brown, p. 182.
21. Capp, *The Fifth Monarchy Men*, p. 199.
22. *MW*, vi, p. 127.
23. *MW*, vi, pp. 49, 50.
24. *MW*, vi, pp. 72–73.
25. *MW*, iii, p. 94.
26. *MW*, iii, p. 81.
27. *MW*, iii, p. 130.

will be shaking the sharp end of their weapons against the Son of God, continually labouring to keep him . . . from having . . . rule in the Church, and in the World'. Ultimately, through the endurance of the saints, 'God will take hold of Kings' and make them yield to his reign.[28] From the saints, however, kings have nothing to fear, for the church is not 'a Rebellious City, and destructive to Kings, and a Diminisher of their Revenues'.[29] The saints would indeed figure prominently in the building of the millennial city, but not with worldly weapons. Unwilling to accept the view of revolutionary Fifth Monarchists that the saints, following a divine command, would engage in violent activity to usher in the millennium, Bunyan wrote only of the godly using 'the Gunshot . . . of the Word and Spirit of God'.[30] On the one hand there would be no brash insurrections of the Venner type, but on the other the coming of the millennium and the triumph of Christ and the saints were inevitable: 'The return of *Zion* from under the Tyranny of her Afflictors, and her recovery to her Primitive Purity, is no head-strong brain-sick rashness of her own, but the gracious and merciful hand and goodness of God unto her, therefrom to give her deliverance'.[31]

Generally, Bunyan's eschatological ideas in *The Holy City* are in accord with those of other millenarians, including the Fifth Monarchists. Nevertheless, several discrepancies existed between his exposition and the tenets of the more radical Fifth Monarchists, such as John Canne and especially John Tillinghast. Bunyan refused to engage in chronological speculation or the pursuit of historical study for the purpose of charting the unfolding of a divine plan. Nor did he display the keen interest in the conversion of the Jews and their restoration to the Holy Land typical of some Fifth Monarchists. Not one of the signs of Christ's second coming in *Some Gospel-Truths Opened*, for example, mentions the Jews. Most striking, perhaps, is Bunyan's rather consistent repudiation of the use of force by saints to aid in the establishment of Christ's earthly kingdom. Not until *The Holy War* (1682) does the use of force appear, and then only in an allegorical setting and principally under the direct leadership of Emanuel, the barely disguised figure of King Jesus. Bunyan does follow the general Fifth Monarchist tendency to place the second coming of Christ at the end of the millennium, though he apparently changed his mind in *An Exposition of the First Ten*

28. *MW*, iii, p. 166–67.

29. *MW*, iii, p. 96.

30. *MW*, iii, p. 167. Cf. Morgan Llwyd, *Gweithiau Morgan Llwyd*, ed. T. E. Ellis and J. H. Davies, 2 vols. (Bangor, 1899, 1908), ii, p. 237.

31. *MW*, iii, p. 98. Capp correctly observes that most of the violence espoused by the Fifth Monarchists was only verbal; *The Fifth Monarchy Men*, p. 134.

Chapters of Genesis. Simpson's espousal of a premillennial return had caused considerable disruption in the Fifth Monarchist community on an earlier occasion.[32] In most respects, Bunyan's millenarian ideology was compatible with Fifth Monarchist thinking.

According to some millenarians, the year 1666 was the time for the millennium to commence.[33] This expectation may account for the stream of millennial ideas that flowed from Bunyan's pen in 1665. But the next year brought neither deliverance for the church — no millennium, no fall of the Antichrist — nor freedom for Bunyan from his prison, except momentarily. For six years Bunyan published nothing, and when he did resume writing in 1672, he did so only in the context of theological and sectarian disputes. Millenarian themes are surprisingly absent in his *Confession of My Faith*, despite its sections on the Second Coming, the Resurrection, and future rewards.[34] The millenarian expectations that had preoccupied Bunyan in 1665 are not in evidence in the polemical writings of these post-imprisonment years, perhaps because the political situation was conducive neither to the psychology of martyrdom and desperation nor to the chiliastic excitement typical of the 1650s. Yet the influence of the earlier millenarian expectations lingered. In *The Pilgrim's Progress* God the King, not God in his paternal role, awaited Christian at the end of his pilgrimage. Heaven was a monarchy.[35] The allegorical device of a pilgrimage did not, however, provide an opportunity for the development of millenarian themes.

Bunyan experienced no comparable limitation when he developed the allegory of *The Holy War* (1682), although the primary focus was on conversion and the Christian life. Nevertheless, he clearly borrowed the physical description of Mansoul from *The Holy City*, and with that portrayal he also carried forward his earlier millenarian ideology. Though such themes are readily apparent and are even buttressed with the standard references to the book of Revelation, the allegory as a whole does not reflect the usual millenarian schema. For one thing, Emanuel returns twice, the first time apparently to establish the millennium by setting up 'new Laws, new Officers, new motives, and new ways', and by binding Diabolus in chains.[36] From Emanuel the

32. Capp, *The Fifth Monarchy Men*, pp. 190–94. For Canne and Tillinghast see *BDBR*, s.vv.

33. See, e.g., John Canne, *A Voice from the Temple* (1653), pp. 24–25; John Rogers, *Ohel or Beth-shemesh* (1653), p. 24.

34. *MW*, iv, pp. 137–38, 142–43.

35. *PP*, pp. 359–63. For Bunyan's activities in this period see *MW*, viii, pp. xvii–xxiv.

36. *HW*, pp. 85, 92.

saints receive a charter giving them earthly supremacy, but eventually they begin to backslide, forcing Emanuel to come again to restore his authority.[37] 'Behold *Emanuel* came, and he came with Colours flying, Trumpets sounding, and the feet of his men scarce toucht the ground'.[38] '*For yet a little while*' the saints would remain in their earthly kingdom and then Emanuel would rebuild Mansoul in '*the Kingdom of my Father*'.[39]

The figure of Emanuel is of the same cast as the militant King Jesus in Fifth Monarchist literature. 'So *Emanuel* came upon him [Diabolus] on the one side, and the enemies place was betwixt them both; then again they fell to it afresh, and now it was but a little while more but *Emanuel* and Captain *Credence* met, still trampling down the slain as they came.' Emanuel is 'the Prince', the head of a vast royal army that vanquishes 'the *Bloodmen*', those forces of the Antichrist depicted in Revelation 19:17-21, as well as a lawgiver and a sovereign.[40] Perhaps more than any other work of Bunyan's, *The Holy War* evokes a spirit akin to that in the Fifth Monarchist writings of the 1650s. The allegory may therefore reflect not only his personal religious experience and his days in the parliamentary army but an indebtedness to the radical ideology of that chiliastic era.

The revival of millenarian concerns in 1682 after an apparent hiatus of seventeen years requires some explanation. Possibly Bunyan was not motivated by the expectation of some millenarians that Antichrist would fall in 1688, yet Bunyan's later millenarian writings specifically rejected attempts to set any date. More important, therefore, must have been the trips Bunyan made to London in the 1670s and 1680s. In the City his principal associates were George Cokayne, John Owen, George Griffith, Anthony Palmer, and Matthew Meade.[41] Of these men, perhaps the most important influence on Bunyan was Cokayne, who had resumed his Fifth Monarchist convictions in the 1660s and who associated with such radicals as John Vernon, Thomas Glasse, and John Simpson, all of whom had Fifth Monarchist ties. Cokayne was arrested in 1664, investigated for sedition in 1678, and fined for illegal preaching in 1682 and 1683. Unfortunately, it is impossible to know whether he was still espousing Fifth Monarchist views in these years, but the tenor of his preaching clearly alarmed the government. During this period his Independent congregation in London was an approved

37. *HW*, p. 138.
38. *HW*, p. 222.
39. *HW*, p. 247. See Tindall, chap. 7.
40. *HW*, pp. 222, 228–29.
41. See chap. 9, infra.

place of transfer for members of Bunyan's church. Moreover, in 1672 an elder in the Bedford congregation received a licence to preach in Cokayne's house at Cotton End, Bedfordshire, and in 1688 Bunyan died in the house of a member of Cokayne's congregation.[42] This sometime Fifth Monarchist was probably a major influence in the revival of Bunyan's interest in millenarian principles.

Of Bunyan's other close associates in London, Palmer, too, had been a Fifth Monarchist. For his religious activities he was suspected of plotting against the state in 1661, arrested in 1664, and fined for illegal preaching in 1670. His church was also an authorized place of transfer for members of Bunyan's congregation. Owen, Griffith, and Meade were not Fifth Monarchists, but at least Owen and perhaps the others were millenarians. Owen and Griffith helped ordain Meade in 1671, and both men worked closely with Cokayne. The government was spying on Griffith in 1663, his home was searched for arms and suspicious papers in 1671, the state was concerned about his and Meade's activities in 1682, he was convicted of *praemunire* in 1683, and he was fined for illegal preaching in 1684. Meade, too, was often persecuted and was linked to the Rye House plotting; the tutor in his home, John Nisbet, was an agent of the United Societies, a highly militant group of extreme Covenanters in Scotland.[43] Bunyan's associations with these men were probably responsible for his renewed millenarian concerns, particularly since he placed considerable stress in his eschatological pronouncements on the ugly fate that awaited those who persecuted the saints.

Curiously, the revival of millenarian conceptions in *The Holy War* was hardly reflected in the remainder of the books Bunyan published prior to his death. Among his posthumous works, however, are several which are strongly millenarian. Possibly these were composed in the 'silent period' after the publication of *The Holy City* in 1665, when Bunyan might have had difficulty getting works with such obvious political overtones published. To have had them printed following his release in 1672 would have been risky; as it was, he was incarcerated again in 1676-77. Bunyan authorities have traditionally regarded these posthumous writings as coming from the period immediately preceding his death. Yet in that year he published several substantive (but not millenarian) works, including *The Advocateship of Jesus Christ, Good News for the Vilest of Men*, and *The Acceptable Sacrifice*. If, then, the posthumous apocalyptic works do not come from the late 1660s, they must have

42. For Cokayne, Vernon, and Glasse see *BDBR*, s.vv.

43. *BDBR*, s.vv. Palmer, Meade, Owen; Peter Toon, *God's Statesman: The Life and Work of John Owen, Pastor, Educator, Theologian* (Exeter, 1971).

been written in the early and mid-1680s, in which case *The Holy War* signalled the commencement of a major revival of millenarian ideals on Bunyan's part.[44]

Certainly Bunyan was not alone in expressing millenarian concerns in the early and mid-1680s, for during this period the conservative Nonconformist Richard Baxter devoted considerable attention to this subject. Particularly while in prison in 1686, Baxter corresponded on eschatological matters with Thomas Beverley, Drue Cressener, and Increase Mather. Yet Baxter's concern was strikingly different from Bunyan's, for Baxter wrote in the context of his determination to preserve both a national church and a system of ecclesiastical discipline. Moreover, he did not look for a coming millennium but regarded the Apocalypse as proof that Christ had already established a Christian empire. With Constantine, Christ had begun to reign visibly through civil magistrates, whom Baxter therefore exalted. The Apocalypse is significant not as a key to the future but as a testimony to the importance of the exercise of Christ's power by the civil magistrate. For Baxter, obedience to a civil magistrate and acceptance of a state church were necessary for the establishment of godly discipline. It was precisely in this respect that a national church fulfilled its apocalyptic role.[45] Bunyan, too, was very concerned in the 1680s with the role of sovereigns in an apocalyptic setting, but his millenarian tenets were significantly different from those of Baxter, as will be seen. Yet, if Baxter did not believe in a coming millennium, he was at least convinced that the advent of Christ was at hand. The revival of eschatological issues in the 1680s, then, was shared by a broad religious spectrum, but those concerns were developed in manifestly different ways.

The early and mid-1680s were the Indian summer of the Fifth Monarchy movement. In 1682, the year of *The Holy War*, Fifth Monarchists were meeting with members of the earl of Shaftesbury's political organization, the Green Ribbon Club, with a view to toppling the government. Fifth Monarchists were also suspected of complicity in the Rye House plotting in 1683. Two years later the Fifth Monarchist Henry Danvers, one of Bunyan's Baptist critics in the 1670s, was supposed to raise London for Monmouth's uprising, but he failed

---

44. After *The Holy War* (1682), Bunyan's publications were *The Greatness of the Soul* (1683), *A Holy Life* (1684), *Seasonable Counsel* (1684), *A Caution* (1684), *The Pharisee and the Publicane* (1685), and *A Book for Boys and Girls* (1686). These were not millenarian works.

45. William M. Lamont, *Richard Baxter and the Millennium: Protestant Imperialism and the English Revolution* (London, 1979), chaps. 1 and 4.

to do so, thereby contributing to the duke's demise. The disaster at Sedgemoor marked not only the defeat of Monmouth but the collapse of the Fifth Monarchy cause.[46] If Bunyan was working on his last millenarian works at this time, it is not difficult to see why they remained unpublished, or why he was so careful to eschew any manifestation of disloyalty to the state. The atmosphere in the aftermath of the insurrection was not conducive to the acceptance of anything with Fifth Monarchy overtones.

For millenarian principles, the most significant of the posthumous works was Bunyan's discourse *Of Antichrist, and His Ruine*. One of its striking qualities is its candid repudiation of attempts to speculate on the year of the Antichrist's fall, for Bunyan believed that erroneous calculations had only spurred the ungodly to sneer. Instead, he concentrated on the signs that would herald the imminent fall of the Antichrist, whose destruction was assured because 'he standeth in the way of the setting up of the kingdom of Christ in the world'.[47] Again, the conversion and restoration of the Jews are not included among these signs. Unlike the more radical Fifth Monarchists, Bunyan now asserted that monarchs, with the certain assistance of the church, were the divinely appointed agents to destroy the Antichrist. 'Antichrist shall not down, but by the hand of kings. The preacher kills her soul, and the king kills her body', though some monarchs will in fact bewail his fall and yet be helpless to stop it.[48] Like the rulers of the ancient Persians who liberated the Hebrews, the chosen kings, as God's ministers, must deliver the church. '*Kings*, I say, must be the men that must down with Antichrist', but to do this they must be weaned from their loyalty to him and protected from the advice of their evil counsellors: 'There are so many Sanballats and Tobias's to flatter with them and misinform them'.[49] For Bunyan the model sovereign was Artaxerxes, a godly monarch. Bunyan exhorted the saints to pray for their sovereigns and deplore all conspiracies against the state: 'Be not angry with them, . . . but consider, if they go not on in the work of reformation so fast as thou wouldest they should, the fault may be thine'.[50] In *The Holy City* Bunyan had depicted most sovereigns as adherents of the Antichrist, but now at least some of them were the instruments of his destruction. The saints still retained a hand in that task, but their

46. Capp, *The Fifth Monarchy Men*, pp. 220–21.
47. Offor, ii, pp. 58–59, 79.
48. Ibid., ii, p. 61.
49. Ibid., ii, p. 73.
50. Ibid., ii, pp. 44, 74. Cf. *MW*, vii, pp. 172–73; Vavasor Powell, *The Bird in the Cage* (1661), p. 35.

role was restricted to the exercise of faith and the offering of prayers. Only when the Antichrist had been destroyed would the kingdom of Christ be set up in the world.[51] Bunyan's later millenarianism was thus candidly quiescent even as it dealt with the apocalyptic images of the beast, the ten horns, and the seven vials, which had been grist for the mills of Fifth Monarchist insurrectionaries in earlier decades.

This quiescent millenarianism also appears in *A Discourse of the House of the Forest of Lebanon*, published posthumously, where Bunyan clearly affirms the peaceful deportment of the saints. Explicitly denying that the kingdom of Christ will be introduced with physical weapons, Bunyan insisted that before Christ returns personally he will destroy the Antichrist through the power of his Word. Through the same means, monarchs will be informed and the church quieted. The proper demeanour for the saints is consequently patience.[52]

Bunyan reiterated his opposition to predicting dates for millennial events in *An Exposition of the First Ten Chapters of Genesis*, another posthumous work. 'Let Christians beware that they set not times for God, lest all men see their folly.'[53] The coming of the millennium, however, was beyond dispute. The sabbath was an indication that the thousand years would commence after God had perfected 'his works and providences that concern this world' in a period of 6,000 years (beginning with the creation).[54] The four rivers which flowed from the river in the Garden of Eden were 'a type of the four great monarchies of the world', and Adam's life of nearly a thousand years was a type of Christ, prefiguring the millennium, 'that sabbath when Christ shall set up his kingdom on earth'.[55] Some of Bunyan's contemporaries, he hoped, would live to see this, for he believed it was imminent.[56]

By his own admission in 1688, then, Bunyan had once been an apparent adherent or sympathizer of Fifth Monarchist ideology, quite possibly at Bedford in the later 1650s when he was an associate of the Fifth Monarchist agent John Child in the gathered church. In this period Bunyan knew of the congregation's links to the millenarian Henry Jessey, the Fifth Monarchist John Rogers, and the ex-Fifth Monarchist John Simpson. Bunyan's earliest works reflect millenarian views. Imprisoned in 1660, he denounced the Venner insurrection the following year, as did many Fifth Monarchists, including George

51. Offor, ii, pp. 72, 78.
52. *MW*, vii, pp. 172–73.
53. Offor, ii, p. 480.
54. Ibid., ii, p. 424.
55. Ibid., ii, pp. 426, 456.
56. Ibid., ii, p. 457.

Cokayne. After a lapse of some six years, Bunyan's millenarian interests strongly revived in 1665, as reflected in *The Holy City*. Perhaps the anticipated fall of the Antichrist in 1666 sparked this interest. Unless several of his posthumous publications date from the late 1660s, Bunyan did not return to millenarian themes until 1682, when they appear in *The Holy War*. By this time he had established close relations with a number of London radicals, including the one-time Fifth Monarchists George Cokayne and Anthony Palmer and the millenarian John Owen. He was also close to George Griffith and Matthew Meade, who, like the others, were regularly harassed by the government for illegal preaching and suspected plotting against the state. Either in the late 1650s or now, in the first half of the 1680s, Bunyan was attracted to the Fifth Monarchists. Perhaps in the 1680s, Bunyan returned to the Fifth Monarchy views to which he had been drawn as a younger man. Probably at this time, in the aftermath of *The Holy War*, Bunyan wrote *Of Antichrist, and His Ruine*, *A Discourse of the House of the Forest of Lebanon*, and *An Exposition of the First Ten Chapters of Genesis*. These works make it abundantly clear that his millenarianism did not embrace political insurrection; whatever republican inclinations he apparently had in the 1650s, he now expressed patience with kings, whom he regarded as divine agents to usher in the millennium. No evidence suggests that Bunyan was ever a Fifth Monarchist of the politically active type such as Thomas Venner or Henry Danvers. Like his friend George Cokayne, Bunyan looked for the establishment of the millennial reign of the saints under the ultimate sovereignty of King Jesus, but the way to the attainment of this vision was not by insurrection against the established authorities. Bunyan's self-proclaimed attraction to the Fifth Monarchists, whether in the late 1650s or the early and mid-1680s, did not make him a political revolutionary.

9

The Holy War and London Nonconformity

In the opening paragraphs of *The Holy War*, Bunyan, explaining how it was his 'lot to travel', came upon 'a *fair* and *delicate Town*, a Corporation, called *Mansoul*: a Town for its Building so curious, for its Situation so commodious, for its Priviledges so advantageous . . . that I may say of it, . . . *There is not its equal under the whole Heaven*'.[1] As the allegory of Mansoul unfolds, it obviously refers in part to the spiritual struggle depicted by Bunyan in *Grace Abounding to the Chief of Sinners*.[2] The unequalled city with its commodious location, however, also contains reflections of post-Restoration London with its stormy history of Nonconformity. The Cromwellian era, when Bunyan gained some knowledge of the City through his connections with the printers John and M. Wright,[3] is blissfully recalled in his depiction of London as 'so goodly a Town' with 'Dominion over all the Country round about. . . . Ay, the Town it self had *positive* commission, and power from her King [Shaddai] to demand service of all, and also to subdue any, that any ways denied to do it'.[4] The city was fortified by defences so secure that they 'could never be broken down, nor hurt, by the most mighty adverse Potentate, unless the Towns-men gave consent thereto'.[5]

1. *HW*, pp. 7–8.
2. For a synopsis of other views of the sources of *HW*, see Tindall, chap. 7; Daniel Lamont, 'Bunyan's *Holy War*: A Study in Christian Experience', *Theology Today* 3 (1946–47), 459–72; and the Marxist interpretation by Alick West, '"The Holy War" and "The Pilgrim's Progress"', *Modern Quarterly* 8 (Sumer 1953), 169–82. For other studies see James F. Forrest and Richard L. Greaves, *John Bunyan: A Reference Guide* (Boston, 1982); E. Beatrice Batson, *John Bunyan: Allegory and Imagination* (London, 1984), pp. 71–86.
3. *MW*, ii, p. 3.
4. *HW*, p. 8.
5. *HW*, p. 8.

While Cromwell ruled, 'they were all true men, and fast joyned together', but after Captain Resistance was slain, the forces of Diabolus took the city.[6] Mr. Conscience, the recorder, 'a man well read in the Laws of his King, and also a man of courage and faithfulness, [who would] . . . speak truth at every occasion', was 'put out of place',[7] as were the clergy who refused to conform to the restored Church of England. A new oath, indicative of the purpose of the Clarendon Code in the eyes of the Nonconformists, was imposed on the city, which was soon filled with 'Odious Atheistical Pamphlets and filthy Ballads & Romances full of baldry'.[8] The tone of Restoration morality is unmistakable. The challenge to Shaddai could not be ignored; hence he dispatched an army under the command of Captains Boanerges, Conviction, Judgment, and Execution, whom Bunyan identifies as 'Gods Ministers' who 'will set Mansoul against him [Diabolus]'.[9] The ensuing struggle of the captains and their forces for control of the city is described at length, until finally the forces of righteousness take possession.[10] At this point the allegory apparently becomes millenarian in its expectation of a godly triumph, but Diabolus' recapture of the city may reflect the temporary lapse of persecution in 1672 and the ensuing attempt to reimpose Anglican exclusivity commencing in 1673.

Behind the allegory lie Bunyan's activities in London as well as his inner religious experience. His associations with London Nonconformists in the years prior to his writing of *The Holy War* (1682) can be determined, and they show him cooperating with the most influential Dissenting ministers, several of whom had held high positions — as Bunyan's 'true men' — in the Cromwellian era. The struggles of these men in an era of persecution and occasional indulgence are reflected in the pages of *The Holy War*, which therefore represents not only the spiritual conflict of one man but also the historical experience of an underground faith.

The ministers depicted in the allegory as the four captains can tentatively be identified as George Cockayne, George Griffith, Anthony Palmer, and John Owen. A key to their identity is found in letters of dismission from the church at Bedford to the London congregations of which these men were ministers. On 19 June 1671 the Bedford church took up the matter of Mary Tilney, who had moved to London and requested a letter of dismission. The reply, signed by Bunyan and

6. *HW*, pp. 9, 17.
7. *HW*, p. 18.
8. *HW*, p. 31.
9. *HW*, pp. 36–40.
10. *HW*, pp. 90–93.

three colleagues, authorized her to join the congregation of George Cockayne, George Griffith, or Anthony Palmer. It also gave her the option of selecting another congregation if any of these men or John Owen would write a commendatory epistle setting forth 'the faith and principles' of the church in question. When this plan did not meet with her approval, the Bedford church reaffirmed its position in September.[11] In November 1671 the church sent a commendatory epistle on behalf of another member, Martha Grew, to the London church of 'our dearly beloved brother Anthony Palmer'. The Bedford Nonconformists 'beseech you to receive her to the Lord's table with you, and to grant her those Gospell priviledges which, by the testament of Christ, are bestowed upon you'.[12] On 29 May 1674 the Bedford congregation sent a letter 'to that church of whom brother [Henry] Jesse once was pastor, to know whether it be their church principle still to hold communion with saints as saint[s] though differing in judgment about watter baptizm'.[13] The Bedford letter was in response to a request from London, dated 12 May 1674, asking for the approval of Bedford to admit Martha Cumberland to membership in the London congregation. The Bedford church had previously authorized her to join the church of Cockayne, Palmer, or Owen, a fact called to the attention of Jessey's former church. The Bedford members were noticeably upset because Cumberland was not content with these churches, 'the which we have taken very ill, especially since those of our members which are in London are receaved by and hold communion with them, they being also of that Christian principle afore mentioned, to hold communion with saints as saints'. Bedford refused to recommend her to Jessey's former church because of her attitude toward the congregations of Cockayne, Owen, and Palmer, as well as other demeaning behaviour. Bunyan was among those who signed the letter.[14]

Bunyan's ministerial contacts in London in the late 1660s and 1670s thus focus on four men. A closer look at Cockayne, Griffith, Palmer, and Owen will establish the heart of the circle in which Bunyan moved when he visited London. This circle broadened before his death in 1688, as will be noted. Those who comprised this circle were closely interrelated and were normally involved in illegal religious activities — actions Bunyan viewed as part of the holy war against Diabolus.

Cockayne, who received his B.A. degree in 1639 from Sidney Sussex

---

11. *Minutes*, pp. 65–67, 68–69.
12. Ibid., p. 71.
13. Ibid., p. 77.
14. Ibid., pp. 77, 79–80.

College, Cambridge, had been rector of St. Pancras, Soper Lane, from 1648 to 1660. While serving in this position he received a letter from the Bedford church in 1659 seeking someone to assist John Burton, Bunyan's minister, in the pastoral work. 'The adjacent churches' recommended that Bedford contact Cockayne, Jessey, and John Simpson, rector of St. Botolph, Bishopsgate (1652-55, 1659-62).[15] This advice presumably came from John Donne of Pertenhall, William Wheeler of Cranfield, and John Gibbs of Newport Pagnell, all neighbouring ministers, whose help was sought when Burton was disabled the following year (1660). What recommendations Cockayne made, if he replied, are not known.

Some of Cockayne's activities after the Restoration are noted in the 'Spy Book' of Joseph Williamson, a Privy Council secretary, who compiled alphabetically-indexed extracts from informers' reports to provide information on persons to be watched for violation of the penal statutes against Nonconformity or for seditious activity. The informers reported that Cockayne was living at Soper Lane, where several conventicles met.[16] One of these brought together several well-known Independents: 'Mr. [Joseph] Carrall [Caryl,] Mr. [Matthew] Barker[,] Mr. Cockaine[,] Mr. [George] Grefeth[,] all pastors[,] they all joyne there Churchs sometymes together, and mete sometymes in *Soper laine*, sometymes *Mr. Willetts* in St. Laurence laine', near the Guildhall.[17] Caryl was closely associated with Owen, who was to succeed him as minister of the Congregationalist church in Leadenhall Street in 1673. The meetings reported to Williamson occurred in 1663, a year before Cockayne is thought to have visited Bunyan in prison.[18]

Cockayne's activities are difficult to follow during the next eight years, though by 1672 a regular congregation was worshipping in his home in Red Cross Street. Like Bunyan he took advantage of the 1672 Declaration of Indulgence to apply for a licence. As has been noted, his congregation was one of those in London to which Bedford was willing to dismiss members in the 1670s. This relationship did not change in the next decade. In 1682 a letter of commendation signed by Bunyan and others was sent to Cockayne's church on behalf of William

15. Ibid., p. 34; *CR*, s.v.; Geoffrey F. Nuttall, *Visible Saints: The Congregational Way, 1640–1660* (Oxford, 1957), p. 36. For the possibility of relations between Bunyan and Simpson, see Tindall, pp. 30, 125–26, 230 n., 255 n.

16. G. Lyon Turner, 'Williamson's Spy Book', *Transactions of the Congregational Historical Society* 5 (1912), 247.

17. Ibid., p. 314; cf. p. 247.

18. C. Bernard Cockett, 'George Cokayn', *Transactions of the Congregational Historical Society* 12 (April 1935), 229–30.

Breeden, a tradesman and lay preacher.[19] *A List of the Conventicles or Unlawful Meetings Within the City of London*, published in 1683, one year after Bunyan's *Holy War*, indicates that in that year Cockayne's church was meeting between White Cross Street and Red Cross Street, near the Peacock Brew-House.[20] In September 1688 Cockayne wrote a preface to Bunyan's posthumous *The Acceptable Sacrifice*, in which he described himself as 'a lover and honourer of all saints as such' and implied that he had known Bunyan well. Cockayne remarked that God 'was still hewing and hammering him [Bunyan] by his Word, and sometimes also by more than ordinary temptations and desertions' late in his life. Bunyan 'always needed the thorn in the flesh, and God in mercy sent it him, lest, under his extraordinary circumstances, he should be exalted above measure; which perhaps was the evil that did more easily beset him than any other'.[21]

Griffith, a friend of Cockayne's, was another London minister known to and approved by Bunyan, and may have been a model for one of the captains in *The Holy War*. Born in Montgomeryshire in 1619, Griffith was a fellow of Trinity College, Cambridge, in 1646, and a preacher at the Charterhouse in London from 1648 until his ejection in 1661. In 1654 he obtained an appointment as a lecturer at the St. Bartholomew Exchange, and he also served as one of Cromwell's Triers. Williamson learned that Griffith was ministering to a conventicle in St. Laurence Lane, near the Guildhall, in 1663, where Joseph Caryl also preached. Griffith's and Caryl's association with Cockayne and Matthew Barker here and in Soper Lane has been noted. In 1672 Griffith received a licence as a Congregationalist to preach at his own house in Addle Street. He was preaching at Plaisterers' Hall as of March 1684. From sometime after that date to about 1694 his congregation met at Girdlers' Hall in Basinghall Street. Baxter thought well of him because of his conciliatory attitude and open meetings, which would also have appealed to Bunyan.[22]

Griffith was closely associated with the likely prototype for another

19. *Minutes*, p. 87.

20. 'London Conventicles in 1683', *Transactions of the Congregational Historical Society* 3 (1907–8), 364–66.

21. Cited in Offor, i, pp. 686, 688.

22. *CR*, s.v.; *Rel. Bax.*, ii, p. 193; iii, p. 19; Walter Wilson, *The History and Antiquities of Dissenting Churches and Meeting Houses in London, Westminster, and Southwark* (1808–14), ii, p. 517. 'Mr. Griffith and afterward Mr. Tate had a Church who met in an afternoon at Girdlers hall, and upon Mr. Tate's death which was about 1710 wholly dispersed.' 'A View of the Dissenting Intrest in London of the Presbyterian & Independent Denominations from the Year 1695 to the 25 of December 1731', DWL MSS RNC 38.18, fol. 76.

captain in *The Holy War*, John Owen, who has also been linked to the meetings in Soper Lane in the 1660s.[23] Owen was undoubtedly the leading Congregationalist of the period. He had served as a chaplain to Oliver Cromwell; as dean of Christ Church, Oxford (1651–60); and as vice-chancellor of the university (1652–57). In 1663 Williamson learned that he 'dwells in the Fields on the left hand neer Moregate where the Quarters hang, & meets often with [Thomas] Goodwine'.[24] This was Moorfields, and 'the Quarters' referred to the place where the drawn and quartered bodies of animals were hanged in chains. Anthony Palmer and Laurence Wise also lived in this area. The informants indicated that Owen met often with Thomas Goodwin and Henry Jessey 'in the fields neer to Moore Gate'.[25] In 1669 Owen was preaching not only in White's Alley, Moorfields, but also at a combined Congregational-Presbyterian lecture at Hackney. In the same year he and Griffith advised the Nonconformist church at Hitchin, which later requested the services of John Wilson from Bunyan's church in 1674.[26]

There is no record of Owen's being licensed in 1672, when the Congregationalist John Crouch obtained a licence to teach at White's Alley.[27] The next year Owen succeeded Caryl as pastor of the church in Leadenhall Street, 'with which he joined his previous meeting'.[28] Bunyan's congregation approved both the previous congregation and the Leadenhall church as a place of transfer for its members. Bunyan, moreover, was in contact with Owen before the publication of his *Differences in Judgment about Water Baptism* in 1673. 'The sober Dr. *Owen*, though he told me and others at first, he would write an Epistle to my Book, yet waved it afterwards; . . . it was through the earnest solicitations of several of you [Henry Danvers, Thomas Paul, or William Kiffin and possibly other Baptists] that at that time stopped his hand.' Bunyan was philosophic about the fact that his polemic was not '*seconded by so mighty an Armour-bearer as he*'. Owen's opinion would have been helpful, inasmuch as Bunyan's position was attacked not only by leading Baptists but also by 'some of the sober Independents'.[29] That Owen had been asked to draft an epistle for Bunyan was not unusual,

23. R. Tudor Jones, *Congregationalism in England, 1662–1962* (London, 1962), p. 72.

24. Turner, 'Williamson's Spy Book', p. 253.

25. Ibid., pp. 249, 251.

26. *CR*, s.v.

27. *CR*, s.v.

28. *CR*, s.v.

29. *MW*, iv, p. 272.

given the number of epistles Owen wrote for other authors, including Bunyan's possible friend at Sudbury, Samuel Petto; Francis Holcroft's colleague at Cambridge, Samuel Corbyn; and numerous others.[30]

Owen's stature in London Nonconformist circles is reflected in a letter of George Vernon, rector of Bourton-on-the-Water, Gloucestershire, depicting him as the centre of a Congregational spy ring.[31] Eleven of his 'under-Officers' are listed, and at least three of these are associated in some way with Bunyan. Palmer and Griffith ministered to congregations approved by Bunyan, and Vavasor Powell compiled a concordance used by Bunyan, and may have known Bunyan personally and corresponded with him.[32] Thomas Goodwin worked closely with Owen and perhaps knew Bunyan. The other seven 'under-Officers' are Philip Nye, Francis Howell, Thomas Brooks, Stephen Ford, John Chester (Collins?), John Loder, and a Mr. Barrow. They contributed to the Nonconformist cause in London, though there is no direct evidence that Bunyan knew them. Nye's church met at Cutlers' Hall and later at Tallow-chandlers' Hall. Loder was Nye's assistant, and Howell worked with John Collins, a Pinners' Hall lecturer, at the Lime Street church. Brooks, like Goodwin and Owen, preached in Moorfields after his ejection, and Ford ministered to a congregation in Miles Lane, Cannon Street.[33] Vernon's depiction of Owen as the chief of these men aptly reflects his place in the centre of the web of London Congregationalism. Vernon, it should be remembered, was no supporter of this movement. To him it was comprised of '*Enthusiastick Sectaries* . . . [who] are men generally of illiterate minds, unpolished manners, and hearts full fraught with malice, impatience, discontent, pride, vain-glory and all those mental vices, which render them the Incendiaries of humane Societies'.[34]

Anthony Palmer, one of Owen's 'under-Officers' — and probably one of Bunyan's captains — was viewed by Bunyan and his colleagues at Bedford as 'our dearly beloved brother'[35]; his London congregation

30. These included Thomas Gouge, *The Surest and Safest Way of Thriving* (1674); Henry Scudder, *The Christian's Daily Walk* (1674); James Durham, *The Law Unsealed* (1676); Patrick Gillespie, *The Ark of the Covenant Opened* (1677); and Elisha Coles, *A Practical Discourse of God's Sovereignty* (1678).

31. *DNB*, s.v.

32. Tindall, pp. 125, 126–27, 261 n. Powell, who died in October 1670, spent nine of his last years in prison. Nuttall, *The Welsh Saints, 1640–1660* (Cardiff, 1957), p. 51. See also *BDBR*, s.v.

33. Jones, *Congregationalism in England*, p. 80. For Nye, Howell, Collins, Brooks, and Ford see *DNB*, s.vv. and *BDBR*, s.vv; for Loder see *BDBR*, s.v.

34. [Vernon], *A Letter to a Friend Concerning Some of Dr. Owens Principles and Practices* (1670), p. 51.

35. *Minutes*, p. 71.

was another approved place of transfer for members leaving Bedford. Born in 1616 at Great Comberton, Worcestershire, Palmer had been a fellow of Balliol College, Oxford, before resigning to become rector of Bourton-on-the-Water. After his ejection in 1660, he moved to London and was living at Little Moorfields in 1663. Williamson discovered that Palmer met 'often at one Shawes[,] Sailemaker in Tower Wharfe, and likewise at Palmers, [the Baptist Laurence] Wise, & Mr. [Carnsew?] Helmes [who had been ejected from Winchcombe, Gloucestershire[36]] who all dwell in the fields on the left hand neer Moregate where the Quarters stand[,] where there are severall noted persons supposed to lurke', including Owen, Goodwin, Brooks, and Jessey.[37] The authorities issued a warrant for Palmer's arrest on 25 February 1664. About five years later he was pastor of a mixed congregation of Independents and Baptists at Pinners' Hall, where he remained until his death on 26 January 1679. He was fined £20 in May 1670 for illegal preaching, but acquired a licence as a Congregationalist in 1672 to preach at a house on London Bridge.[38] The government issued a similar licence to Palmer's assistant, George Fownes, former vicar of High Wycombe, Buckinghamshire (1656–57); he too was a Cambridge graduate (M.A., Emmanuel College, 1659). Fownes had been a Presbyterian, but adopted Baptist views in 1657. After Palmer's death he accepted the pastorate of the Baptist church at Broadmead, Bristol in September 1679. Two years later he was imprisoned at Bristol; he died in a Gloucester gaol in 1683.[39] Palmer and Fownes were succeeded at Pinners' Hall by Richard Wavel, who had probably been responsible for Bunyan preaching a sermon there in 1682, the year *The Holy War* appeared; the sermon was later published as *The Greatness of the Soul*. The 1683 *List of Conventicles* identifies Pinners' Hall as Presbyterian,[40] but this is essentially incorrect. The congregation formerly ministered to by Palmer and Fownes continued to use the hall, but shared it with others. On Tuesdays lectures were given, usually by Presbyterians. On Saturdays from 1681 to 1684 the Seventh-Day Baptists, led by Francis Bampfield, met there.[41] No evidence indicates that Bunyan attended or gave one of the Tuesday lectures, but knowledge of Bampfield's Saturday endeavours may have prompted him to write his *Questions About the Nature and Perpetuity of*

---

36. *CR*, s.v.; *BDBR*, s.v. He died in 1669.
37. Turner, 'Williamson's Spy Book', p. 253; see pp. 246, 314, 346.
38. *CR*, s.v.; *BDBR*, s.v.; *DNB*, s.v.; Wilson, *History and Antiquities*, ii, pp. 256–58.
39. *CR*, s.v.; Wilson, *History and Antiquities*, ii, pp. 258–60.
40. 'London Conventicles in 1683', pp. 364–66.
41. Greaves, *SAR*, chap. 7; W. T. Whitley, 'Thompson's List of Conventicles in 1683', *Transactions of the Congregational Historical Society* 7 (1916–18), 300–301.

the Seventh-Day Sabbath, which Nathaniel Ponder published in London in 1685.

The reasonable accuracy of Vernon's letter citing Owen as the leader of such Nonconformists as Palmer, Griffith, Goodwin, Nye, Brooks, Cockayne, and Loder is substantiated in the correspondence of London Nonconformists with colleagues in Boston, Massachusetts, between 1669 and 1672. These letters shed further light on the circle of Nonconformists with which Bunyan came in contact on his visits to London. The correspondence grew out of actions in Boston surrounding the organization in May 1665 of a Baptist church, whose members included people excommunicated by the established Congregational church. The General Court passed laws to restrain the Baptists, prompting concern among the English Nonconformists. Owen, Goodwin, Nye, Caryl, and nine others sent a letter expressing their disapproval on 25 March 1669.[42] A letter from the magistrates and ministers of Massachusetts, dated 21 August 1671, dealt with the affairs of Harvard College and was addressed to an even broader group of English Nonconformists centred in London. The addressees included the four men just named as well as Griffith, Brooks, Cockayne, Palmer, Loder, William Greenhill, Nicholas Lockyer, John Knowles, William Hooke, Matthew Barker, (Ralph?) Venning, Matthew Meade, Samuel Lee, John Collins, and Leonard Hoare.[43] A reply to this letter, dated 5 February 1672, carried the names of thirteen leading London Nonconformists, namely Owen, Palmer, Caryl, Griffith, and Cockayne (all of whom were almost certainly known to Bunyan), as well as Brooks, Loder, Nye, Collins, Hooke, Knowles, Barker, and John Rowe.[44]

Among these men another person with whom Bunyan was probably

---

42. *The Correspondence of John Owen*, ed. Peter Toon (London, 1970), pp. 145–46.

43. Ibid., pp. 149–51. Greenhill (1591–1671) was pastor of a Congregationalist church at Stepney, where Bunyan later preached; Lockyer (1611–1685) formerly preached at St. Pancras, Soper Lane, and was ejected in 1662 as rector of St. Benet Shorehog; Knowles (1600?–1685) was co-pastor of a Presbyterian church that met in the parish of St. Catherine-in-the-Tower; Barker (1619–1698) was pastor of an Independent church in Miles Lane; Venning (1621?–1674) was pastor of a Congregationalist church at Pewterers' Hall; Lee (1625–1691) became a member of Owen's Leadenhall Street church, and in 1677 succeeded John Rowe (infra, n. 44) as a co-pastor at Baker's Court, Holborn; Collins (1632?–1687) was pastor of an Independent church in Lime Street; and Hoare (1630?–1675) succeeded Charles Chauncy as president of Harvard College. For all these men see *DNB*, s.vv.

44. *Correspondence of Owen*, ed. Toon, pp. 151–53. After the Restoration Rowe ministered to churches in Bartholomew Close and Baker's Court, Holborn. *DNB*, s.v.

acquainted was Matthew Meade, a fellow Bedfordshire man. Born about 1630 at Leighton Buzzard, Meade had been a fellow of King's College, Cambridge, from 1649 to 1651. In 1669 he went to the Congregationalist church at Stepney to assist William Greenhill, succeeding him when Greenhill died in 1671. Owen and Caryl were present at Meade's ordination on 14 December 1671. In 1674 a new meetinghouse was completed, where Bunyan almost certainly preached. Meade had the largest congregation in the London area. In 1683 he replaced Owen as a lecturer at Pinners' Hall, and may have associated with Bunyan in this connection.[45]

Bunyan and his colleagues had contact with one more London congregation — that of Henry Jessey (1601-1663). Jessey, who had been pastor of a Separatist congregation in Southwark in 1637, adopted Baptist views eight years later. He subsequently became the teacher of a Baptist church at Swan Alley, Coleman Street, but he staunchly advocated open membership and open communion.[46] Bunyan recorded his agreement with Jessey on this matter. When Bunyan came to London in 1673 to give his manuscript for *Differences in Judgment about Water Baptism* to his printer, John Wilkins, he '*providentially . . . met with*' a copy of Jessey's views on open membership and communion.[47] Jessey's influence had been 'a prime factor' in getting others to adopt such tenets,[48] and had he lived another decade or two he might have been instrumental in persuading more Baptist and Congregational churches to embrace this position. He died, however, in September 1663, the year in which Williamson learned that he often met with Goodwin and Owen in the fields near Moregate.[49] Jessey had maintained contacts with people whose eminence declined at the Restoration; the 'Spy Book' has this entry for Hertfordshire and Middlesex: 'Coll: [Henry] Danvers. Navington, where Mr. Jessey, Mr. Ward, Mr. Strainge mettes at the *Lady Hartop*'.[50] This was the home at Stoke Newington of Lady Elizabeth Hartopp, daughter of General Charles Fleetwood and Bridget Ireton (née Cromwell), and wife of Sir John Hartopp of Freeby, Leicestershire, where Lady Elizabeth endowed a Nonconformist church.[51] Jessey's death marked

45. *DNB*, s.vv. Meade and William Greenhill; Tindall, pp. 211, 241 n., 284 n.

46. *CR*, s.v.; *DNB*, s.v.; A. C. Underwood, *A History of the English Baptists* (London, 1947), pp. 57ff., 97.

47. *MW*, iv. p. 193.

48. Nuttall, *Visible Saints*, p. 119.

49. Turner, 'Williamson's Spy Book', p. 251.

50. Ibid., p. 315.

51. Ibid., pp. 248, 352–54.

the end of Bedford's fellowship with his congregation, for the church, encouraged by William Kiffin, adopted traditional Baptist views.[52] This congregation did not play a central role in London Nonconformity after Jessey's death. The signatories of the 1674 letter from this church to Bedford are little known men: Henry Forly, James Fitton, William Nutall, Walter Thomas, Thomas Flud, and Henry Crumpt.[53]

Thus the circle in which Bunyan moved when he travelled to London in the 1670s to preach and to deal with his publishers — notably Nathaniel Ponder, Francis Smith, and Benjamin Harris — is reasonably clear. Cockayne's church at Red Cross Street had been a regular place to visit, as implied by Cokayne's posthumous remarks about Bunyan. Cockayne may have written *A Continuation of Mr. Bunyan's Life*, which has this to say about his work in London:

> When he was at leisure from Writing and Teaching, he often came up to *London*, and there went among the Congregations of the Nonconformists, and used his Talent to the great good liking of the Hearers; and even some, to whom he had been misrepresented, upon the account of his Education, were convinced of his Worth and Knowledge in Sacred Things, as perceiving him to be a man of sound Judgment, delivering himself, plainly and powerfully; insomuch that many who came meer Spectators, for novelty sake, ... went away well satisfied with what they heard.[54]

Cockayne lived near Owen in these years, and his associations with the latter would surely have brought Owen and Bunyan together. This would give credence to the tradition that Owen heard Bunyan preach, possibly in Red Cross Street or in Owen's Leadenhall Street congregation. Bunyan would also have gone to Addle Street, where Griffith lived and preached to a congregation Bedford approved. The homes of Palmer and Fownes, or their church at Pinners' Hall, would have been visited as well. There Bunyan would have learned about the work of Francis Bampfield, whose views on the Saturday sabbath he repudiated.

In the later 1670s and 1680s Bunyan's fame spread in London. Following his final release from prison in 1676, 'he preached the Gospel publickly at *Bedford*, and about the Countries [i.e. counties], and at *London*, with very great success, being mightily followed every where.'

52. Tindall, p. 240.
53. *Minutes*, p. 79.
54. Ad cal. *GA*, pp. 170–71.

> When *Mr. Bunyan* preached in *London*, if there were but one days notice given, there would be more people come together to hear him preach, than the Meeting-house would hold: I have been to hear him preach . . . [to] about twelve hundred at a Morning-Lecture by seven a clock, on a working day, in the dark Winter time.
>
> I also computed about three thousand that came to hear him one Lords day at *London*, at a Townsend Meeting-house.[55]

The latter place must have been Meade's church at Stepney, built in 1674. Among the other likely sites for Bunyan's London sermons are Plaisterers' Hall and Girdlers' Hall (where Griffith preached) and Pinners' Hall (where Palmer and Fownes, and later Richard Wavel, preached, and where Bunyan definitely spoke in 1682). Contacts with London Nonconformists naturally increased in these years. Bunyan associated across the Thames with Stephen More at Winchester Yard, Southwark, where the cobbler Samuel How had once preached.[56] He also knew John Gammon of Boar's Head Yard, the author of *Christ, a Christian's Life*. Both Gammon and More were adherents of open communion. Bunyan preached his last sermon in Gammon's church near Whitechapel on 29 August 1688.[57] He died at the home of the grocer John Strudwick, a member of Cockayne's church.

Cockayne, Griffith, Palmer, and Owen thus apparently provided the inspiration for Captains Boanerges, Conviction, Judgment, and Execution. The struggles of these men in the 1660s and 1670s are poignantly expressed by Bunyan in a speech by Prince Emanuel to the people of Mansoul:

> O ye inhabitants of the now flourishing Town of *Mansoul*, . . . carry it not ruggedly, or untowardly to my Captains, or their men; . . . for though they have the hearts and faces of Lions, when at any time they shall be called forth to ingage and fight with the King's foes, and the enemies of the Town of *Mansoul*; yet a little discountenance cast upon them from the Town of *Mansoul*, will deject and cast down their faces, will weaken and take away their courage.[58]

Such was the likely tenor of the London sermons preached by Bunyan in the 1670s and early 1680s.

Written against the background of the exclusion controversy, *The Holy War* carried political overtones. Indeed, two of the Nonconformist

---

55. Doe, pp. 873–74.
56. Tindall, p. 87. For Wavel and How see *BDBR*, s.vv.
57. Sharrock, *JB*, p. 47; Tindall, p. 210.
58. *HW*, p. 143.

ministers who may have inspired Bunyan's captains, Owen and Griffith, would soon be accused by the duke of Monmouth of complicity in his plans for a general insurrection to compel Charles to exclude James from the line of succession. On his visits to London Bunyan must have discussed the controversial political and religious issues that confronted the nation, particularly the perceived Catholic threat, with men such as Owen, Griffith, and Meade. Written in a highly charged political and religious atmosphere, *The Holy War* conveyed Bunyan's message of firmness and resolve to all Nonconformists in the early 1680s: '*Remember therefore, O my* Mansoul, *that thou art beloved of me; as I have therefore taught thee to watch, to fight, to pray, and to make war against my foes, so now I command thee to believe that my love is constant to thee.* . . . Behold, I lay none other burden upon thee, than what thou hast already, hold fast till I come.'[59]

59. *HW*, p. 250.

10

Amid *The Holy War*: Bunyan and the Ethic of Suffering

The decade 1678–1688, spanning the period from the Popish Plot to the Revolution of 1688–89, was one of the most turbulent in British history. Coincidentally the last decade of Bunyan's life, it is the period in which his reputation was firmly established by the publication of all of his major works with the exception of *Grace Abounding to the Chief of Sinners*. Because relatively little biographical information about Bunyan is available for these years, specialists have concentrated on the literary masterpieces while devoting minimal attention to his reaction to contemporary events. Too many commentators have written as if Bunyan lived in virtual isolation from the great political events that swirled around him — a Protestant Franciscan devoted to the pursuit of piety and the conversion of souls. Such was not the case, although Bunyan's cautious temperament necessitates a close reading of his works to ascertain his views on contemporary events. In this essay I am primarily interested in exploring his position vis-à-vis the state in the context of the Rye House plotting, with special attention to his enunciation of an ethic of suffering.

As we have seen, Bunyan's periodic visits to London brought him into contact with influential Nonconformist ministers, including George Cokayne, Anthony Palmer, George Griffith, and John Owen. Palmer died in January 1679, but Bunyan knew his successor as pastor of the Pinners' Hall congregation, Richard Wavel. At some point Bunyan also met Matthew Meade, a fellow Bedfordshire man whose ordination Owen and Griffith had attended in 1671; given the links between Meade, Owen, and Griffith, Bunyan probably made Meade's acquaintance in the 1670s.[1] The names of three of these men — Meade, Owen, and Griffith — surfaced during the investigation of the Rye House conspiracy in 1683.

---

1. *Minutes*, pp. 66, 71, 79–80; Greaves, *SAR*, pp. 92–93; chap. 9, supra.

There were actually two conspiracies, one calling for a general insurrection by the English and the Scots to pressure Charles into securing traditional liberties and a Protestant succession, the second for the assassination of the king and the duke of York, with the aim of putting the duke of Monmouth on the throne or re-establishing a commonwealth. The conspiracies overlapped to some degree in terms of their personnel, particularly the Scottish minister Robert Ferguson, who had been Owen's assistant from 1674, and who seems to have been a member of Owen's Leadenhall Street congregation until he fled to the Netherlands with the earl of Shaftesbury in 1682.[2] Owen, of course, helped procure Bunyan's release from prison in 1677, and may at some point have introduced him to Ferguson.

The evidence linking Meade and Owen to the plotting is sketchy, and in the case of Griffith quite weak. By his own admission, Meade, who used the alias Richardson, had retained the Scot John Nisbet as a tutor in his home for eight or nine months. Nisbet, a member of the United Societies, a militant, extremist sect of Covenanters, had come to London with one of that group's ambassadors, Alexander Gordon of Earleston. When the authorities arrested Gordon in May 1683, they found a coded letter to him from Nisbet dated 20 March, apprising him of discussions concerning a general insurrection in which the earl of Argyll figured prominently. Neither Nisbet nor Gordon directly implicated Meade in the conspiracy, although Gordon admitted having met with Meade at the house of a London merchant.[3] Meade acknowledged that Ferguson had visited him in his home, but also claimed that he had once criticized Ferguson for writing against the government.[4] When Ferguson returned from the Netherlands in February 1683, he told the attorney and conspirator Robert West that Meade was 'Zealous in the Business of an Insurrection'; West claimed that he had received the same information from another plotter, the lawyer Richard Nelthorpe.[5] More incriminating was the testimony in September 1684 of the Scot William Carstares, a covert agent of William of Orange, who confessed that he had informed Meade, Owen, and Griffith of the planned insurrection, all of whom purportedly concurred with the scheme. Earlier, in November 1683, Monmouth

2. Peter Toon, *God's Statesman: The Life and Work of John Owen, Pastor, Educator, Theologian* (Exeter, 1971), p. 156.

3. PRO SP 29/427/25, 98; Bodleian Library, Tanner MSS 34, fols. 286r–287r; *Copies of the Informations and Original Papers Relating to the Proof of the Horrid Conspiracy*, 3rd ed. (London, 1685), pp. 136–37, 142, 146; Michael Sheilds, *Faithful Contendings Displayed* (Glasgow, 1780), pp. 18, 43–44, 58, 65–66.

4. PRO SP 29/427/98, 111.

5. *Copies*, p. 92.

himself had admitted to the king that Meade, Owen, Griffith, 'and all the considerable Nonconformist Ministers knew of the Conspiracy'.[6]

After the Baptist oilman Josiah Keeling informed the government of the cabal, Meade, Nisbet, and the conspirator Zachary Bourne, a brewer, were arrested as they attempted to flee to the Netherlands. In June, Bourne had suggested to an inner circle of militant plotters that they include Meade and another Congregationalist minister, Stephen Lobb, in their planning; at that point the proposal was rebuffed, although Lobb was subsequently recruited. Bourne, however, later insisted that he had never discussed the plot with Meade, and would admit only that West had once told him that Meade had enlisted 'a couple of Sea Captains', and that Meade claimed he had met with William Lord Russell, a key associate of Monmouth's.[7] After providing sureties for good behaviour, Meade obtained his release in late July despite the fact that, in Ferguson's words, 'positive Information [had been] given in against him'. Three years later Meade contended that he had not been guilty of anything more than Nonconformity, although this proclamation of relative innocence was made in the context of his efforts to obtain a pardon that would enable him to return to England from his exile in the Netherlands.[8]

The most significant evidence against Owen was Carstares' admission that he had told Owen as well as Griffith and Meade of the projected insurrection. Moreover, West testified that Ferguson had informed him that Owen had sanctioned both insurrection and assassination as lawful and necessary. In addition, Francis Charlton, one of Shaftesbury's political intimates, had met with Ferguson at Owen's house. When Owen, whose brother Henry was also allegedly involved in the plotting, was arrested and interrogated, he denied any knowledge of a conspiracy.[9] That he had sanctioned the assassination of Charles and James is

6. *The Deposition of Mr. William Carstares* (Edinburgh, 1684), p. 4; Robert Herbert Story, *William Carstares: A Character and Career of the Revolutionary Epoch (1649–1715)* (London, 1874), p. 91; *Copies*, p. 191; PRO SP 29/434/98.

7. BL Add. MSS 4,107, fol. 38v; Nottingham University Library, MSS PwV 95, fol. 251; PRO SP 29/427/25, 98, 127; SP 44/68, p. 300.

8. PRO SP 44/54, p. 185; SP 29/429/168; BL Add. MSS 4,107, fol. 39r; Robert Ferguson, *A Letter to Mr. Secretary T[renchard]* (1694), in *A Choice Collection of Papers Relating to State Affairs* (London, 1703), p. 383; BL Add. MSS 41,813, fols. 113v–114r; 41,819, fol. 240r. Cf. Matthew Meade, *The Vision of the Wheels* (London, 1689), sigs. A3v–A4r.

9. *Deposition of Carstares*, p. 4; *Copies*, pp. 91–92; *Historical Manuscripts Commission* 29, Portland, ii, p. 236; PRO SP 29/425/102; 29/430/34. The houses of Owen, Meade, and Francis Smith, one of Bunyan's publishers, were searched for weapons and seditious material in July 1683. PRO SP 29/429/184. For Colonel Henry Owen see PRO SP 29/425/132; 29/427/16; 63/341/154, 155; 63/343/149.1; BL Lansdowne MSS 1152, fols. 171r–172v, 174r.

inconceivable from all we know of his views, but behind the accusations of Carstares and Monmouth may lie Owen's general blessing for a plan to secure the Protestant interest and alter the succession from James to Monmouth.[10] After all, in a tract published in 1682, Owen had embraced a doctrine of active resistance in cases where religious and civil rights were threatened. Since the Reformation, he argued,

> the Protection and Preservation of Religion was taken up by sundry Potentates, free Princes and Cities, who had a legal Right and Power to protect themselves and their subjects in the Profession of it. It hath been and is at this day incorporated into the Laws, Rights and Interests of sundry Nations, which ought to be defended. And no instance can be given of any people defending themselves in the Profession of the Protestant Religion by Arms, but where together with their Religion their Enemies did design and endeavour to destroy those Rights, Liberties and Priviledges.[11]

The Nonconformists, of course, saw the events of the years 1678-82 as an attempt to destroy their rights through the establishment of tyrannical government and a Catholic succession. In Owen's judgment, active resistance, as his assistant Ferguson also asserted,[12] was therefore legitimate, and his support for the sort of insurrection planned by Russell, the earl of Essex, and their associates is conceivable, if not incontestably demonstrable.

Bunyan was in London while planning for the insurrection, originally scheduled for 19 November 1682, was underway. His sermon at Pinners' Hall was probably preached in early 1682, and he apparently returned to London in the autumn to check proofs for *The Greatness of the Soul*. Little information survives about his activities in 1683, even in the Bedford church book. In July the government ordered the arrest of various booksellers for allegedly printing and publishing treasonable and scandalous books. Among them were Dorman Newman and Benjamin Alsop, who had published *The Holy War*; Alsop had also brought out *The Greatness of the Soul*, and had agreed to issue *A Holy Life*. All of the publishers fled, which may explain why *A Holy Life* was delayed; it appeared in the Stationers' Register on 10 August and again on 6 October. In any case, Alsop's 'Advertisement' for the book referred to Bunyan's 'inconvenient distance' from London, perhaps

　　10. Cf. PRO SP 29/431/108.

　　11. John Owen, *A Brief and Impartial Account of the Nature of the Protestant Religion* (London, 1682), p. 12.

　　12. [Robert Ferguson], *The Second Part of No Protestant Plot* (London, 1682), pp. 1–2.

an indication of his fear to return to the City while the Rye House investigation was at its peak.[13]

Against this background, we can turn to the key Bunyan works of this period. *The Holy War*, written in 1681, must be read in the context of the exclusion controversy and reflects the militant mood of Whigs and Nonconformists in the face of a perceived Catholic threat. Bunyan's next work, *The Greatness of the Soul*, belongs to early 1682, after which there is a gap until the appearance of *A Holy Life* and *A Case of Conscience Resolved* in October 1683. Another gap follows until the second part of *The Pilgrim's Progress* is recorded in the Stationers' Register on 22 November 1684. During each of these hiatuses Bunyan almost certainly wrote a crucial work with political overtones. He probably drafted *Of Antichrist, and His Ruine* in 1682, though the work was published only posthumously. That this treatise belongs to the early 1680s is suggested in part because it refers to two decades of religious degeneration (presumably 1660-80) and reflects the supercharged atmosphere stemming from the alleged Popish Plot. But it also urges readers to pray for the king's long life and seeks divine assistance to enable him to 'discover all plots and conspiracies against the government' and to 'drive away all evil and evil men from his presence'.[14] The latter point in particular was shared by men such as Lord Russell, who saw an insurrection as the only means to liberate Charles from his 'evil' advisers. Once the government began arresting alleged conspirators, including some of Bunyan's friends, in June 1683, it would have made no sense for him to endorse a campaign to discover plots; *Of Antichrist* therefore cannot have been written any later than the early spring of 1683.

The other key work, *Seasonable Counsel: or, Advice to Sufferers*, which Alsop published, reflects Bunyan's response to the discovery of the Rye House plotting. He probably commenced work on it in the autumn of 1683, and it appeared in 1684, a year largely devoted to writing the second part of *The Pilgrim's Progress*.

The tone for the works of the early 1680s was set in the complex levels of allegory that comprise *The Holy War*. Although the most basic reading must be soteriological — the struggle for the salvation and sanctification of the individual soul — the political allusions and the

---

13. *MW*, ix, pp. xvii–xviii; *Minutes*, p. 88; Nottingham University Library, MSS PwV 95, fols. 255–56; *A Transcript of the Worshipful Company of Stationers* (London, 1913–14), iii, p. 180.

14. *Transcript*, iii, pp. 197, 199, 262; *MW*, ix, pp. xxiii–xxiv; W. R. Owens, 'The Date of Bunyan's Treatise *Of Antichrist*', *The Seventeenth Century* 1 (July 1986), 153–57; chap. 6, supra; Offor, ii, pp. 45, 74.

militant imagery combine in an unmistakable indictment of Charles II's government during the bitter conclusion to the exclusion controversy. Diabolus, after all, tyrannized Mansoul as its king, remodelling the corporation, making havoc of the statutes of Shaddai, and spoiling the law books. In response, '*Emanuel* resolved to make, at a time convenient, a war upon the Giant *Diabolus*, even while he was possessed of the Town of *Mansoul*'. The bedrock supporters of Diabolus, the notorious Bloodmen, symbolized the more militant Tories who led the campaign to crush Nonconformity and political opposition to absolute monarchy. Their ranks included, in Bunyan's words, the '*Tyrannical* and *Incroaching*', the '*Devilishly furious*', and those determined to have private vengeance on their enemies. Emanuel therefore had to instruct his supporters '*to watch, to fight, to pray, and to make war against my foes*'. Despite Emanuel's recapture of Mansoul at the end of the allegory, which in political terms could only be an expression of hope, the struggle was hardly over, for Emanuel's last words were an exhortation to 'hold fast till I come'.[15]

Despite the secondary level of political criticism in *The Holy War*, Bunyan does not seem to have been endorsing an insurrection, at least not if his other writings are used as the primary basis for interpreting the allegory. Conditions in the country had not improved in 1682 when he wrote *Of Antichrist, and His Ruine*. If, by this point, he had received any information from his London friends about the plans for an uprising, he was probably unsympathetic, even though such plans originally intended only to liberate Charles from his 'evil' advisers, not overthrow him. In *Of Antichrist* Bunyan accords monarchs a crucial apocalyptic role as divine agents in the destruction of the Antichrist, particularly the deliverance of the saints. Such rulers will be divinely trained 'by the light of the gospel, so that they might be expert, like men of war, to scale her walls, when the king of kings shall give out the commandment to them to do so'. The imagery, of course, is precisely that of *The Holy War*. While the church too has an apocalyptic role in the overthrow of the Antichrist, its weapons are solely spiritual: 'the church . . . , as a church, must use such weapons as are proper to her as such; and the magistrate, as a magistrate, must use such weapons as are proper to him, as such'.[16]

15. *HW*, pp. 17, 24–27, 29 (quoted), 228–30 (229 quoted), 250 (quoted). The suggestion that *The Holy War* tilts at the establishment in the post-Rye House period is, of course, an error. *HW*, p. 274.

16. Offor, ii, pp. 61–62, 72–74. Owen had been concerned about the Antichrist in 1681. *An Humble Testimony unto the Goodness and Severity of God* (London, 1681), pp. 53–54.

Some monarchs, Bunyan argued, will be excluded from this apocalyptic function and will remain loyal to the Antichrist. Whether Bunyan
included Charles II in this category is impossible to ascertain, but he
clearly did not endorse a revolution against him. On the contrary, the
Antichrist can only be toppled *after* Christianity has been almost totally
devastated: 'there will for a time scarce be found a Christian spirit, or
a true visible living church of Christ in the world'. Thus despite the
influence of corrupt advisers on Charles — the flattering Tobiases —
Bunyan exhorted the godly to be patient and honour the king. Under
Charles, England was manifestly more hospitable to Protestants than
the France of Louis XIV; Charles 'is a better saviour of us than we
may be aware of, and may have delivered us from more deaths than
we can tell how to think'.[17]

While others plotted to alter the succession or assassinate Charles
and James, Bunyan pursued a different course, insisting that the
appropriate conduct for those with 'cold and chill frames of heart'
was to 'be up and doing' in the quest for godly living. He prefaced
A Holy Life with a jeremiad that reflected the plight of Nonconformity
in 1683: God, Bunyan thundered, is *'angry with this Land'* because of
'the sin of the Professors that dwell therein'. Owing to their iniquity, he will
'give them over to the hand of the Enemy, and . . . deliver them to the
tormentors'.[18] By the time Bunyan wrote this, the first discoveries of
the Rye House conspiracies may have appeared in the press, but his
principal reaction to the abortive plotting was expressed in *Seasonable
Counsel*.

Bunyan's denunciation of the plotting was scathing. It was the work
of spirits commissioned by the devil to disturb not only individuals
but entire nations by inciting division and rebellion, enticing even
'the looser sort of Christians' to participate. In an implicit although
unmistakable reference to Monmouth, he observed how Absalom had
conspired against his father with the support of two hundred simple,
ignorant men. Beware of such evils, Bunyan warned, for they are as hot
as a burning iron and will cause the Christian to suffer as an evil doer,
the greatest blemish that can befall the godly. Reflecting published
reports of how the conspirators had met in taverns and coffee-houses to
scheme and condemn the government, Bunyan offered this advice:

> Take heed of *hearing of any thing spoken that is not according to
> sound Doctrine*: thou must withdraw thy self from such, in whom
> thou perceivest not the words of knowledge. Let not talk against
> Governours, against Powers, against Men in Authority be admitted;

17. Offor, ii, pp. 61, 66, 73–74, 77.
18. Offor, ii, p. 74; *MW*, ix, pp. 256–57, 265.

> keep thee far from an evil matter. *My son*, says Solomon, *fear thou the Lord, and the King, and meddle not with those that are given to change.*

There could be no comfort, Bunyan maintained, for those who conspired against the king or refused to give the state its due.[19]

As the scaffold relentlessly claimed its victims, Bunyan demonstrated little pity, convinced that each rebel had shamed his faith and given evil people reason to rejoice. 'His *cause* will not bear him out, his heart will be clogged with guilt, innocency and boldness will take wings and fly from him. Though he talketh of Religion upon the stage or ladder, *that* will blush to hear its name mentioned by them that suffer for evil-doing.' In fact, however, some of the plotters demonstrated neither remorse nor qualms of faith as they went to their deaths. Bunyan's assertion that 'such an one must have combats and conflicts at the last, who carry in their consciences the guilt and condemnation that is due to their deeds', does not square with the execution speeches of Lord Russell and Algernon Sidney.[20] Bunyan, it seems, overstated his case either in his disgust with the conspiracy or, as I suspect, in an attempt to distance himself from friends implicated, however tenuously, in the plotting.

The case for the latter hypothesis is strengthened by his denial in *Seasonable Counsel* of any knowledge of the cabal — a denial he felt constrained to make not once but twice. Following his pointed reference to Absalom's conspiracy against David, he added: 'I thank God I know of no such men, nor thing', which, if true, meant that he had learned nothing of the projected insurrection from his London associates. Later in the same work he reiterated his innocence: 'I speak not these things, as knowing any that are disaffected to the Government: (for I love to be alone, if not with godly men, in things that are convenient)'. He mentioned this, he averred, only because he did not know into whose hands his work would fall, and he wanted everyone to know of his loyalty to the king.[21] Given Bunyan's association with dissidents such as Francis Smith and Benjamin Alsop, who would shortly take up arms with Monmouth, and probably with Meade, his claim not to know anyone disaffected to the government

19. *MW*, x, pp. 32 (quoted), 33, 38–39 (quoted), 75–77, 102–104. Cf. Thomas Grantham, writing in 1684: 'Many have undone themselves by itching after Changes in Worldly Government'. *The Loyal Baptist* (London, 1684), p. 39.

20. *MW*, x, pp. 33 (quoted), 104 (quoted); W. Cobbett, T. B. Howell, et al., *Cobbett's Complete Collection of State Trials and Proceedings*, 34 vols. (London, 1809–28), ix, pp. 683, 907–16.

21. *MW*, x, pp. 32, 40.

rings false. Bunyan was clearly distancing himself from the militancy that had given birth to the Rye House plotting.

Moreover, had Bunyan admitted knowledge of the conspirators and their work, he would have been subject to arrest and pressure to testify against his ministerial colleagues for allegedly treasonable conduct. Those who accept his denial of plotting at face value should bear this in mind. Would he have placed a higher value on absolute honesty than the lives of Nonconformist ministers? I think not, but this is a matter on which we can only speculate.

Bunyan's sincerity in expostulating an ethic of suffering in *Seasonable Counsel* cannot, however, be questioned, for such a theme runs throughout most of his writings, and indeed is common to the Judaeo-Christian tradition. What makes Bunyan's treatment in this work unusual is its timing and its extensiveness. His contemporaries often referred to tribulation in their writings, none more so than the Quakers, who repeatedly depicted themselves as sufferers and regularly recounted the stories of their persecution in print.[22] But as important as suffering was, Nonconformists habitually treated it only in passing. It is, nevertheless, possible to piece together the general thrust of a Nonconformist ethic of suffering against which Bunyan's view can be evaluated. Three basic themes prevailed: the necessity of suffering; the resulting benefits; and the correct way to suffer.

Widespread agreement existed among Nonconformists that the godly must suffer, although to varying degrees. 'Affliction is their portion', said George Swinnock; 'They must not be Christians, if they would not take up their Cross'. 'No cross, no crown' was William Penn's succinct expression of this verity, and Joseph Alleine advised believers to covenant with God to accept their lot, knowing that suffering was the prerequisite of reigning with Christ. Suffering was also, Swinnock added, 'a *Messenger* sent by the great God to us, about business of concernment' and must not therefore be slighted. It served both as a means to test a believer's willingness to obey divine commands and as a device to impose corrective discipline on the godly. Suffering was also essential because of the example of Christ, which gave the godly,

---

22. Petition of Herefordshire Quakers, 22 November 1680, Harley Papers, BL MSS Loan 29/183, fol. 52r; George Fox, *The Protestant Christian-Quaker a Sufferer* (London, 1680), pp. 3, 14–19; Isaac Penington, *Concerning Persecution* (London, 1661) pp. 17, 30; *A Short Relation of Some Part of the Sad Sufferings* (1670); William Brend, *A Loving Salutation to All Friends* (London, 1662); [Daniel Baker], *This Is a Short Relation of Some of the Cruel Sufferings* (London, 1662); Richard Crane, *A Hue and Cry After Bloodshed* (1662); C[rane], *The Cry of Newgate* (London, 1662), p. 3; George Whitehead, in F[rancis] H[owgill], *A Testimony Concerning . . . Edward Burroughs* (London, 1662), p. 17.

as Penn noted, 'a tast of what his Disciples must expect to drink more deeply of; namely, *The Cup of Self-denyal, cruel Tryals, and most bitter Afflictions*'.[23]

The notion that suffering was necessary raised casuistic questions as to whether one could legitimately flee persecution or deliberately seek it. The advice, cautiously rendered, proposed a sort of *via media*: the saint should neither go in quest of a cross nor flee persecution 'without just *Cause*, and *Call*'. As Richard Alleine put it, 'I would not go to a Prison without a *Mittimus* from Heaven, lest if my suffering be of my self; I be there left to shift for my self'. The godly were more likely, he noted, to err by trying to escape divinely ordained tribulation. If confronting persecutors would glorify God, or if one was specially emboldened to suffer by God (as Stephen and Paul had been), then Vavasor Powell regarded flight as unlawful. In the end, the decision to flee or stay was essentially a matter of conscience, for even the Biblical record offered varying examples.[24]

For those who suffered, the promised benefits were extensive, and included a greater revelation of God, 'a more plentiful diffusion of special Grace', and a pledge of spiritual blessing for those who persevered. Nonconformists perceived suffering as a token of divine love and election, a means 'to drink deep of his Love and Free-Grace', and a device to increase holiness, humility, and conformity to Christ's image. From his cell Joseph Alleine told his fellow prisoners to 'cast up your accounts. . . . If your Souls go forward in Grace by your Sufferings, blessed be God that hath brought you to such a place as Prison is'.[25] Suffering was also widely seen as a purgative to cleanse

23. George Swinnock, *The Christian Man's Calling*, 3 vols. (London, c. 1660–65), ii, pp. 350, 362–64, 384; *Mr. Joseph Alleines Directions, for Covenanting with God* (London, 1674); Thomas Goodwin, *Patience and Its Perfect Work* (London, 1666), p. 91; Zachary Crofton, *The Hard Way to Heaven* (London, 1662), p. 1; Matthew Meade, *The Good of Early Obedience* (London, 1683), p. 87; John Corbet, *The Remains of . . . John Corbet* (London, 1684), pp. 254, 257; Nathaniel Vincent, *A Funeral Sermon* (London, 1679), p. 13; R[ichard] A[lleine], *Godly-Fear* (London, 1674), p. 148; William Penn, *No Cross, No Crown* (1669), pp. 37–39; William Dyer, *Christs Famous Titles* (Cambridge, 1672), p. 100.

24. Vavasor Powell, *The Bird in the Cage, Chirping* (London, 1661), pp. 38–39; R[ichard] A[lleine], *Heaven Opened* (London, 1666), pp. 52–53; Edmund Calamy, in *The London-Ministers Legacy to Their Several Congregations*, 2nd ed. (1662), p. 11; *The Life & Death of . . . Joseph Alleine* (London, 1672), pp. 77–78.

25. R. Alleine, *Heaven Opened*, pp. 55–58; R. Alleine, *Godly-Fear*, p. 154; [Arthur Annesley, earl of Anglesey], *The King's Right of Indulgence in Spiritual Matters* (London, 1688), p. 64; Dyer, *Titles*, pp. 54, 204; Swinnock, *Calling*, ii, pp. 371, 374–75; Ralph Venning, *Mr. Ralph Venning's Alarm to Unconverted Sinners* (London, 1675); John Griffith, *Some Prison-Meditations and Experiences* (1663), sig. A2r–v; Thomas Watson, *Religion Our True Interest* (London, 1682), pp. 218–19; *Life & Death of Alleine*, pp. 71–76; Penington, *Persecution*, pp. 14–15.

the believer of sin, a means of refining spiritual gold by purging dross, and a medicine for religious ills. 'Suppose, Christian', mused William Dyer, 'the furnace be heat[ed] seven times hotter, its but to make you seven times better; fiery trials make golden Christians'. For the Nonconformists in general, the most important benefit of suffering was the resultant sense of spiritual peace. Repeatedly, they referred to a heightened awareness of Christ's presence that transformed their prison cells into palaces. Despite the deplorable conditions of London's Newgate prison, Francis Bampfield could write: 'My Lord is with me, to the sweet feeding and full satisfaction of my whole man, [and I am] greatly rejoycing, overcomingly-Triumphing, Abasing of self, and Advancing of *Jehovah Elehim*'. Similar statements are legion and represent a psychological steeling to withstand the rigours of state repression.[26]

The Nonconformist ethic also deemed it important to suffer properly. Above all, that meant suffering patiently. While the Quaker Katherine Evans was in the custody of the Inquisition in Malta in 1662, she wrote to her husband and children, exhorting them to 'bear the Cross with patience . . . ; for it is through the long-suffering and patient waitings, [that] the Crown of Life and Immortality comes to be obtained'. Patient suffering was so important to John Owen that he made it, along with holy living, one of the two basic duties of a Christian. Suffering must also be borne cheerfully, humbly, and willingly.[27]

26. Dyer, *Titles*, p. 146; Watson, *A Divine Cordial* (London, 1663), pp. 36, 40–43; Thomas Jollie, BL Add. MSS 54,185, fol. 42v; Swinnock, *Calling*, ii, pp. 393–99; Elias Pledger, *Of the Cause of Inward Trouble*, in *The Morning-Exercise at Cripple-Gate*, 4th ed. (London, 1677), pp. 307, 315; Thomas Jacomb, in *London-Ministers Legacy*, pp. 84–86; *The Life of the Reverend Mr. George Trosse*, ed. A. W. Baker (Montreal and London, 1974), p. 128; James Janeway, *Heaven upon Earth*, 3rd ed. (London, 1671), p. 73; Griffith, *Prison-Meditations*, pp. 11, 18; *Letters of Eminent Men, Addressed to Ralph Thoresby, F.R.S.*, 2 vols. (London, 1832), i, p. 34; Joseph Alleine, *Christian Letters* (1672), p. 36; [Francis Bampfield], *The Lords Free Prisoner* (London, 1683), p. 4; Isaac Clifford, in *Letters of John Pinney, 1679–1699*, ed. Geoffrey F. Nuttall (London, 1939), p. 1; *Diaries and Letters of Philip Henry, M.A.*, ed. Matthew Henry Lee (London, 1882), p. 175; John Audland, *The Suffering Condition of the Servants of the Lord* (London, 1662), p. 19.

27. Katherine Evans, in Baker, *Short Relation*, p. 54; John Owen, *A Discourse Concerning the Holy Spirit* (London, 1674), p. 572; Goodwin, *Patience*, pp. 19–21, 25; Pledger, *Diary*, DWL MSS 28.4, fol. 30r; Richard Baxter, *The Cure of Church-Divisions* (London, 1670), p. 247; Annesley, *Right*, pp. 63–64; Bampfield, *Prisoner*, p. 1; Bampfield to Charles II, PRO SP 29/99/52; Swinnock, *Calling*, ii, pp. 362, 365, 370; Watson, *The Duty of Self-Denial Briefly Opened and Urged* (London, 1675), p. 43; R. Alleine, *Godly-Fear*, pp. 158–59; R. Alleine, *Heaven Opened*, p. 54.

In most respects, Bunyan's ethic of suffering harmonized with that of other Nonconformists. The Christian does not suffer by chance or human will but divine appointment; for those called to undergo it, suffering is a duty. Although Bunyan believed it was the will of God 'that they that go to heaven should go thither hardly or with difficulty', he exempted some Christians from the necessity of the most grievous suffering by making it a special badge of honour. Not all saints, he suggested, were deemed worthy 'to suffer shame for . . . [Christ's] Name'.[28]

On the enigmatic question of confronting or fleeing from persecution, Bunyan embraced the *via media*. 'A man, though his cause be good, ought not by undue ways to run himself into suffering for it', a course that is contrary to both nature and divine law. The latter, Bunyan insisted, does not require the believer to put herself or himself 'into the mouth of his enemy', for on occasion both Jesus and Paul escaped magistrates. To flee because of slavish fear or to deny the Gospel is wrong, he explained, yet under appropriate circumstances 'flying is an ordinance of God, opening a door for the escape of some' by providence. For Bunyan this principle justified a minister who fled from a magistrate in order to preach elsewhere. But when suffering was divinely ordained, no Christian could escape. 'It remaineth then that we be not much afraid of men, nor yet be foolishly bold, but that we wait upon our God in the way of righteousness, and the use of those means which his providence offereth to us for our safety.'[29] A more mellow Bunyan was less willing to seek a confrontation than he had been when he deliberately courted arrest at Lower Samsell, Bedfordshire, in 1660. He would suffer rather than relinquish his right to preach and worship as his conscience dictated, and he would do this as a duty, but he refused to sanction reckless bravado.

Like other Dissenters, Bunyan extolled the benefits of suffering, the '*bitter pills*' of which purged the saints of impurities. '*I still have need of these Tryals*', he remarked in a personal aside. Despite having spent more time in prison than almost any other Dissenter, he could still aver that God could make a gaol more beautiful than a palace by the honeyed sweetness of his Word and the glory of his presence. Suffering is a manifestation of divine love, not wrath, and through it spiritual graces are experienced in greater intensity; there is, for instance, 'a rejoycing *in hope, when we are in tribulation, that is, over*

28. *MW*, x, pp. 11–13, 41–42, 69–71, 72–73 (quoted).
29. *MW*, x, pp. 8–9, 33–34, 49, 50 (quoted), 65–69 (p. 67 quoted), 73–75, (p. 74 quoted).

and above that which we have when we are at ease and quiet'. Through persecution in this world, the saint can 'shine' in the life to come as well as manifest greater holiness here. 'Righteousness thriveth best in affliction, the more afflicted, the more holy man; the more persecuted, the more shining man'. Bunyan clearly intended to make suffering less forboding, thereby decreasing the likelihood that those who experienced it would react violently to their persecutors.[30]

For Bunyan it was not enough to say that one must suffer patiently, meekly, and contentedly, though that was true enough. Reflecting the charged atmosphere of the Rye House investigations, he also insisted that they suffer quietly. 'Sit still and be quiet, and reverence the ordinance of God: I mean affliction.' By this he did not mean a retreat from Christian responsibility as he perceived it, but a willingness to accept the consequences of worshipping as a Dissenter without complaining. He especially wanted Nonconformists to avoid the impression that they would persecute others if they attained power: 'What will men say, if you *shrink* and *whinch*, and take your sufferings unquietly: but that if you your selves were uppermost, you would persecute also? . . . Be quiet then', and turn the other cheek.[31]

Bunyan distinguished himself from most other Nonconformists by the rigid conditions he imposed for efficacious suffering. One must suffer in the correct manner. Simply to suffer patiently if one lacks 'that word of the Holy One that alone can make his cause good *as to matter'* is not enough. The cause itself must be worthy or suffering is meaningless; by a good cause Bunyan meant morality (for which tribulation was rare) or evangelical righteousness and worship. Even dying in the flames for the Gospel is not enough to ensure effectual suffering if the victim lacks the grace that enables him or her to die properly. Suffering must be 'not only for *truth*, but of love to truth; not only *for* God's word, but *according* to it: to wit in that holy, humble, meek manner as the word of God requireth'. Implicitly, then, this ruled out any recognition of the executed Rye House plotters as martyrs; they may have acted in defence of God's Word, but not, in Bunyan's judgment, in the manner it stipulated.[32]

Suffering meekly, patiently, quietly, and in a Biblical manner was only part of a Christian's duty. The saint was also expected to suffer *willingly*. Bunyan distinguished between passive suffering, as inflicted on the murdered children of Ireland, France, and Piedmont because

30. *MW*, x, pp. 6 (quoted), 21–23, 61 (quoted), 80, 94–98.
31. *MW*, x, pp. 11–12, 36, 37 (quoted), 71–72, 102 (quoted).
32. *MW*, x, pp. 30 (quoted), 42–46.

of their parents' religion, and active suffering, which required the victim's approval. 'Active suffering, must be by the consent of the will'; the believer must kiss the chastising rod and love it, knowing that tribulation is divinely imposed. In effect, suffering was a fundamental aspect of worship. As any reader of John Foxe's *Acts and Monuments* knew, it was also a telling pedagogical act. With his flair for the dramatic, Bunyan expressed it thus: 'A man when he suffereth for Christ, is set upon an *Hill*, upon a *Stage*, as in a *Theatre*, to play a part for God in the World'.[33]

Bunyan's sensitivity to the plight of Nonconformity in the wake of the Rye House discoveries is evident in his efforts to calm feelings toward persecuting magistrates as well as to depict true Christianity as being no threat to the state. Christianity, he disarmingly observed, 'is so harmless a thing, that be it never so openly professed, it hurts no man'. In fact, however, Protestant principles provided much of the motivation for the Rye House conspirators, a fact Bunyan obviously knew. Bunyan found it necessary, then, to insist that Christians '*must imbrace nothing but harmless Principles*'. With an obvious eye to wary magistrates as well as his readers, he reiterated the commonplace doctrine that magistrates were ministers of God to whom the godly must be subject for the sake of conscience.[34] Repeatedly Bunyan urged his readers not to reproach their governors or condemn their acts, for all their '*ways are Gods*, either for thy help or the tryal of thy graces'. To complain when one is persecuted by the state is to love the flesh and distrust God to manage everything for the church's good. Magistrates who persecute do so as agents of God even if they are ignorant of the fact. '*Persecutors* as well as the *persecuted* are his, and he has his own designs upon both.' Like many other Dissenters, Bunyan tried to placate his readers by promising that at some point God would avenge himself on persecutors, but in the meantime the godly must shun revenge, concentrate on self-denial, and prepare themselves for more suffering by seeking the spiritual graces of meekness and patience that will enable them to endure.[35]

Whatever Bunyan may have known of the plotting for an insurrection in 1682–83 — if anything — his response to the government's discovery of the conspiracies indicates a degree of nervousness presumably occasioned by his association with Owen, Alsop, Newman, Francis

---

33. *MW*, x, pp. 34–35, 41, 42 (quoted), 62 (quoted).
34. *MW*, x, pp. 5 (quoted), 33, 39–40, 51 (quoted). Cf. Grantham, *Loyal Baptist*, sig. A3r; pp. 35–36, 61; Corbet, *An Account Given of the Principles & Practises of Several Nonconformists* (London, 1682), p. 11; Baxter, *Cure*, p. 242.
35. *MW*, x, pp. 8–9, 33–34, 71 (quoted), 94–95, 99 (quoted).

Smith, and probably Meade, all of whom were in trouble with the state. This would explain why Bunyan went out of the way to claim he knew no one disaffected to the government, and why, in espousing an ethic of suffering, he made a special point of asking his readers not to condemn persecuting magistrates. The threat posed to Nonconformity by the abortive plotting explains why Bunyan felt it essential to devote an entire tract to the duty of suffering — a tract that reveals a significant departure from the militant imagery of *The Holy War*. The discovery of the Rye House conspiracies may also explain why Bunyan did not publish his treatise on *Antichrist, and His Ruine*, which, though not anti-monarchical, was unrelenting in its insistence that the Antichrist must be destroyed. In the charged atmosphere of the Rye House discoveries, when Nonconformists were widely castigated as seditious, the more appropriate theme was suffering.

11

The Authorship of *Reprobation Asserted*

Reprobation Asserted: or the Doctrine of Eternal Election & Reprobation Promiscuously Handled, in Eleven Chapters was, according to its title-page, written by 'John Bunyan of Bedford, a Lover of Peace and Truth'. The authenticity of this claim has been a matter of dispute since Bunyan's principal biographer, John Brown, argued that the book was pseudonymous.[1] Subsequent critics have been divided on the issue: Henri Talon and G.B. Harrison rejected Brown's arguments and instead affirmed Bunyan's authorship, whereas Roger Sharrock, while rejecting Brown's arguments as inconclusive, decided after a more intensive analysis that the work was, in fact, not Bunyan's.[2]

Reprobation Asserted, as the title indicates, is an attempt to prove by logic and Biblical argument the Calvinist doctrine of reprobation, which in essence states that some people have been predestined by God from eternity to damnation, although this damnation is the result not of God's act of reprobation but of human sin. Divine grace elects only the chosen few, and the remainder are left to damnation because of their sin — helpless and unable to accept the offer of salvation in Christ. The purpose of *Reprobation Asserted* is to defend this doctrine against the attacks of the Arminians, who contended that God reprobated people only after their refusal of his grace, and not from eternity.

The treatise is undated, but Charles Doe has suggested that it appeared in 1674.[3] Unfortunately, in spite of his personal acquaintance

---

1. Brown, p. 228.
2. Talon, *John Bunyan: The Man and His Works*, trans. Barbara Wall (London, 1951), p. 261, n. 10; G. B. Harrison, *John Bunyan: A Study in Personality* (London, 1928), pp. 125–26; and Sharrock, personal correspondence, 27 March 1963. In *A Bibliography of the Works of John Bunyan* (Oxford, 1932), F. M. Harrison lists the treatise as 'repudiable' (p. 34).
3. Doe, p. [871].

with Bunyan, Doe was sometimes inaccurate. He also dated *Christian Behaviour* in 1674, when in fact it was first published in 1663. He dated *Come, & Welcome, to Jesus Christ* between 1679 and 1683, but Bunyan published it in 1678. *Mr. Badman* appeared in 1680, although Doe ascribed a date of 1684 to it. Doe, then, is not a reliable source for dating.

The first independent claim of Bunyan's authorship appeared in a catalogue of his works printed by Nathaniel Ponder in the third edition of *One Thing is Needful: or, Serious Meditations upon the Four Last Things* in 1688. Ponder's criterion for attribution was whether or not a title-page printed Bunyan's name in full. *Reprobation Asserted* therefore qualified, in Ponder's judgment, as a genuine work of Bunyan. Although Ponder's reasoning is not compelling, it is a point in favour of Bunyan's authorship of *Reprobation Asserted* that the publisher of at least eight of his works regarded it as his. Ponder's testimony is additionally important in view of the fact that he published *The Pilgrim's Progress* (1678 and 1684) and was therefore acquainted with Bunyan's concern about pseudonymous imitations.[4]

Doe did not include *Reprobation Asserted* in the partial edition of Bunyan's works he published in 1692, although the treatise un- doubtedly would have been had that undertaking been completed. Doe specifically stated that those works which he had listed but not included in the first 'folio' would be published in the second, which unfortunately never appeared. The first 'complete' edition of Bunyan's works, published in 1736–37, omitted *Reprobation Asserted*. This does not, however, necessarily imply that its editor, Samuel Wilson, regarded it as pseudonymous, for his collection did not include *A Discourse of the . . . House of God* (which Ponder had listed in his 1688 catalogue), *A Case of Conscience Resolved*, or *Profitable Meditations*. *Reprobation Asserted* was first incorporated in the 1784 edition of Bunyan's works edited by William Mason and John Ryland, and it was also published by George Offor in his edition of 1852–53.

The title-page of *Reprobation Asserted* states that the book was printed for G.L. and that copies were 'to be sold in Turnstile-Alley in Holbourn'. The initials almost certainly mean — or were intended to give the impression of meaning — that the book was printed for George Larkin. In the period between 1659 and 1688 there is no record of another bookseller with the initials G.L.[5] Prior to

4. See his preface to *The Pilgrim's Progress* (London, 1684).
5. Cf. H. R. Plomer, *A Dictionary of the Booksellers and Printers . . . from 1641 to 1667* (London, 1907); and *A Dictionary of the Printers and Booksellers . . . from 1668 to 1725* (London, 1922).

that period George Latham (d. 1658) sold books in London, but he conducted his business at the Brazen Serpent as well as the Bishop's Head, both in St. Paul's Churchyard.[6] At this time, John and M. Wright were selling Bunyan's books, namely *Some Gospel-Truths Opened* (1656), *A Few Sighs from Hell* (1658), and *The Doctrine of the Law and Grace Unfolded* (1659). Furthermore, if Latham had published *Reprobation Asserted*, it would have been, at the latest, Bunyan's fourth book — unlikely in view of its theological and philosophical context and his minimal education and writing experience. At this early date, of course, it is also highly improbable that someone would have used Bunyan's relatively unknown name for a pseudonym. The initials G.L. must therefore refer to George Larkin.

Larkin, who sold, among other things, *Grace Abounding to the Cheif of Sinners* (1666), *Good News for the Vilest of Men* (1688), *Solomon's Temple Spiritualiz'd* (1688), *A Discourse of the . . . House of God* (1688), and *The Acceptable Sacrifice* (1689), usually did business at Two Swans without Bishopsgate. He also sold books in at least three other locations, although none of these was Turnstile Alley.[7] Furthermore, Larkin customarily printed his name in full rather than using his initials. According to Brown, therefore, Larkin is not the true bookseller, nor is Bunyan the author.[8] However, the magistrates prosecuted Larkin for selling various books,[9] and he may therefore have temporarily sold his wares in Turnstile Alley, using only his initials, to evade further trouble.

That pseudonymous works were published in Bunyan's name is an established fact. Barring the possible exception of *Reprobation Asserted*, however, these pseudonymous works did not appear until after the publication of *The Pilgrim's Progress* in 1678. If Doe's date of 1674 for the publication of *Reprobation Asserted* is correct, this treatise came out four years before the book that occasioned the publication of the (other) pseudonymous works. If Doe erred in his dating, the mistake was probably like his others in that he dated it too late; *Reprobation Asserted* might therefore have appeared even more than four years prior to *The Pilgrim's Progress*. The description of Bunyan on the title page as 'a Lover of Peace and Truth' indicates that the book was almost certainly published before 1678, for after that date a pseudonymous author would presumably have described Bunyan — as he himself usually did — as the author of *The Pilgrim's Progress*. Thus if *Reprobation*

---

6. Plomer, *A Dictionary . . . 1641 to 1667*, p. 113.
7. Ibid., and *A Dictionary . . . 1668 to 1725*, pp. 183–84.
8. Brown, p. 228.
9. Plomer, *A Dictionary . . . 1668 to 1725*, p. 184.

Asserted is pseudonymous, a book other than Bunyan's famous allegory persuaded the author to use his name.

Among Bunyan's earlier works were *The Doctrine of the Law and Grace Unfolded*, *Christian Behaviour*, *The Holy City*, *Grace Abounding*, and *A Defence of the Doctrine of Justification, by Faith in Jesus Christ* — certainly enough major works to have established a reputation. In the period between 1672 and 1674 he was involved in a controversy over the necessity of baptism for church membership and communion, and the final volume of his trilogy on this subject, published in 1674, was *Peaceable Principles and True*. This work must have provided Bunyan — or the pseudonymous author — with the inspiration to describe the writer as 'a Lover of Peace and Truth'.[10] Perhaps an admirer of Bunyan in this debate (an open-membership, open-communion Particular Baptist), knowing his reputation, wrote *Reprobation Asserted* and published it in Bunyan's name. This would explain the existence of a pseudonymous work prior to the publication of *The Pilgrim's Progress*. Yet the external evidence neither proves nor disproves that Bunyan wrote *Reprobation Asserted*.

Stylistically *Reprobation Asserted* is manifestly different from Bunyan's theological treatises and homiletic and expository works. Its logical and well-ordered structure, involving eleven chapters in forty-four pages, is essentially without parallel in Bunyan's (other) writings. The customary 'use' or 'application' with which he concludes most of his works is also absent. *Reprobation Asserted* is dryly written,[11] at times distinctly philosophical,[12] and does not display the popular language and illustrative material characteristic of Bunyan. As John Brown aptly remarked, Bunyan 'writes not long before he either melts with tenderness or glows with fire'.[13] Only when Bunyan was directly embroiled in a theological controversy did he tend to omit popular phraseology, a direct appeal to the audience, and use of colourful metaphors. In *Reprobation Asserted* Roger Sharrock has found only one

10. Doe was probably accurate in his dating of *Reprobation Asserted*.

11. The author is 'hard and cold in style, thin in scheme and substance, and he is what Bunyan never was—pitiless in logic, without being truly logical', according to Brown, p. 228. G. B. Harrison admits that 'Bunyan and his religion at its worst is shown in *Reprobation Asserted*, a piece of cold-hearted casuistry, inspired partly by religious hate', referring to Bunyan's unjust condemnation in the Agnes Beaumont affair. Yet he also believes that 'the same hard, logical style is to be found in *Questions about the Nature and Perpetuity of the Seventh-day Sabbath*, wherein Bunyan was again arguing a point of doctrine'. *John Bunyan*, pp. 122, 125.

12. *Reprobation Asserted*, pp. 8–9, 15.

13. Brown, p. 228.

fully developed metaphor[14] and three phrases typical of Bunyan's style: 'Lazarus ... stunk in his Grave'; 'the Reprobate then doth ... run himself upon the Rocks of eternal Misery'; and 'How is the Word buried under the Clods of their Hearts?'[15] To this can be added a brief reference to similitudes. Bunyan, of course, was not the only writer of his period who used such graphic language, and the presence of only three phrases and one metaphor typical of his style in an entire treatise so uncharacteristic of his writing is sufficient reason to doubt his authorship.

The doctrine of reprobation presented in the treatise is essentially harmonious with that taught by Bunyan. The author defines reprobation as non-election, although Bunyan was not nearly so emphatic on this point.[16] He also refers to the unchangeableness of reprobation, in that the precise number to be elected and reprobated has been determined by God,[17] and stresses the idea that people have been condemned for their sins rather than as the consequence of their reprobation.[18] Mention is also made of God's 'Distinguishing Love'[19] and of the offer of salvation and grace to the greatest sinners — the latter being one of Bunyan's favourite homiletic themes.[20] None of these ideas was unique to Bunyan; all were generally accepted doctrine among contemporary Calvinists. Yet in general the doctrines of election and reprobation set forth in *Reprobation Asserted* are compatible with the statements of those doctrines found in Bunyan's (other) works.

Several important discrepancies exist between the theology of *Reprobation Asserted* and that set forth in Bunyan's (other) writings. The most important difference is the affirmation of a general atonement in *Reprobation Asserted*, which conflicts with Bunyan's concept of a limited atonement.[21] According to the author of the disputed treatise, 'Christ

14. *Reprobation Asserted*, pp. 13–14. Sharrock observes that this metaphor 'lacks the colour and the energetic quality that one is accustomed to in Bunyan's imagery'. imagery'.

15. *Reprobation Asserted*, pp. 32, 36, 39. Sharrock has also examined the Scripture references used in this tract for the presence of texts concerning promises or threatenings which, because of their autobiographical significance for Bunyan, occur both in *Grace Abounding* and in various doctrinal treatises. Only two such examples were found: Jer. 31:3 (p. 43) and the phrase 'to binde them fast in Chains of Darkness, unto the Judgement of the great day' (p. 11).

16. *Reprobation Asserted*, pp. 4, 13–14. Cf. Doe, p. 46; *MW*, viii, pp. 217–18.

17. *Reprobation Asserted*, p. 12. Cf. *MW*, vii, p. 113.

18. *Reprobation Asserted*, p. 14. Cf. *MW*, iii, pp. 281–82; viii, pp. 319–20, 325–26; ix, p. 174.

19. *Reprobation Asserted*, pp. 9, 40. Cf. *MW*, ix, p. 57.

20. *Reprobation Asserted*, pp. 24–25. Cf. *MW*, xi, pp. 13–92.

21. Cf. *Reprobation Asserted*, pp. 25–26.

died for all [2 Cor. 5:15], tasted death for every man [Heb. 2:9]; is the Saviour of the World [1 John 4:14], and the Propitiation for the sins of the whole World [1 John 2:2]'.[22] The writer employs these verses to support a doctrine of general atonement. Elsewhere, Bunyan quoted Hebrews 2:9 and 1 John 2:2 when referring to the extent of the atonement, but he qualified the latter verse by stating that Christ 'as a Propitiation' is 'not ours only, but also for the Sins of the whole World; to be sure, for the Elect throughout the World'.[23] Furthermore, the author of *Reprobation Asserted* clearly stated that

> the death of Christ did extend itself unto them [that is, the reprobate]: for the offer of the Gospel cannot, with Gods allowance, be offered any further then the death of Jesus Christ doth go; because if that be taken away, there is indeed no Gospel, nor Grace to be extended.[24]

According to Bunyan, however, Christ 'died for all his Elect'[25] and 'doth but petitionarily ask for his own, his purchased ones, those, for whom he died before, that they might be saved by his Blood'.[26] Bunyan may, of course, have changed his mind on this issue; most of the statements expressing his belief in a limited atonement come from a period subsequent to that when *Reprobation Asserted* was written. Yet he made at least two comments reflecting the concept of a limited atonement in 1672 and 1674, so that such a possibility is remote.[27]

In an astute defence of Bunyan's authorship of *Reprobation Asserted*, Paul Helm has argued that the author of this tract did not teach a doctrine of general atonement. Much of Helm's case rests on the seeming incompatibility of such a doctrine with the unmistakable teaching in this work that some persons have been elected to salvation. Yet Helm rightly acknowledges that nowhere in this tract does the writer explicitly indicate that Christ died for the elect alone; on the contrary, he clearly states that Christ's death 'did extend itself unto them', that is, the reprobate. Moreover, the author contends that the Gospel is offered to all people in good faith: 'it must needs be that the gospel was with all faithfulness to be tendered unto them; the which it could not be unless the death of Christ did extend itself unto them'.

22. Ibid., p. 25.
23. *MW*, xi, p. 145.
24. *Reprobation Asserted*, p. 26.
25. *MW*, xi, p. 216.
26. Doe, p. 370.
27. Cf. *MW*, iv, p. 64 (but cf. a statement on the same page: 'So he dyed for all'); viii, p. 61.

Helm contends that this passage means only that the benefits of the atonement are offered to the reprobate 'in the sense that if they were to believe then Christ's death would suffice for their salvation'. However, if Christ died for the elect alone, any offer of the benefits of his death to the reprobate would be fraudulent. The author of *Reprobation Asserted* attempts to avoid this problem by affirming a general atonement, which therefore legitimates the offer of grace.[28]

Two other doctrinal points should be noted. The important explanation that sin came into the world by being 'offered' to humankind and 'prevailing' over people does not appear (elsewhere) in Bunyan's writings, even when he is discussing the fall and humanity's responsibility for its sin.[29] Secondly, the argument that the divine will is the rule both of mercy and of righteousness is typically Calvinist and therefore compatible with Bunyan's theology, but this was a subject with which he was not particularly concerned.[30]

When all the facts are analysed it is possible to argue plausibly either for or against Bunyan's authorship of *Reprobation Asserted*. Yet the discrepancies in style and theology, coupled with the uncertain external evidence and the distinct possibility that the treatise was written shortly after the publication of *Peaceable Principles and True* by an open-membership, open-communion Particular Baptist who admired Bunyan's role in that debate, point to the likelihood that *Reprobation Asserted* is a spurious, pseudonymous work.

28. Paul Helm, 'John Bunyan and "Reprobation Asserted"', *Baptist Quarterly* 28 (April 1979): 87–93. The fact that Bunyan did not specifically repudiate this work as his own proves nothing; he did not make a point of renouncing all spurious attributions of authorship.
29. *Reprobation Asserted*, p. 17. Cf., e.g., Doe, pp. 13–15.
30. *Reprobation Asserted*, pp. 20–21.

12

Tercentenary Reflections

Three-hundred years after Bunyan's death, scholarly interest in his life and writings has never been greater. Under the direction of Roger Sharrock, the first critical edition of his complete works has nearly been completed; what Bunyan, who sneered at Oxford and Cambridge, would think of his new publisher, Oxford University Press, can only be a matter of conjecture. Christopher Hill has written a magnificent social biography of Bunyan[1] in the tradition of William York Tindall's 1934 classic, *John Bunyan: Mechanick Preacher*. International symposia to celebrate the tercentenary were convened at the Vrije Universiteit in Amsterdam, and at Durham University and the Open University's Milton Keynes campus in England. Select proceedings of the Vrije Universiteit and Open University conferences have now been published, as have scholarly collections edited by Neil Keeble and Robert Collmer.[2] In addition, a host of articles have been published and addresses given.

Although appreciation of Bunyan in scholarly circles has never been higher, especially considering the superb quality of current Bunyan scholarship,[3] ignorance of his works among the general population is probably at an all-time high. In a survey of what seventeen-year-old American students know, less than one in seven could identify *The Pilgrim's Progress*.[4] Few American university students read the allegory.

Bunyan scholarship has changed our understanding of him, particu-

1. Hill, *JB*.
2. Keeble, *JB*; *John Bunyan Today*, ed. Robert Collmer (Kent, Ohio, 1988).
3. Richard L. Greaves, 'Bunyan Through the Centuries: Some Reflections', *English Studies: A Journal of English Language and Literature* 64 (April 1983), 113–21; *John Bunyan: A Reference Guide*, ed. James F. Forrest and Richard L. Greaves (Boston, 1982), pp. ix–xvii.
4. Diane Ravitch and Chester E. Finn, Jr., *What Do Our 17-Year-Olds Know?* (New York, 1987), cited in Hill, *JB*, pp. 372–73.

larly as historians and literary scholars have taken greater cognizance of the significance of his lesser works and his associations in the wider Nonconformist community. While interest in *The Pilgrim's Progress* continues to hold pride of place in Bunyan studies, no Bunyan student can henceforth ignore the minor works, including the critical books published posthumously. Writings such as *Of Antichrist, and His Ruine* and the commentary on Genesis reveal much about Bunyan's millenarian convictions, his overarching concern with persecution in his later years, and his views on church-state relations. Although more work must be done to date the posthumous works, the establishment of a reasonably firm chronology is crucial if we are to understand how Bunyan's thought evolved and how he reacted to contemporary events. This is especially important given the relative scarcity of biographical data for Bunyan's years as a prisoner and for his subsequent ministerial career.

The primary source for Bunyan's life, his magisterial spiritual autobiography, *Grace Abounding to the Chief of Sinners*, is in fact a work that professional historians should use only with the greatest caution. Written while Bunyan was in prison and first published in 1666, *Grace Abounding* recalls — often in great detail — spiritual struggles that occurred more than a decade earlier. His memory sometimes failed him, he was uncertain about the chronological sequence of some events, and he recalled others as he expanded the work in subsequent editions. Just as importantly, it is essential to consider the purpose of the book, which was intended in part as a spiritual guide to others, and in part as a demonstration of his credentials as a religious leader. Lacking the traditional education at Oxford or Cambridge, he stressed the drama of his own conversion — the miraculous regeneration of history's greatest sinner, or so he boasted — to document his divine calling. Thus biography was expanded to include spiritual counsel and to claim divinely bestowed authority. Bunyan, in other words, almost certainly exaggerated the scope and intensity of his conversion experience, partly to encourage struggling readers, partly to assure them of his ministerial qualifications. Because he wrote the work in prison, it also reflects his re-examination of his conversion and calling, which, after all, were the source of his defiance of the state and his resulting incarceration. Attempts to psychoanalyze Bunyan are often therefore misguided because they fail to understand the nature of *Grace Abounding*.

Standing alone, Bunyan's spiritual autobiography suggests that he, like some other Nonconformists, was keenly interested in the process of spiritual self-examination. For some, this was indeed a duty of paramount importance. 'Examine, and try, and search your selves', exhorted William Dyer, 'how do your pulses beat after Christ?' John Owen similarly proclaimed that 'there is not any thing in our whole Course that we ought to be more awake unto, than a diligent Observation of the *Progress* and *Decayes* of Grace; . . . they are very hardly and difficultly to be discerned'. The significance of this duty was espoused throughout the spectrum of Nonconformity, from the 'meer Nonconformist' Richard Baxter and the Presbyterian Thomas Watson to radicals such as Vavasor Powell and the Quaker Margaret Fell.[5]

To assist the saints, as we have seen, some ministers prepared broadsheets, suitable for tacking on a wall, that provided questions for this exercise in autoinquisition. The Presbyterian Christopher Jelinger's included twelve questions as well as a general directive: 'I will . . . examin my self every evening before I go to bed (besides praying, reading, singing, which at that time must be done also, with my family and apart), what evils have I thought, done, and spoken, and what good have I done?' Those who took this duty seriously had no trouble occupying their evenings. The list provided by the Presbyterian Joseph Alleine included a hefty twenty-nine questions to be asked each evening, and another five each morning.[6]

Those who took this duty seriously undoubtedly became intensely introspective. Some preachers recommended that the godly keep spiritual diaries to record the results of their daily examinations. No evidence indicates that Bunyan used such a diary as a source for the composition of *Grace Abounding*, although it too reveals, retrospectively, a similar spiritual stock-taking. Extant diaries, which are by their very nature more reliable historical records than spiritual autobiographies, reflect varying degrees of intensity and consistency. Unmistakable parallels exist between some of the statements in the diaries and *Grace Abounding*, a fact that tends to authenticate the general thrust of Bunyan's religious experience. There is, for instance, Owen Stockton's rueful entry: 'About 4 days before[,] I had felt the sin of my heart overpowering of me. I was cast down that I should yet sin against

5. William Dyer, *Christs Famous Titles, and a Believers Golden-chain* (Cambridge, 1672), p. 54; John Owen, *A Discourse Concerning the Holy Spirit* (London, 1674), p. 351; Owen, *The Grace and Duty of Being Spiritually-Minded* (London, 1681), p. 29; Richard Baxter, in *The London-Ministers Legacy to Their Several Congregations*, 2nd ed. ([London?], 1662), p. 180; Thomas Watson, Funeral Sermon for Elizabeth Knolles, DWL MS 24.13, fol. 5v; Vavasor Powell, *The Bird in the Cage Chirping* (London, 1661), p. 54; Margaret Fell, *The Evident Demonstration to Gods Elect* (London, 1660), p. 11.

6. Christopher Jelinger, *The Resolution-Table* (London, 1676); *Mr. Joseph Alleines Directions, for Covenanting with God* (London, 1674).

God'. Like Bunyan, Elias Pledger struggled against temptations of the flesh as well as the spirit: 'I have many times temptations to Indecent action, which I thank god have cold entertainment with me'. Another diarist fretted that 'I have not had such Manifestations of his Love as I have had at other times'. Sometimes, as in *Grace Abounding*, spiritual relief appears in the diaries as Bible verses that bolt into the conscience. Thus Eleanor Stockton recounted her concern that God might never have mercy on 'shuch a vile wretched unholy creature that have so dishonoured him as I have don', but then happily added that 'it pleased God suddenly to give in an answer to those sad thoughts by bringing to mind & seting hom[e] upon my soul these following scriptures', namely Luke 12:32 and Romans 4:5.[7]

We have no evidence that Bunyan himself engaged in such self-interrogation once he had finished *Grace Abounding*, nor was he preoccupied with urging his readers to examine themselves intensively each day. Admonitions to perform spiritual duties and to be on constant watch against evil predators are common in his writings, and no student of Bunyan can doubt his interest in the spiritual welfare of the godly. Bunyan's answer to the demand for religious interrogatories was probably *The Pilgrim's Progress*. Here, in convenient, appealing, memorable format, was a synopsis of the spiritual life in which readers could easily ascertain the state of their souls by reflecting on the allegorical episodes. For three centuries readers have readily grasped the element of common experience in such scenes as the Slough of Despond, Doubting Castle, Vanity-Fair, amd the Valley of the Shadow of Death. The Doubting Castle episode, in fact, reflected one aspect of self-examination, namely the soul-wrenching experienced by saints who left the designated spiritual path and became victims of despair. Judging from the spiritual diaries, such experiences were relatively common. 'I find Unbelief prevailing', a concerned relative of Philip Henry wrote, while Owen Stockton worried when 'I saw the plaug of my heart breaking out; I argued against my corruption yet it overcame me & lead me captive'.[8] Those who experienced such crises could find their spiritual states mirrored in *The Pilgrim's Progress*, which presumably offered comfort in light of Christian's happy ending.

The Pilgrim's Progress, of course, was also intended to lure readers to the Gospel; Bunyan likened himself to an angler in quest of fish,

7. Powell, *Bird*, p. 120; Owen Stockton, Diary, DWL MSS 24.7, fol. 10r; Elias Pledger, Diary, DWL MSS 28.4, fol. 29v; Diary of a Member of the Henry Family, BL Add. MSS 42,849, fol. 78r; Eleanor Stockton, Diary, DWL MSS 24.8, fol. 12r.

8. Henry, Diary, BL Add. MSS 42,849, fol. 78v; Owen Stockton, Diary, DWL MSS 24.7, fol. 10r.

although simultaneously he had a view to those seeking knowledge of their spiritual estate:

> *Would'st read thy self, and read thou know'st not what*
> *And yet know whether thou are blest or not,*
> *By reading the same lines? O then come hither,*
> *And lay my Book, thy Head and Heart together.*[9]

The allegory was a book calculated not only to appeal to the heart but to provide a simple means by which to gauge the soul's religious condition.

Recent suggestions that *The Pilgrim's Progress* is not faithful to Bunyan's strict Calvinist orthodoxy are mistaken. Gordon Campbell, an astute Bunyan scholar, rightly stresses the fact that the allegory is an imaginative work rather than a theological treatise, but he mistakenly argues that the doctrine of election 'does not affect the Christian of *The Pilgrim's Progress*'.[10] If this were so, the allegory would have little use for a reader seeking to ascertain whether he or she was 'blest or not'. Election is depicted allegorically as the wicket gate to which Christian (initially his name, not an indication of his spiritual state) was directed by Evangelist, a godly preacher, and through which he could pass only after it was opened for him. Christian had the capacity in his pre-conversion state to run toward the gate and knock when he reached it, but this is an allegorical reference to the Puritan-Nonconformist concept of preparation. Similarly, in the second part of the allegory the gate had to be opened for Christiana and her companions. This was simply Bunyan's way of underscoring the absolute necessity of electing grace. No would-be pilgrim had the ability to open the gate; 'I am not a free-willer', Bunyan reiterated in his last sermon, 'I do abhor it'.[11]

Despite Bunyan's best efforts to build a sense of drama in *The Holy War*, it too rests, when interpreted soteriologically, on a Calvinist foundation. There is never any real doubt about the fate of Mansoul, nor does Mansoul's destiny rest in the hands of anyone other than God. The contest for the soul is really fought between Emanuel and Diabolus, with the latter either too stubborn or too ignorant to realize that his cause is hopeless. In case the allegory as a whole did not make this point abundantly clear, Bunyan conspicuously placed the Election-Doubters, Vocation-Doubters, Grace-Doubters, Faith-

9. *PP*, pp. 3, 7.

10. Gordon Campbell, 'The Theology of *The Pilgrim's Progress*', *The Pilgrim's Progress: Critical and Historical Views*, ed. Vincent Newey (Totowa, N.J., 1980), p. 257.

11. Offor, ii, p. 756.

Doubters, and Perseverance-Doubters in Diabolus' army. When a representative Election-Doubter was captured and tried, the judge sentenced him to death, but only after explaining that 'to question Election is to overthrow a great Doctrine of the Gospel, to wit, the *Omnisciency*, and *Power*, and *Will* of God, to take away the liberty of God with his Creature, to stumble the faith of the Town of *Mansoul*, and to make Salvation to depend upon works, and not upon Grace'.[12] To Bunyan the Election-Doubter thus represented the intolerable face of Popery and Arminianism. A man so conscious of the value of his own liberty and, in the context of the exclusion struggle, the liberties of English subjects, was inevitably sensitive to anything he thought deprived God of freedom.

The fact that Perseverance-Doubters were similarly condemned should have cautioned recent interpreters who argue that *The Holy War* manifests a double conversion.[13] The source of the confusion is simple enough: Mansoul is captured by Emanuel, retaken by Diabolus, and finally recaptured by Emanuel. But this does not necessarily ensure safety from Diabolus in the future, as the allegory's last line reveals: 'Hold fast till I come'. The struggle, in other words, is not over. Perhaps more to the point is the fact that any notion of double conversion is diametrically opposed to Bunyan's Calvinist principles, and specifically to the tenet that the soul elected by grace will persevere to the inevitable heavenly reward.[14] For the elect the end is certain, no matter how rocky the road; we are back to the theme of *The Pilgrim's Progress*. Advocates of a notion of double conversion have also missed the point that Puritans and Nonconformists had long looked to the Biblical story of David as one model of conversion. Notwithstanding David's faith, he seduced Bathsheba and arranged her husband's murder, yet despite the heinous nature of his action he remained, according to these interpreters, one of the elect. His subsequent remorse, repentance, and forgiveness did not amount, they argued, to another conversion. David was thus a model for believers who succumbed to serious temptations, but who, through grace, were assured of perseverance to glory. Mansoul's temporary reconquest by Diabolus was an example of Davidic backsliding, the solution to which was not a second conversion but repentance.

12. *HW*, pp. 240–41.

13. Anne Hawkins, 'The Double Conversion in Bunyan's *Grace Abounding*', *Philological Quarterly* 61 (Summer 1982), 259–76: for *The Holy War*, see pp. 271–72.

14. Greaves, *John Bunyan* (Appleford, Berks., 1969), pp. 89–94.

Election and its corollary, perseverance, were not, according to Bunyan, an excuse for licentious living. Do not, he warned, 'take courage to live loose lives, under a supposition, that once in Christ, and ever in Christ, and the covenant cannot be broken, nor the relation of Father and Child dissolved'.[15] The supposition as a whole was invalid, not because the covenant could be broken or the father-child relationship terminated, but because anyone who used the doctrine of perseverance to justify the pursuit of evil had never been one of the elect. Bunyan thus drove readers back, at least implicitly, to some form of self-examination — to 'a *spiritual inquisition*; a bringing ones self to trial', as Thomas Watson said.[16]

Although Bunyan obviously wanted believers to remain sensitive to their spiritual condition, he stressed action rather than introspection as the key to godly living. Pilgrimage and warfare are, after all, metaphors more conducive to activity than reflection. His writings are peppered with admonitions to do, to act, to suffer, to deny oneself. One of the dominant themes of *Christian Behaviour* (1663) is 'that every Believer should not only be careful that their works be good, and for the present do them, but should also be careful to maintain them; that is, They should carefully study to keep in a constant course of Good Works'.[17] The core of Christian living could be summed up as the performance of religious duties, but even the best of saints, Bunyan admitted, sometimes sinned 'in their most exact and spiritual performance of Duties; they pray not, they hear not, they read not, they give not Alms, they come not to the Lord's Table, or other holy Appointments of *God*, but in, and with much coldness, deadness, wandrings of heart, ignorance, mis-apprehensions, *&c*'.[18] Right things must be done in the right spirit.

This emphasis on intent as well as deed, common among Nonconformists, had the practical effect of making religious life both intensive and, in ideal terms, uncompromising. Moderation was tantamount to indifference.[19] Bunyan urged his readers to ponder their death

15. *MW*, ix, p. 43.

16. Watson, *Heaven Taken by Storm* (London, 1669), p. 56.

17. *MW*, iii, pp. 11–12.

18. *MW*, viii, p. 209.

19. Watson, *The Godly Mans Picture, Drawn with a Scripture-Pensil* (London, 1666), pp. 159–60, 164; Watson, *Heaven Taken*, pp. 8–9, 14; Matthew Meade, *The Good of Early Obedience* (London, 1683), p. 194; Zachary Crofton, *The Hard Way to Heaven* (London, 1662), p. 5; Owen, *A Discourse Concerning the Holy Spirit*, pp. 157, 160; Thomas Manton, *How May We Cure Distractions in Holy Duties?*, in *The Morning-Exercise at Cripple-Gate*, 4th ed. (London, 1677), p. 392.

frequently: 'Bring thy last day often to thy bed-side, and ask thy heart if this morning thou wast to die, if thou be ready to die or no'.[20] This was less a revival of the medieval *ars moriendi* than a convenient means to order spiritual inventory. Other preachers, including Richard Baxter and the Congregationalist Bartholomew Ashwood, issued exhortations similar to Bunyan's.[21] At least some of the laity took this advice to heart, thereby reinforcing their sense of spiritual commitment. Of death Edward Harley wrote: 'The continual having of it before our eyes, should not only serve for water to quench the hottest temp[t]ations, but every fresh instance of it, should make us fit'. In her diary Eleanor Stockton asked, 'Soule what if thou wast this day to die[,] couldst thou bid death welcome'? Her positive response would have earned Bunyan's approval.[22]

The intensity of conviction that was the bedrock of Nonconformity inspired the courage with which Bunyan and his fellow Dissenters withstood demands to conform. His short tract, *I Will Pray with the Spirit* (1662?), though written in prison, breathed defiance against those who would require him to use the Book of Common Prayer. 'Thus is the Spirit of Prayer disowned, and the Form imposed; the Spirit debased, and the Form extolled: they that pray with the Spirit, though never so humble and holy, counted *Phanaticks*; and they that pray with the Form, though with that only, counted the *Vertuous*.'[23] He had already been incarcerated for holding a conventicle at Lower Samsell, Bedfordshire, in November 1660, at which time he had opted to confront the magistrates rather than escape.[24] Much later in his career, he reflected on the quandary that faced those about to be persecuted. Should they too flee, or should they stand fast to defy their persecutors? His advice, perhaps tempered by age and more than a dozen years in prison, was ambivalent: both natural and divine law, he argued, demonstrate that 'a man, though his *cause* be good, ought not by undue ways to run himself into suffering for it'. As in every other area of life, *how* one suffers is far more significant than the mere fact of suffering. 'A man may be a Christian, *and suffer*, and yet not suffer . . . *according to the will of God*.' The key is intent: one who suffers while professing the Gospel, that is, one who 'walk[s so] as

20. *MW*, viii, p. 44.

21. Baxter, in *The London-Ministers Legacy*, p. 187; Bartholomew Ashwood, *The Best Treasure* (London, 1681), p. 419.

22. Harley Papers, Portland MSS, BL Loan 29/183, fol. 111r; Eleanor Stockton, Diary, DWL MSS 24.8, fol. 21r. Cf. Matthew Henry, BL Add. MSS 42,849, fol. 27r; *MW*, i, p. 376.

23. *MW*, ii, p. 284.

24. 'A Relation of the Imprisonment of Mr. John Bunyan', ad cal. *GA*, pp. 105–107.

to make my profession of it more apparent', acts properly. The decision was ultimately left to each person: 'If it is in thy heart to fly, *fly*: if it be in thy heart to stand, *stand*'.[25]

The ethic of suffering was particularly necessary for those who, like Bunyan, espoused passive resistance. Whereas Bunyan was radical in many respects, such as his open-membership policy, his pronounced dislike of most rich and powerful people,[26] and his determination to hold conventicles, we have no evidence that he ever asserted the right of Christians to take up arms against an antichristian government. In this respect he deviated from a tradition previously advocated by such Protestant stalwarts as John Knox and Christopher Goodman, and in his own day by men such as John Milton and Robert Ferguson. Bunyan probably never met Milton or read any of his works, but Ferguson was John Owen's assistant from 1674 to about 1682, and may have made Bunyan's acquaintance when the latter visited London. Ferguson, an intimate of Shaftesbury, was heavily involved in the earl's plans to mount a general insurrection in 1682 to terminate the duke of York's right of succession. As we have seen, he was also a key figure in the plot to assassinate Charles II and his brother near the Rye House in Hertfordshire the following year. Owen would never have approved of assassination, but he was probably privy to the plans for an uprising.[27]

Whether Bunyan was aware of the projected insurrection or not, he was indisputably frequenting the company of prominent dissidents in the London area. Nor was this the first time, as he had previously had links to Fifth Monarchists and had perhaps been attracted to their extreme millenarianism. By the 1680s his circle of friends included Griffith and Meade, both of whom were accused, like Owen, of complicity in Monmouth's plans. Moreover, Bunyan's printers were habitually in trouble with the government for illegal and allegedly seditious activities. Benjamin Alsop, in fact, even participated in Monmouth's rebellion in 1685.[28] Given these associations, Bunyan was probably watched by informers when he visited London. Awareness of that fact may help to explain why he was not in London in the latter half of 1683 to examine the proofs of *A Holy Life*; this was also, of course, the period during which the government was furiously investigating the Rye House plotting.[29]

25. *MW*, x, pp. 30 (quoted), 50–51 (quoted), 73 (quoted), 74–75.
26. Hill, *JB*, pp. 87–89.
27. Chap. 10, supra.
28. Hill, *JB*, pp. 283–91.
29. *MW*, ix, p. xviii.

Bunyan was not opposed to monarchical government *per se*, and in fact envisioned a role for kings in the overthrow of the Antichrist. This is not, however, to say that he refused to sanction violence, for he fully expected these monarchs to utilize physical weapons in their task. He denied the church a similar right, insisting that it be restricted solely to the use of spiritual weapons, including prayer and preaching. These weapons were not as harmless as they appear to modern readers, a fact fully appreciated by government supporters who waged a relentless campaign to quash conventicles. Francis Wingate, the magistrate who issued a warrant for Bunyan's arrest in 1660, was not altogether unjustified in his apparent suspicion that those who met 'did intend to do some fearful business, to the destruction of the country'. John Eston and John Grew, both prominent members of the congregation, had been interrogated in April 1657 for supporting a petition opposing the assumption of the crown by Oliver Cromwell, and in October 1659 the Bedford church celebrated the defeat of Sir George Booth's royalist rebellion.[30] This clearly was a church known for its pro-commonwealth views, hence Bunyan's determination to continue preaching after the monarchy had been restored raised legitimate concern; he was already on record as having warned that the saints would ultimately 'slight' their persecutors as much as the latter 'slighted them'. He followed this with a quotation from Psalm 58:10, 'The Righteous shall rather rejoyce when he seeth the vengeance of God upon thee', but he prudently did not quote the last half of that verse, 'he shall wash his feet in the blood of the wicked'.[31]

Throughout most of Charles II's reign, a minority among the Nonconformists engaged in seditious activities, sometimes using conventicles as their base. Thomas Venner's Fifth Monarchist congregation rebelled in London in January 1661, and in the spring of 1663 Presbyterians and Congregationalists in Dublin made preparations to seize the castle, arrest the duke of Ormond, and join forces with rebellious Scots in Ulster. The mastermind of the northern rebellion in October 1663, which involved dissidents in Durham, Westmorland, and Yorkshire, was Edward Richardson, a Congregationalist minister. 'Soberer Fanatiques' dissuaded another minister, the Particular Baptist and Fifth Monarchist Nathaniel Strange, from attacking Whitehall Palace in early 1665. That August sympathetic Londoners rescued the Particular Baptist Henry Danvers, with whom Bunyan would subsequently debate the necessity of baptism for church membership,

30. Chap. 6, supra; Hill, *JB*, pp. 93–94.
31. *MW*, i, p. 284.

after Danvers had been arrested on suspicion of seditious activity. Reports of plotting, many of which were almost certainly groundless, were rampant throughout the 1660s. In 1670 the Presbyterian Thomas Blood, the Fifth Monarchist Richard Halliwell, and others briefly kidnapped the duke of Ormond with a view to hanging him for his alleged crimes. The plotting died down only when persecution abated because of the indulgence the king issued in 1672.[32] When persecution resumed and the country faced the prospect of a Catholic sovereign, some Nonconformists not only supported the abortive exclusion campaign but, as we have seen, allegedly approved Shaftesbury's proposed insurrection.

At one time or another, most of Bunyan's principal associates, including Owen, Meade, Griffith, Palmer, and Cokayne, were suspected of seditious activity. Bunyan understood that a similar suspicion was behind his arrest. Yet like many Nonconformists he distinguished between conventicles held as a cover for evil purposes and those in which God was properly worshipped. From the government's standpoint, this was not a useful distinction, since it would require constant monitoring of all conventicles. With many other Nonconformists, Bunyan denounced Venner's futile insurrection, insisting that it was his duty to behave himself as a Christian.[33] His subsequent statements on church-state relations are generally consistent with this principle of obedience. In *Seasonable Counsel* (1684), for instance, he proclaimed that '*we must fear God, and honour the King*'. Because this was written as the government investigated the Rye House plotting, including accusations against Owen, Meade, and Griffith, he urged his readers not to speak against those in power or to '*meddle . . . with those that are given to change*'.[34] Aside from a resolute determination to preach in defiance of the law and a willingness to publish unlicensed works, Bunyan was a cautious man, particularly when discussing political affairs. That fact undoubtedly explains why some of his works, which manifest his hostility not only to Catholicism but to absolute monarchy, were only published posthumously.

One of the more important aspects of Bunyan's outlook with respect both to political affairs and to the life of the individual Christian is providence. Bunyan scholars have paid relatively little attention to this concept, despite its prominence in Protestant and especially

---

32. Greaves, *DUFE*, chaps. 2, 4–6; Greaves, *EUHF*, chaps. 1, 6.
33. 'Relation', pp. 119–20.
34. *MW*, x, pp. 38–41 (p. 39 quoted), 98 (quoted).

Puritan and Nonconformist thought, probably because he seldom used the term. Yet the doctrine itself informs much of his theology. As explained by John Owen, providence is 'the effectual working of his [God's] Power, and Almighty Act of his Will, whereby he sustaineth, governeth, and disposeth of all things, Men, and their Actions, to the ends which he hath ordained for them'. Though the outworking of providence was attributed, in Meade's words, to God's 'immutable Decrees', providence always operated in conformity with Biblical principles rather than whim. This did not, however, mean that the workings of providence could always be understood. 'In all cases where you are not able to reconcile Gods Providences with his Promises', explained Owen Stockton, 'you must steadfastly believe that God is faithful and righteous, although you cannot apprehend how such or such a Providence should be consistent with his faithfulness, or with his righteousness'.[35] In practical terms, belief in providence provided an explanation for events, both personal and public, that on the surface seemed to contravene divine sovereignty. God ruled even when it appeared he did not.

At the personal level providence was thus a comforting doctrine. 'All the *Providences of God*, though never so *dark* and *mysterious*, and *seemingly contrary* to his *Promises*', wrote the Presbyterian Edmund Calamy the elder, 'shall all of them at last concur to the fulfilling of his *Promises*'. William Kiffin and Elias Pledger attributed the hardships they experienced to providence, while Matthew Henry hoped it would prevent a trip to London if the journey did not suit God's purposes. Henry's father held providence responsible for the Great Fire of London, and others used it to explain their movements and activities. 'Providence removes me from my desired Pastures', Dr. William Guy told his stepfather.[36] We are immediately reminded of Bunyan's famous statement, 'upon a day, the good providence of God did cast me to *Bedford*'. Bunyan also spoke of 'providences', by which

35. Owen, *The Principles of the Doctrine of Christ* (London, 1684), p. 18; Matthew Meade, *The Vision of the Wheels Seen by the Prophet Ezekiel* (London, 1689), p. 30; Owen, *An Humble Testimony unto the Goodness and Severity of God* (London, 1681), p. 69; Owen Stockton, *A Treatise of Family Instruction* (London, 1672), p. 333.

36. Edmund Calamy, *The Happinesse of Those Who Sleep in Jesus* (London, 1662), sig. A2v; William Kiffin, *Remarkable Passages in the Life of William Kiffin*, ed. William Orme (London, 1823), p. 50; Elias Pledger, Diary, DWL MSS 28.4, fol. 26r; Matthew Henry, BL Add. MSS 42,849, fol. 22r; *Diaries and Letters of Philip Henry, M.A.*, ed. Matthew Henry Lee (London, 1882), p. 192; George Swinnock, *The Christian Man's Calling*, pt. 1 (London, '1668' [i.e. *c*. 1660]), sig. D2v; Dr. William Guy, DWL MSS 12.63.(13).

he meant the good and bad things that befell a person; they occurred because of the outworking of providence itself.[37]

The concept of providence was especially useful to Bunyan as he attempted, on the one hand, to condemn the spirit of the Antichrist and its manifestation in any repressive state (including late Stuart England), and, on the other, to counsel his followers not to take up arms against the government but to suffer for the cause of the Gospel. 'When, by providence I am cast for my profession into the hands of the enemies of God and his truth, then I am called to suffer for it what God shall please to let them lay upon me'. Through providence God 'engaged us in his work', and thus in the face of persecution providence either offers a way of legitimate escape or enables the believer to suffer righteously. Because providence appoints some to suffer, Bunyan concluded that providence also assigns others to inflict punishment. '*Persecutors* as well as the *persecuted* are his, and he has his own designs upon both.' The saints were therefore exhorted to pity their persecutors, who were divinely delegated to do this work and yet would ultimately be punished for it.[38]

Providence enabled Bunyan to castigate antichristian persecutors without calling on the saints to overthrow them. However, if providence directed monarchs to take up arms on behalf of Christ, Bunyan was prepared to support such efforts; he was no pacifist. Had he lived to see the Revolution of 1688-89, he would undoubtedly have welcomed William of Orange with as much zeal as did Matthew Meade. 'There is', Meade said while reflecting on the revolution, 'no altering the course of Providence; no art, no power, no policy, can turn . . . [God] out of the way, his Providence is setled in its motion'.[39] In short, providence was a very pragmatic doctrine, useful in justifying either quiescent suffering or rebellion.

The Bunyan of history was a more sophisticated, shrewd, and politically concerned minister than has generally been recognized. He was not above stretching the truth: we cannot take seriously his claim to have derived his views solely from Scripture,[40] or his depiction of himself as the greatest sinner, or his professed dislike of controversy with other saints.[41] He withheld various manuscripts from

37. *GA*, p. 14; Offor, ii, p. 11; cf. *MW*, x, pp. 8, 87.
38. *MW*, x, pp. 52–53 (quoted), 54, 69–72 (p. 71 quoted).
39. Meade, *The Vision of the Wheels*, p. 29.
40. Campbell, 'Fishing in Other Men's Waters: Bunyan and the Theologians', in Keeble, *JB*, pp. 137–51.
41. Underwood, 'It Pleased Me Much to Contend: Bunyan as Controversialist', a paper presented at the 'Bunyan and Puritanism' Tercentenary Conference, Durham University (March 1988).

the press because they were potentially explosive, but he published others without having them licensed. His allegory of *The Holy War* was not only technically sophisticated but full of subtle criticism of Charles II's government, and although he was no critic of kingship per se, he had no use for absolute monarchy or Popery. He was pragmatic enough to welcome the indulgence of Charles and to endorse a modest degree of cooperation with James. Like his friends Owen, Meade, and Cokayne, Bunyan was far more concerned with contemporary events than most biographers have suggested, particularly as he expounded on Christian duties in an age of recurring persecution. To honour him properly on the tercentenary of his death, we can do no less than study him in his proper historical context, recognizing the full range of his concerns, including his radical associations.

13

Conventicles, Sedition, and the Toleration Act of 1689

The original version of the Declaration of Rights, known as 'the Heads of Grievances', called specifically for religious freedom for Protestants, stating that 'effectual provision [was] to be made for the liberty of Protestants in the exercise of their religion and for uniting all Protestants in the matter of public worship as far as may be possible'. The House of Commons excluded this provision from the revised Declaration because, like certain other articles, it required new legislation as distinct from the simple reassertion of ancient rights. In its stead, the House passed the bill 'for Exempting Their Majesties' Protestant Subjects, Differing from the Church of England, from the Penalties of Certain Laws' in May 1689, and included only exemption from certain penal laws, not civil disabilities. The bill provided, in other words, minimal toleration, and even then only under strict conditions. Places of worship had to be registered with bishops, Nonconformist clergy had to subscribe to all but five of the Thirty-nine Articles, and those who worshipped in Dissenting meetings had to subscribe to the Oaths of Allegiance and Supremacy and the Oath against Transubstantiation.[1]

The act included two other provisions that help to explain the reticence with which toleration (a word never mentioned in the act) was bestowed. One of these provided for the punishment of 'any person or persons at any time . . . [who] willingly and of purpose maliciously or contemptuously come into any Cathedrall or Parish Church Chapell or other Congregation permitted by this Act and disquiet or disturbe the same or misuse any Preacher or Teacher'. This was directed not only at the Quakers, who had an irritating habit of disrupting the worship services of others, but also at those Dissenters who had manifested

---

1. 'The Heads of Grievances', reprinted in Lois G. Schwoerer, *The Declaration of Rights, 1689* (Baltimore, 1981), pp. 299–300; 1 Gul. & Mar,, c. 18, *The Statutes of the Realm*, vi (London, 1963), pp. 74–76.

disrespect for the established church by desecrating the altar or physically abusing the Book of Common Prayer. Reference to the 'misuse' of preachers may have been prompted by physical assaults on conforming clergy in Scotland. Even more revealing was the provision that places of Nonconformist worship must not have 'the doores locked barred or bolted dureing any time of such Meeting'.[2] Behind this provision lay the most important reason why limited toleration was bestowed so reluctantly: the deep-seated belief that conventicles had historically been nurseries of sedition. This suspicion was not without foundation.

The events of the period 1660-88 demonstrated an unmistakable link between Nonconformity and seditious activity, though only on the part of a minority within the Dissenting community. During this period it became apparent that the only effective way to pacify the Nonconformists was through a policy of toleration. The years of effective indulgence, both in the early 1670s and again in 1687, were devoid of serious plotting by Dissenters. By comparison, significant conspiratorial activity had occurred in the 1660s and the early 1680s when major efforts were underway to curb conventicles.

As early as January 1661 the London congregation of the Fifth Monarchist Thomas Venner launched a violent campaign to inaugurate the reign of King Jesus. Combining religious zeal, antimonarchical fervour, and a plea for radical social reform, the Vennerites fought valiantly but were crushed in a matter of days. Some forty persons died, about half of them rebels, and the government responded by cracking down on conventicles.[3] Meetings of Baptists, Quakers, and Fifth Monarchists were specifically prohibited. Although most Dissenters, including Bunyan, moved quickly to denounce the insurrection, they were nevertheless tarred with the brush of sedition. Throughout England dissidents went to prison or had to post bonds to assure peaceful behaviour. From Hull Sir Robert Hildyard wrote that 'upon inquirie into the humours of people wee have discovered more fanaticks both in this towne & also in the Country then I did imagine there had beene: wee have disarmed them'.[4] The monarchy had been

2. *Statutes of the Realm*, vi, pp. 74–76.

3. Greaves, *DUFE*, pp. 50–57.

4. Joseph Caryl, Philip Nye, et al., *A Renuntiation and Declaration of the Ministers of Congregational Churches and Publick Preachers* (London, 1661); White Kennet, *An Historical Register and Chronicle of English Affairs* (London, 1744), p. 383; Thomas Crosby, *The History of the English Baptists*, 4 vols. (London, 1738–40), ii, pp. 35–42, 98–144; *Kingdomes Intelligencer* (14–21 Jan. 1661); *Mercurius Publicus* 2 (10–17 Jan. 1661); *Historical Manuscripts Commission* 78, *Hastings*, ii, p. 141; iv, p. 219; PRO SP 29/28/99 (quoted); 29/29/104.

restored less than a year, and already the spectre of renewed civil war, spearheaded by radical Nonconformists, had been raised.

The loyalists' suspicion of conventicles was undoubtedly intensified by the deep undercurrent of popular hostility toward the Stuart regime that continued throughout the period from the Restoration to the Revolution of 1688-89. The stereotypical picture of universal happiness at the return of Charles II in May 1660 was a myth fostered by royalists. From the beginning the disaffected made hate-filled predictions of the king's imminent death. A Yorkshire labourer, for example, allegedly warned that 'the King is a rogue, and if he does not depart the land presently hee shall die the sorest death that ever King died'.[5] 'Lett this younge Rogue take heed', warned a Somerset man of Charles, 'that his head be not cutt of[f] as his fathers was.' Weymouth dissidents refused to observe a day of fasting in memory of Charles I, and others repeatedly evoked the Good Old Cause and the glorious days of Oliver Cromwell. Accusations that Charles II was a tyrant and lecher were commonplace.[6]

Sermons from Nonconformist pulpits fanned hostility toward the Stuart regime. The majority of such discourses were undoubtedly harmless, but historians, by focusing on printed material, have underestimated the importance of sermons with a radical content. As early as May 1660 the Presbyterian John Milward called for the saints to 'gird every man his sword upon his thigh, and sheath it in his neighbour's bowell, for I doe believe too many of us have Popes in our bellies'. John Wesley urged God to extirpate the Stuarts, 'for they were an Antichristian generation'. The Fifth Monarchists John Vernon and Nathaniel Strange used their pulpits to reassert their fidelity to the Good Old Cause, and the Presbyterian Thomas Horrockes preached in the spring of 1664 that the Cavalier Parliament would 'lye in the dust' before the year's end. George Cokayne reportedly predicted that Charles II deserved to be beheaded as his father had been.[7]

The publications of the underground press, most of which were from the pens of Nonconformists, added to the attack. The best efforts of Roger L'Estrange, who devoted much of his career to

---

5. *Depositions from the Castle of York, Relating to Offences Committed in the Northern Counties in the Seventeenth Century*, ed. J. Raine (Surtees Society, vol. 40, 1861), p. 88; cf. pp. 85, 94; *Middlesex County Records*, ed. John Cordy Jeaffreson, 4 vols. (London, 1886–1892), iii, pp. 304–305, 311.

6. PRO SP 29/58/17 (quoted); 29/97/91; 29/111/103; 29/159/7.1; 29/178/92; *Depositions from the Castle of York*, pp. 93–94.

7. *Depositions from the Castle of York*, p. 83 (quoted); PRO SP 29/30/32 (quoted); 29/91/22; 29/99/7.

suppressing these publications, ultimately failed. Among the host of early underground works were the *Mirabilis Annus* tracts of 1662, probably by Cokayne or Henry Danvers. Recounting colourful signs and prodigies, the tracts carried unmistakable warnings of divine judgment against a persecuting state and the established church. Illegal publications ranged from direct attacks on the Church of England, such as John Goodwin's *Prelatique Preachers None of Christ's Teachers* (1663), to Captain Roger Jones' *Mene Tekel; or the Downfal of Tyranny* (1663), in which the right of the people to overthrow a tyrannical sovereign was asserted along with the people's right to choose their own rulers.[8]

In the face of such attacks, conventicles, it seemed, could easily foster renewed attempts to overthrow the government. Plots — and, more numerously, rumours of plots — were rife throughout the reign of Charles II. Although most of the allegations were probably baseless, or in a few cases even planted by the government in 'sting' operations, some conspiracies were real enough. In 1663, for instance, dissident Presbyterians and Congregationalists in Ireland plotted to seize Dublin Castle, imprison the duke of Ormond, secure the city, and march north to join rebellious Scots in Ulster. The leaders included not only ex-Cromwellian officers such as Lieutenant Thomas Blood and Colonels Thomas Scott and Edward Warren, but such ministers as the Presbyterian William Lecky and the Congregationalist Edward Baines. As the plotters prepared to act in May, three Nonconformist churches in Dublin prayed for their success. The conspirators' declaration explained that they intended to secure the English interest in the three kingdoms and reform the established church in accord with the principles of the Solemn League and Covenant. This rebellion was not republican in intent, but it manifestly linked secular and religious grievances and was firmly tied to the Nonconformist community in Ireland. That community was in turn in touch with sympathetic Dissenters in England and Scotland, thus underscoring the seriousness of the threat to the Stuart regime.[9]

An insurrection more broadly based than that of the Vennerites occurred in October 1663 in Yorkshire, Westmorland, and Durham, but it collapsed owing to inclement weather, a preemptive strike by the government, and poor planning and leadership. The government had in any event infiltrated the conspirators' inner circle and was ready. The mastermind, Edward Richardson, a Congregationalist minister, had been arrested in August, though he soon escaped and fled to

8. Greaves, *DUFE*, chap. 7.
9. Ibid., pp. 140–50.

the Netherlands. Among the other key figures were ex-Cromwellian officers such as Captain Roger Jones and Colonel John Mason, and the Congregationalist ministers Jeremiah Marsden and Thomas Palmer. Their declaration, *A Door of Hope Opened in the Valley of Achor for the Mourners in Sion out of the North*, proclaimed that temporal realms had to be overthrown before the kingdom of God could be inaugurated, and called for a religious reformation in keeping with the example of the best Reformed churches. Sectaries of all stripes, including Quakers, were involved in planning the uprising; hence its aftermath saw renewed repression of conventicles and fresh attacks on Dissenters.[10] Loyalists disagreed on how dangerous the Nonconformists actually were, but there was general concurrence that their discontent had not abated. The 'hot spurs, Annabaptists and Quakers goe on more fearse', fretted Sir Brian Broughton, adding that they still thought a rebellion was feasible if their allies in Scotland and Ireland would revolt. In Sir William Morice's judgment, 'there are still many ill humors in these bodyes, and though quiet for the present, yet [they are] not abated in their malignancy'.[11]

Finding an effective way to deal with religious dissent was thus essential for the security of the state. At first the government had recourse to an Elizabethan statute (35 Eliz. I, c. 1) to prosecute Nonconformists (including Bunyan), although this law had been primarily aimed at recusants rather than illegal assemblies. Alternatively, Dissenters could be cited for riotous assembly, assuming the meeting was less than peaceful, or for refusing to take the Oath of Allegiance. Once the 1662 Act of Uniformity was in place, the House of Commons prepared a bill designed specifically to curb unlawful religious gatherings. Although it was approved by a two-to-one margin in the Commons in June 1663, the House of Lords delayed passage until May 1664 in a successful effort to implement limitations on the search of their own houses by magistrates seeking conventicles. The resulting act (16 Car. II, c. 4) imposed a penalty of up to three months in prison or a fine of up to £5 for first offenders who attended an unlawful religious service; the statute doubled penalties for the second offence, though magistrates had considerable latitude in imposing them. Third offenders were subject to a fine of £100 or deportation, and magistrates who refused to punish violators could themselves be fined.

10. Ibid., chap. 6.

11. PRO SP 29/83/7; 29/90/101 (quoted); *Historical Manuscripts Commission* 71, *Finch*, i, p. 297.

If anything, the imposition of tighter controls on conventicles intensified hostility toward the government and encouraged illegal activity, even during the Second Dutch War. Plotting occurred throughout this period, including contacts between radical exiles and the Dutch. Many of those involved were Nonconformists, particularly ex-Cromwellian officers, though such ministers as the Congregationalists George Cokayne and Nicholas Lockyer were also under suspicion. Some of these purported plots had republican aims and were more radical in scope than the Dublin conspiracy; the conspirators allegedly intended to seize the Tower of London, burn the City, and assassinate the king. Whether based on fact or rumour, such allegations reinforced the notion that conventicles were nurseries of sedition and a clear and present danger to established government in church and state.[12]

The government's efforts to repress illegal religious assemblies by force were unsuccessful, especially in Scotland. The heavy-handed actions of Sir James Turner and his troops in the southwest triggered a major uprising for which planning had already been underway. Prominent Covenanters such as Lieutenant-Colonel James Wallace and the minister Gabriel Semple were among those participating in secret meetings in Edinburgh on the eve of the insurrection. But the government was already wary, Lieutenant-General William Drummond, for example, having warned the earl of Lauderdale that conventicle preachers 'had disposed the people to be in radiness to ryse in armes when the opportunytie showld offer'.[13] The rebellion started by accident when a laird and his friends went to the rescue of an elderly peasant whom Turner's men had threatened to broil alive. Eventually the rebel forces numbered as many as 2,000, among them such fiery Presbyterian ministers as Andrew McCormack, John Carstares, and John Crookshanks. But dissidents in Edinburgh failed to rebel, nor was support forthcoming from south of the Tweed, hence at Rullion Green, near the capital, government troops routed the Covenanters in the snow on 28 November 1666. The rebellion failed, but the very fact that it had been attempted was widely blamed on conventicles. The

12. Greaves, *EUHF*, chap. 1.

13. *Memoirs of Mr. William Veitch and George Brysson*, ed. T. McCrie (Edinburgh and London, 1825), p. 381; Julia Buckroyd, *Church and State in Scotland, 1660–1681* (Edinburgh, 1980), pp. 66–67; *The Lauderdale Papers*, ed. Osmund Airy, 2 vols. (Camden Society, n.s., 34 and 36, 1884–85), i, pp. 262–63 (quoted).

authorities made renewed efforts to repress them, but with minimal success.[14]

Assassination attempts against religious and political leaders by a handful of Nonconformists rendered the Dissenting tradition even more suspect. On 11 July 1668 the Presbyterian firebrand James Mitchell attempted to shoot James Sharp, archbishop of St. Andrews, as he distributed alms on an Edinburgh street. Instead he wounded Dr. Andrew Honeyman, bishop of Orkney, and then escaped as onlookers sneered, 'It's but a Bishop'. Mitchell was eventually apprehended and executed.[15]

No successful political assassinations took place in England, yet a spectacular attempt was made in 1670 against the duke of Ormond while he was visiting London. The architect of the plan was the Presbyterian Thomas Blood, leader of the abortive 1663 Dublin conspiracy. Among the other would-be assassins were Blood's son Thomas, also a Presbyterian, and the Fifth Monarchist Richard Halliwell, who regarded Charles II as the beast of the Apocalypse. The conspirators stopped the duke's coach in St. James's Street, forced him onto a horse, and tried to spirit him to the waiting gallows at Tyburn.[16] Ormond, however, escaped. With some of his cohorts, Blood subsequently claimed that he had almost shot the king as he swam in the Thames River near Battersea, but that he changed his mind after seeing Charles from his hiding place in the reeds.[17]

The 1664 Conventicle Act expired on 1 March 1669, bringing renewed hope of comprehension for Presbyterians in the state church and of toleration for other Protestant Dissenters. Instead, Parliament passed a new Conventicle Act (22 Car. II, c. 1) in the spring of 1670 that was generally more stringent than its predecessor. A justice of the peace, acting alone and without holding a trial, could impose modest fines on the laity of 5s. and 10s. for first and second offences

14. BL Harleian MSS 4631, i, fol. 137v; [James Stuart and James Stirling], *Naphtali, or the Wrestlings of the Church of Scotland for the Kingdom of Christ* (n.p., 1667), p. 137; PRO SP 29/179/106, 107, 148; *The Register of the Privy Council of Scotland*, ed. P. Hume Brown, 3rd ser. (Edinburgh, 1908–10), ii, pp. 228, 398–99, 466–70, 480, 491, 501; Bodleian, Carte MSS 46, fol. 410r; *London Gazette* 110 (3–6 Dec. 1666); BL Add. MSS 23,125, fol. 161r; *Lauderdale Papers*, ii, pp. 102, 107, 122–23; *CSPD 1667–68*, pp. 516–17.

15. PRO SP 29/243/33; BL Harleian MSS 4631, i, fol. 635r.

16. *London Gazette* 528 (5–8 Dec. 1670); 529 (8–12 Dec. 1670); *Historical Manuscripts Commission 7, Eighth Report*, Appendix, Part 1, pp. 154–57; *Historical Manuscripts Commission 63, Egmont*, ii, p. 24; Thomas Carte, *An History of the Life of James Duke of Ormonde*, 2 vols. (London, 1736), ii, pp. 421–22.

17. Carte, *History of the Life of Ormonde*, ii, p. 423.

respectively, though the corresponding penalties for ministers were £20 and £40. The most pernicious aspect of the new law was a provision that gave informers a third of the fines. Not surprisingly, those who informed were sometimes violently assaulted.[18]

Persecution of Nonconformists under both acts was sporadic, varying considerably from time to time and from place to place. Nevertheless the constant threat of prosecution and the vexing activity of informers, especially after 1670, encouraged many Dissenters to resort not only to civil disobedience but also to defensive measures that sometimes led to violence. Some conventiclers met in the pre-dawn hours, and many posted sentries to warn of coming magistrates and took precautions to delay their entry while worshippers fled through other doors and windows.[19] Special concern was taken to ensure a preacher's escape, not only so he could minister again but because the congregation, from 1670, was liable for his fine if he could not pay. A Dissenting congregation at Broadmead, Bristol, protected their minister by having him preach through a newly-cut window in a house adjoining their meeting-place. The Quakers, however, generally stood their ground, preferring confrontation, though not militancy, to flight.[20]

When the magistrates interrupted a service, the scene could turn ugly, sometimes involving no more than harsh language on the part of conventiclers, but on other occasions physical violence. In Lancashire and Cheshire, Presbyterians resisted arrest, as did Congregationalists at Newcastle upon Tyne. When officials attempted to arrest a conventicle preacher in Staffordshire in May 1669, the women listening to his sermon rescued him and spirited him away. Conventiclers at Deal in 1682 similarly liberated their minister when he defied the magistrates.[21] Violence was rare, though other manifestations of civil disobedience were not. When magistrates tried to prevent illegal services by locking the doors of the meeting-houses, Dissenters broke into the buildings. Others met on the borders of shires, particularly in Somerset and Wiltshire, so as to escape into a neighbouring county when magistrates approached. To prevent their goods from being distrained, conventiclers hid them, sometimes even leasing their houses and lands to others in order to live in simple cottages, virtually barren of anything officials could seize. The spread of civil

18. *CSPD 1682*, p. 272; *True Protestant Mercury* 158 (8–12 July 1682).
19. PRO SP 29/115/40; 29/129/14; 29/276/75; 29/278/163; 29/418/89 (quoted); 29/419/19; 29/432/89.
20. PRO SP 29/276/75; 29/419/118.
21. PRO SP 29/146/68; 29/179/95; 29/261/22; 29/276;82; 29/281/97; 29/421/127; Bodleian Carte MSS 39, fol. 68r.

disobedience placed the magistracy in a difficult position. Failure to punish Dissenters rendered magistrates subject to penalties and the possibility that loyalists would file complaints at Westminster.[22] Yet justices who imposed fines or incarcerated Dissenters risked not only economic and physical reprisal but the loss of esteem from subordinates in the social hierarchy. As long as the problem of Nonconformity was unresolved, the social fabric was subjected to considerable strain.

For this reason, as well as for the more obvious fear that those who met behind locked doors might be scheming against constituted authority, loyalists repeatedly accused the conventicles of breeding sedition. One of Sir Joseph Williamson's correspondents reported from Chester in 1669 that the Dissenters 'vent dangerous tenents & doctrine, tending to sedition if not rebellion', while another wrote from York that the conventicles reminded him of those that had preceded the outbreak of the civil war in 1642.[23] A royal proclamation issued in July 1669 acknowledged that the increasing number of Nonconformist meetings endangered the public peace. Less than two years earlier, Williamson had been warned that dangerous fanatics overwhelmed the country, meeting by the thousands and reproaching the government.[24]

Some of the themes reportedly espoused in the conventicles lent a degree of credibility to such assertions. The Congregationalist Richard Gilpin's London followers sang a metrical version of Psalm 149, which exhorted them 'To binde their stately kings in chains,/ their Lords in iron bands'. The message, though defensibly Biblical, clearly had contemporary overtones. In 1671 a conventicle preacher at Moorfields, London, urged God to convert the royal Councillors or destroy them: 'Let there be Blood, O Lord; let the Land be covered with Blood'. Another London congregation heard the Baptist Nicholas Cox pledge that he and his associates would be true to King Jesus.[25]

Given the antipathy toward the Stuarts in some Nonconformist circles and the radical themes in some Dissenting sermons and underground literature, the authorities were naturally alarmed when conventiclers began bearing arms in their services. As early as the mid-1660s the Baptists at Hertford were armed, as were Baptists who held all-night services in a rented room in the White Lion Prison. The spread of this practice could be potentially inflammatory, especially in light of the fact that by 1670 some 12,000 people attended conventicles

---

22. PRO SP 29/216/133; 29/277/112, 204; 29/287/71; 29/436/55, 55.1, 111.
23. PRO SP 29/129/81; 29/217/15; 29/261/145 (quoted); 29/266/30; 29/415/142; 29/418/27.1, 28; 29/422/110, 142; 29/430/67.
24. PRO SP 29/221/57; 29/263/2.
25. PRO SP 29/249/146.1 (quoted); 29/275/14 (quoted); 29/275/134.1, 2 (quoted).

in London on a single Sunday according to the lord mayor's estimate. With some Presbyterian conventicles in England attracting as many as 3,000 or 4,000 persons in 1670, Sir John Trevor, a secretary of state, was afraid to disperse them with royal guards for fear of the bloodshed that might result. By denying toleration the state had created a situation in which both sides expressed fears of renewed civil war. In Somerset and Wiltshire, armed conventiclers used their weapons to avoid arrest.[26]

The 1672 Declaration of Indulgence temporarily defused the crisis but raised serious doubts about the constitutional implications of a monarch's claim to dispense with statutory law. Although Charles withdrew the indulgence the following year at Parliament's insistence, de facto toleration continued throughout much of England. As late as 1675 some Nonconformists continued to operate as if the indulgence were still in effect, forcing Charles to promise his Privy Council that he would declare 'that his Licences for Preaching are revoked'. With the gradual crackdown on illegal services, the climate of hysteria provoked by the spurious Popish Plot, and the ensuing exclusion controversy, conventicles again became a serious problem. In the summer of 1675 more than 1,500 persons were indicted at Bristol under the Elizabethan Nonconformity statute; when magistrates issued warrants to distrain the goods of several hundred of them, a worried Charles ordered the lord keeper to intervene 'to prevent so warm a Prosecution of such as are Protestant Dissenters'.[27] One staunch loyalist reported in 1677 that Nonconformists were meeting in large numbers at night behind closed doors, perhaps to muster 'as once Venners Crew did in London'. From Yarmouth in January 1678 came a warning that the Dissenters were so bold 'that wee know little difference betweene a King & a protector, the Creatures of the latter doe so ryde the other'.[28] Memories of the sectaries' identification with the revolution lived on.

Long-held suspicions that Charles harboured sympathy for Catholics mushroomed into open accusations with the alleged Popish Plot. Nonconformists played a prominent role in fanning much of this suspicion, particularly that which linked the court to Catholicism and absolutism. During the late 1660s a growing number of tracts had

26. PRO SP 29/115/44; 29/275/174; 29/277/11; *The Parliamentary Diary of Sir Edward Dering, 1670–1673*, ed. Basil Duke Henning (New Haven, Conn., 1940), pp. 4–6.

27. Anthony Ashley Cooper, earl of Shaftesbury, *A Letter from a Person of Quality, to His Friend in the Country* (1675), pp. 3–5; BL Stowe MSS 207, fol. 114r; BL Add. MSS 24,124, fol. 33r.

28. PRO SP 29/392/3; 29/400/19.

associated the Church of England with Rome and generally reflected a virulently antiprelatical and anticlerical strain. Prominent among them was Ralph Wallis' biting satire, *Room for the Cobbler of Gloucester and His Wife: With Several Cartloads of Abominable Irregular, Pitiful Stinking Priests* (1668). Attacks were also launched against the Conventicle Acts, tithes, and anything that smacked of Catholicism. In September 1680 Secretary Leoline Jenkins noted his special concern about wealthier Dissenters who 'pretend the fear of Popery, but under that pretense drive at the change of Government into a Commonwealth'.[29]

The concern of the authorities could only have been intensified by reports from Scotland of enormous field conventicles that periodically erupted into violence between armed worshippers and parties of soldiers sent to disperse them. Some of these meetings drew thousands and were ministered to by some of the most militant Covenanters. In the autumn of 1677, for instance, John Welch had proclaimed that 'the King, the Nobles & Prelates were the Murtherers of Christ. . . . Tell mee what good the King hath done since his home coming, yea hath he not done all the mischeife that a Tyrant could doe both by his Life & Laws?'[30] In East Lothian in 1678 conventiclers killed a soldier and disarmed his compatriots, though the Presbyterians insisted that their recourse to arms was not in defiance of royal authority but simply self-defence. Nevertheless the violence spread and more perished. Referring to the militant conventiclers as 'that ungovernable tribe', the bishop of Edinburgh bitterly protested that 'this spirit of profannes, and blood hath here arrived to the height of Dementation and maddnes'.[31] On 3 May 1679 a party of militant Presbyterians crushed the archbishop of St. Andrews' skull, partly to avenge James Mitchell's death, but primarily because he had 'betrayed Christ and His Church'. The proclamation decreeing the arrest of his assassins warned that similar actions could be expected as long as field conventicles, 'those Rendezvouses of Rebellion, and Forgers of all Bloody and Jesuitical Principles, are as frequent'.[32]

The Covenanters again took up their weapons in May 1679 against a backdrop of armed conventicles and militant sermons. 'I see', thundered John Blackadder, 'a readiness to appear and defend the

29. PRO SP 44/62, p. 87.

30. *CSPD 1678*, pp. 161–62; BL Add. MSS 23,242, fol. 18r–v; PRO SP 29/397/146 (quoted); 29/405/227.

31. PRO SP 29/403/243; 29/406/31, 127; BL Add. MSS 23,242, fols. 96r, 99r; 23,247, fol. 40r (quoted); 35,125, fol. 303r.

32. *A True Account of the Horrid Murther Committed upon His Grace, the Late Archbishop of Saint Andrews* (London, 1679); *London Gazette* 1406 (8–12 May 1679).

cause by instruments of war, which is, indeed, warrantable in its season'. At Rutherglen on 29 May some eighty armed and mounted men not only reaffirmed the Covenant but burned parliamentary statutes they found obnoxious, including the Act of Supremacy and the Act for Establishing Episcopacy. The rebel forces eventually grew to some 6,000 men, and not until 22 June were the royalists able to rout them at Bothwell Bridge.[33] Because preachers again had been actively involved in the rebellion, the government mounted renewed attacks against illegal religious services. A royal proclamation directed that those who attended field conventicles be punished, and that those who bore arms at such assemblies be charged with treason. Yet conventicles which met in houses south of the Tay would be permitted except in Edinburgh, St. Andrews, Glasgow, and Stirling, and only as long as the ministers registered with the Privy Council and forswore the preaching of rebellion. Influenced by the duke of Monmouth, the government was clearly attempting to differentiate between militant and quiescent Presbyterians, even to the point of allowing a degree of toleration to the latter. The militants, however, would not be suppressed; 'how furious their preachers are', one loyalist noted, 'who would be faine at worke againe'. Moreover, the concessionary policy itself lasted only until the summer of 1680, when the duke of York, with the support of the bishops, resumed the policy of suppressing conventicles and garrisoning the west. This change was largely the result of political manoeuvering to reduce Monmouth's influence, not the activities of the conventiclers.[34]

The 1679 Covenanter rebellion erupted just as the House of Commons took up the question of succession, having resolved on 27 April that the probability of James' accession had encouraged the Popish Plot. The ensuing struggle inevitably fed suspicion about the duke of York, whom some dissidents described as a traitor, a pimp, and the son of a whore. 'A Pox take him', said a Chichester radical who also questioned Charles II's legitimacy. John Dutton Colt, M.P. for Leominster in 1681, boasted that he would be hanged at his own door before allowing such a 'Papist dog' as James to succeed to the throne; otherwise "twould be worse then 'twas then [in Mary Tudor's reign]; for we should have Our Children's Limbs cutt off

33. *Memoirs of the Rev. John Blackadder*, ed. Andrew Crichton (Edinburgh, 1823), pp. 229–30; *London Gazette* 1415 (9–12 June 1679); 1420 (26–30 June 1679); Bodleian, Carte MSS 45, fols. 484v–485r; BL Add. MSS 23,244, fol. 16r; 32,095, fol. 190r.

34. *London Gazette* 1424 (10–14 July 1679); BL Add. MSS 23,245, fol. 57r (quoted); Buckroyd, *Church and State*, pp. 132–35.

& thrown into Our Faces'.[35] The numerous Nonconformist sermons denouncing Catholicism contributed to the intensity of dissatisfaction with the government during the exclusion controversy. So too did the underground press. In the words of the author of *Vox Populi, Vox Dei* (1681), 'the people seem to cry out with one Voice, *No Popish Successor, no Idolater*, no Queen *Mary* in Breeches, no Tyrant over the Conscience, no new persecutor of *Protestants* in our Land'.[36] Francis 'Elephant' Smith, who published a substantial amount of radical literature as well as various works of Bunyan's, took pen in hand to castigate those who oppressed Dissenters and accepted the prospect of a Catholic sovereign. Why settle for a Decius or a Titus, he asked, when England could have another Constantine?[37]

The exclusion controversy greatly exacerbated tension between Conformists and Dissenters, especially when the latter became overtly militant. At Bristol in 1680 the radical attorney Nathaniel Wade, a Congregationalist, and his associates organized themselves into 'an armed Company' and resisted magistrates who tried to break up conventicles. The following year a Wiltshire grand jury accused Dissenters of wearing arms and thereby terrorizing loyal subjects. Justices in Monmouthshire and Gloucestershire made similar complaints in 1681 and 1682 respectively.[38] At Taunton in Somerset the sentries posted by the conventiclers in 1682 carried pistols in their pockets. Attempts to suppress London conventicles in June of that year incited tumults throughout the City and physical assaults on informers. Justices at the Gloucestershire quarter sessions in 1682 accused Dissenters of living 'in open disobedience and contempt of his Majesties Lawes by withdrawing his Majesties Subjects from their naturall obedience . . . and corrupting them in their principles and religion as alsoe by holding seditious Conventicles . . . in such great numbers as may be of dangerous consequence to the peace and tranquility of his Majesties Government'.[39] (Thomas?) Taylor prayed with his London congregation to overrule the king and his Council, and in February 1683 a group of 200 to 300 'rabble' attacked a party

35. PRO SP 29/414/159; 29/415/42, 178 (quoted); 29/418/16, 19; 29/420/4 (quoted), 100.
36. BL Egerton MSS 2134, fol. 5r.
37. *Democritus Ridens* 5 (11 April 1681). Cf. Hill, *JB*, pp. 284–88.
38. PRO SP 29/414/54; 29/416/62; 29/417/171; 29/418/26.1.
39. PRO SP 29/418/26.1.

of armed men dispatched to break up conventicles.[40] The ability of the state to maintain law and order increasingly diminished as both sides resorted to violence.

The scheming that eventually culminated in the rebellions of the earl of Argyll and the duke of Monmouth in 1685 began in this heated atmosphere, prior to the discovery of the Rye House plotting in June 1683. Once again the Nonconformists were directly involved. When Argyll invaded Scotland in May, one of his declarations embodied a direct appeal to Presbyterians. Entitled 'The Declaration and Apology of the Protestant People . . . of Scotland, with the Concurrence of the True and Faithful Pastors', it praised the Covenanters of the past, condemned the apostasy and tyranny of Charles II, and accused the government of replacing divine ordinances with human inventions. The rebels aimed, they said, to restore Protestantism, suppress Popery and prelacy, and establish a new government.[41] Yet Argyll himself was no Covenanter, and the popular support he had expected never materialized. If anything, the futility of Argyll's escapade underscored the fact that the militant Covenanting tradition was essentially a spent force by 1685. The repressive measures employed by the government in the early 1680s had been very effective, and the cause of the militant Presbyterians had essentially been reduced to the schismatic Cameronians, who refused to support Argyll because his forces included persons deemed to have been unfaithful to the Covenants. In February 1687 James II informed his Scottish Privy Council that he wanted the remaining field conventicles terminated, but denied any intention 'to incroach on the Consciences of any'. Some field conventicles continued to meet, including one of more than 300 worshippers in the border country near Berwick.[42]

The people of the west country who rallied to Monmouth's banner were mostly from Dissenting churches. 'All the Confideing Dissenters had full Intelligence of Monmouths comeing into the West', exaggeratedly remarked one royalist. Cognizant of the historic links between Nonconformity and sedition (though true only of a minority of Dissenters), James II on 20 June dispatched orders throughout the country to arrest disaffected and suspicious persons, especially Nonconformist ministers and those who had fought against his father

40. PRO SP 29/418/43, 106; 29/422/79; *CSPD 1682*, pp. 255, 272; *True Protestant Mercury* 158 (8–12 July 1682).

41. *London Gazette* 2036 (21–25 May 1685).

42. Ian B. Cowan, *The Scottish Covenanters, 1660–1688* (London, 1976), chaps. 7–8; *London Gazette* 2221 (28 Feb.–3 March 1687) (quoted); BL Add. MSS 41,804, fol. 273r.

and brother. A Dissenting minister — Robert Ferguson — drafted Monmouth's declaration, with its indictment of James as a usurper whose government 'hath been but one continued conspiracy against *Reformed Religion* & rights of the *Nation*'. The declaration demanded the termination of the penal laws against Protestant Dissenters and the provision of liberty of conscience for them.[43] But except for Ferguson and the Baptist preacher Sampson Larke, Dissenting clergy seem not to have played a major role in the uprising, apart perhaps from encouraging their followers to take up arms. Nevertheless the Argyll and Monmouth rebellions had too many unmistakable links to the Dissenting communities in the Netherlands, Scotland, and England not to have reinforced the suspicion that conventicles were potentially seditious.

Ironically, James II's own policies helped make the point that toleration was the best way to sever the link between religious dissent and seditious plotting. Although the 1687 Declaration of Indulgence was primarily intended to benefit Catholics, the king's calculated attempt to win the backing of Protestant Dissenters by extending toleration to them met with some success. Grateful London Baptists pledged 'to give that proof of our Duty and Fidelity to Your Majesty, that You may never have occasion to repent of Your Princely Favour towards us'. Of course, a good deal of suspicion existed among Nonconformists, who urged James to seek parliamentary approval for the indulgence, but it quickly became apparent that religious toleration, properly granted, would calm the Dissenting community. So pleased was the government with the response to the declaration that the earl of Sunderland, citing the calm in all three kingdoms, informed the lord deputy of Ireland that it was no longer necessary to disarm Dissenters.[44]

James' government itself fostered the notion that toleration was conducive to peace and prosperity by regularly publishing declarations of thanks from Nonconformists in the *London Gazette*. One group of London Dissenters likened the king as a deliverer to Moses because the indulgence 'will make Your Government easie and delightful to Your Self and People, augment their Trade, encourage Strangers, encrease Your Subjects, and gain the Empire of all their Hearts'. Reflecting an oft-repeated argument that toleration was good for business as well

43. Peter Earle, *Monmouth's Rebels: The Road to Sedgemoor 1685* (New York, 1977), pp. 5–7; BL Harleian MSS 6845, fol. 286r (quoted); PRO SP 31/2, p. 18; BL Lansdowne MSS 1152, pp. 2 (quoted), 5.

44. *London Gazette* 2234 (14–18 April 1687) (quoted); 2246 (26–30 May 1687); PRO SP 63/340, p. 235.

as security, the clothiers of Worcester credited the indulgence with giving 'a new Life to our decayed Trade'. This carefully orchestrated press campaign even included an address of thanks from clothiers in Taunton, Somerset, one of the hotbeds of radical dissent: 'While interest of Parties are laid aside, the Common Interest, Trade and Safety of the Nation may be advanc'd and promoted by All'.[45]

The problem with James' indulgence policy was not the liberty it allowed to Protestant Dissenters but the granting of toleration to Catholics and the failure to ground the indulgence in statute. The indulgence thus split the Nonconformist community, and such support as Dissenters gave James evaporated in the crisis of 1688. The role of prominent Nonconformists in the overthrow of James is well documented. Politically, therefore, it was impossible not to exempt Protestant Dissenters from at least some religious disabilities. James' own press campaign had demonstrated that, given a modicum of toleration, Nonconformists would live peacefully. When their fundamental rights as English citizens were threatened, however, they were quick to cooperate with Conformists in the defence of their liberties.

Nevertheless, some suspicion concerning the intentions of the more radical Dissenters remained in 1689, particularly in view of events as recent as those of the period 1679–85. A legitimate and understandable reason therefore existed for including a provision against religious meetings behind locked doors in the Toleration Act. Yet the majority of the political nation had also come to realize that Protestant Dissenters were no threat to the security of the realm if allowed to worship openly; hence some concessions were made. The correctness of this decision is demonstrated by the virtual disappearance of Nonconformist conspiracy after the revolution. Republican ideology remained alive but was no longer the potentially revolutionary force it had been when it could be linked to Nonconformist discontent. Dissenters readily adjusted to their new toleration, and some even practised occasional conformity in order to participate fully in the political life of the nation. The power of the Whig magnates in the generation after 1688 is hardly imaginable without the Toleration Act. Having won the right to worship as they pleased, the Nonconformists forswore their militancy, recognized the common bond they shared with Protestants in the state church, and turned their attention to the political and social issues that confronted the eighteenth century.

---

45. *London Gazette* 2270 (18–22 Aug. 1687) (quoted); 2273 (29 Aug.–1 Sept. 1687) (quoted); 2284 (6–10 Oct. 1687) (quoted).

Index

Acts and Monuments (John Foxe), 102, 104, 127, 133, 139, 182
Act of Toleration (1689), 207, 222
Act of Uniformity (1662), 211
Alcock, Nathaniel, 76
Alleine, Joseph, 7n, 23, 177f, 195
Alleine, Richard, 20, 178
Allen, John, 81f, 85
Alsop, Benjamin, 49, 172, 176, 182
Alsop, George, 15, 201
Angiers, Daniel, 94
Anglesey, Arthur Annesley, earl of, 5, 27, 32, 34, 44
Antinomians, Antinomianism, 41f, 60
Argyll, Archibald Campbell, earl of, 170, 220f
Arminianism, 198
Ashley, Gilbert, 77
Ashwood, Bartholomew, 2, 25, 200
Astwood, Luke, 78, 80, 85
Aynsloe, John, 93

Baillie, Robert, 105f
Baines, Edward, 210
Bampfield, Francis, 12, 66f, 162, 165, 179
Bantoft, Samuel, 97
Baptism, 8f, 54, 63f, 84
Baptists: General Baptists, 2, 7-9, 11, 28f, 63, 67, 102, 128; Particular Baptists, 2, 7, 9, 17, 63, 90, 102, 133; Seventh-Day Baptists, 12; other refs., 3, 15, 29, 41f, 52, 66f, 84, 89f, 93, 95, 99, 112, 160, 162-65, 208, 215, 221. *See also* Baptists by name
Barker, Matthew, 158f, 163
Bates, William, 7
Baxter, Richard, 4, 6-10, 22-24, 63, 105-107, 128f, 150, 159, 195, 200

Bedford Church (later Bunyan Meeting), 54f, 60, 62f, 71-87 *passim*, 94-96, 101, 111f, 127, 143f, 149, 152, 156-60, 202
Bedford Corporation, 69, 140
Bedfordshire: Bedford, 13, 63, 71f, 76, 91; Biggleswade, 79; Blunham, 72, 80, 85; Cardington, 78-80, 85f; Chellington, 82; Clapham, 82; Clophill, 86; Cockayne Hatley, 87; Cotton End, 78; Cranfield, 63, 76f, 84f, 87; Dean (Upper or Lower), 82; Edworth, 79, 85-87; Elstow, 86; Felmersham, 82, 86; Goldington, 77, 85; Haynes, 79, 85-87; Houghton Conquest, 86; Kempston, 78, 82, 85f; Kensworth, 97; Keysoe, 63, 73, 76f, 82, 85, 87, 96; Lower Samsell, 52, 180, 200; Luton, 97; Maulden, 79, 85f; Milton Earnest, 82; Northill, 87; Oakley, 78, 82, 85f; Pavenham, 81f, 85f; Potton, 87; Radwell, 81f, 86; Ravensden, 87; Ridgmont, 77, 85; Shefford, 91; Southill, 86; Stagsden, 79, 85; Stevington, 63, 76, 81-83, 85-87; Turvey, 81f, 85; Wilhamstead, 86; other refs., 58, 62f, 71-87 *passim*, 142
Bell, Robert, 38
Berkshire: Newbury, 16; Reading, 74
Bethel, Slingsby, 8
Beverley, Thomas, 150
Bible: Bunyan's use of, 38; Nonconformist views of, 29-31. *See also* Geneva Bible
Blinman, Richard, 9
Blood, Lieutenant ('Colonel') Thomas, 3, 16f, 203, 210, 213
Blount, Charles, 131
Blower, Samuel, 99
Bold, Samuel, 13n, 32n
Bonner, Edmund, 52, 127f
Book of Common Prayer, 15f, 51-53, 107, 127, 200, 208

Booth, Sir George, 202
Boston, Mass., 163
Bourne, Zachary, 171
Bradshaw, Nathaniel, 92
Breeden, William, 72, 83, 158f
Bristol, 2, 12, 14f
Bromley, Thomas, 26
Brooks, Thomas, 161-63
Broughton, Sir Brian, 211
Brown, John, 103, 185, 187f
Browning, John, 83
Bruno of Cologne, 40
Buckinghamshire: Amersham, 11;
    Astwood, 84; Newport Pagnell, 63, 76f,
    82-85, 87, 101; Newton Blossomville, 84;
    Olney, 83-85, 87
Bunyan, Elizabeth, 77
Bunyan, John: life of: and Cambridge
    Nonconformists, 94f; and Essex
    Nonconformists, 97f; and Hertfordshire
    Nonconformists, 95-97; and his printers
    and publishers, 48f; and John Owen, 44;
    and Leicester Nonconformists, 89f; and
    Suffolk Nonconformists, 98f; and the
    authorship of *Reprobation Asserted*, 185-91;
    and the Fifth Monarchists, 141-53; and
    the nature of *Grace Abounding*, 37-41;
    and the Ranters, 41f; arrest (1660),
    51f, 101f, 180, 200; chronology of his
    writings, 44f, 62, 118, 149f, 173, 194;
    contacts in London, 155-67, 169; early
    years in prison (1660-1666), 12f, 52-59,
    110-12, 145-47; later years in prison
    (1666-1672), 59-64; later ministerial
    years (1676-1688), 64-70, 172-77;
    major theological disputes (1671-1675),
    63f, 112; military service, 90, 101;
    organizational work, 13, 62f, 71-87;
    reliance on other authors, 40f, 55;
    religious experience of, 21, 24, 38f;
    second arrest (1676), 65
Bunyan, John: views of: Calvinist
    principles, 197-99; on baptism, 9, 54,
    63f; on Catholicism, 127-30, 132-40; on
    church membership and communion,
    5, 53f, 63f; on denominational
    affiliation and labels, 6, 64; on forms of
    government, 106f; on law, 123-24; on
    millenarianism, 49f, 56f; on monarchs
    and monarchy, 46, 58, 68, 109f,
    118-24, 151, 174f, 202; on providence,
    203-205; on religious experience, 20; on
    resistance, 45-47, 110f, 113, 115f, 125-26,

138; on suffering, 68, 107-109, 115-18,
    126, 177, 180-83, 200f; on the church,
    53f; on the Rye House plotting, 175-77,
    181-83; on the sacraments, 70; on the
    social order, 42-44; on the Stuart state,
    102-26
Bunyan, John: works: *The Acceptable
    Sacrifice*, 44f, 69, 149, 159, 187; *The
    Advocateship of Jesus Christ*, 69, 103,
    141, 149; *A Book for Boys and Girls*, 69;
    A Case of Conscience Resolved, 67, 173,
    186; *Christian Behaviour*, 54, 186, 199;
    A Confession of My Faith, 51, 63, 112,
    147; *Come, & Welcome, to Jesus Christ*, 65,
    69, 97, 186; *A Defense of the Doctrine of
    Justification, by Faith*, 64, 113; *The Desire of
    the Righteous Granted*, 44, 69f; *Differences
    in Judgment About Water-Baptism, No Bar
    to Communion*, 63, 160, 164; *A Discourse
    of the . . . House of God*, 118, 186f; *A
    Discourse of the House of the Forest of
    Lebanon*, 46, 70, 124f, 152f; *A Discourse
    upon the Pharisee and the Publicane*, 66,
    117; *The Doctrine of the Law and Grace
    Unfolded*, 60, 144, 187; *An Exposition of
    the First Ten Chapters of Genesis*, 45-47, 69,
    103, 118, 120-23, 146f, 152f, 194; *A Few
    Sighs from Hell*, 43, 60, 83, 144, 187; *Good
    News for the Vilest of Men*, 69, 149, 187;
    Grace Abounding to the Chief of Sinners,
    24, 37-41, 56, 59-61, 155, 187, 189n,
    194-96; *The Greatness of the Soul*, 66f, 135,
    162, 172f; *The Heavenly Footman*, 60f;
    The Holy City, 41, 48f, 51, 54f, 57f, 63,
    109f, 118, 128f, 136, 145f, 151, 153; *A
    Holy Life*, 66, 115, 135, 172f, 175, 201;
    The Holy War, 38, 41, 43-48, 68, 113-15,
    119f, 123, 125f, 133-36, 140, 146-50,
    153, 155f, 166f, 172-74, 197-99, 206;
    Instruction for the Ignorant, 65; *Israel's Hope
    Encouraged*, 66, 124, 132; *I Will Pray with
    the Spirit*, 48, 52f, 107, 200; *Justification by
    an Imputed Righteousness*, 44; *Last Sermon*,
    70; *The Life and Death of Mr. Badman*,
    41, 66, 133, 186; *Light for Them That Sit
    in Darkness*, 64; *Of Antichrist, and His
    Ruine*, 45f, 50, 68f, 103, 118-20, 122f,
    126, 135-40, 151-53, 173-75, 183, 194;
    One Thing Is Needful, 57, 108-10, 145,
    186; *Paul's Departure and Crown*, 124;
    Peaceable Principles and True, 63, 188;
    The Pilgrim's Progress, 20, 38, 41, 43, 61f,
    65-68, 71, 114, 118, 129f, 140, 147, 173,

187, 194, 196-98; *Prison Meditations*, 55f, 107f; *Profitable Meditations*, 55, 60, 145; *Questions About the Nature and Perpetuity of the Seventh-Day Sabbath*, 66f, 162f, 188n; *The Resurrection of the Dead*, 41, 57; *The Saints' Knowledge of Christ's Love*, 124; *Saved by Grace*, 65; *Seasonable Counsel, or Advice to Sufferers*, 45, 68, 115-17, 119f, 126, 139, 173, 175-77, 180-82, 203; *Solomon's Temple Spiritualized*, 118, 187; *Some Gospel Truths Opened*, 143f, 146, 187; *The Strait Gate*, 65, 69; *A Treatise of the Fear of God*, 66, 133; *A Vindication of Some Gospel-Truths Opened*, 49, 143f; *The Water of Life*, 69; *The Work of Jesus Christ as an Advocate*: see *The Advocateship of Jesus Christ*
Burgess, John, 4
Burrough, Edward, 32, 93, 144
Burton, John, 72, 78, 83, 143, 158

Cain, 121, 135
Calamy, Edmund, the elder, 3n, 26, 128, 204
Calvin, John, 32
Cambridgeshire: Barrington, 92; Cambridge, 12, 64, 80, 85, 90-96, 161; Cottenham, 92; East Hatley, 87; Fenstanton, 11; Fowlmere, 92; Gamlingay, 80f, 85; Haddenham, 91; Hatley St. George, 87; Histon, 91f; Isle of Ely, 92; Landbeach, 92; Litlington, 87; Madingley, 86; Meldreth, 91f; Morden, 86; Oakington, 91f; Orwell, 92, 93n; Over, 91f; Shepreth, 92; Stow cum Quy, 91f; Thriplow, 92f; Toft, 80f, 85f, 94f; Trumpington, 92; Waterbeach, 92; Willingham, 91f, 93n; other refs., 90-96
Cameronians, 220
Campbell, Gordon, 39f, 197
Campion, Edmund, 40, 130n
Canne, John, 146
Care, George, 33
Care, Henry, 5, 130f
Carlton, Peter, 38
Carstares, John, 212
Carstares, William, 170-72
Caryl, Joseph, 24, 158-60, 163f
Cater, Samuel, 93f
Catholicism, Bunyan's view of, 127-30, 132-40
Caton, William, 32

Chambers, Robert, 16
Charles I, 109
Charles II, 46, 57, 68, 73f, 89, 108f, 113-15, 120-22, 124f, 131, 170f, 173-75, 206, 209, 213, 216, 220
Charlton, Francis, 171
Cheevers, Sarah, 13
Cheshire: Chester, 215; other refs., 214
Child, John, 101, 142-44, 152
Christian, William, 90
Clarendon Code, 156
Clarkson, Lawrence, 41
Cleaver, Robert, 40
Cobb, Paul, 103-106, 144
Cokayne, George, 64, 78, 96, 110f, 117, 143f, 148f, 152f, 156-59, 163, 165f, 169, 203, 206, 209f, 212
Coleman, Richard, 90
Coleridge, Samuel Taylor, 37
College, Stephen, 49, 67, 114f
Collier, Thomas, 112
Collins, John, 161, 163
Collmer, Robert, 193
Colt, John Dutton, 218
Common Fund, 4
Congregationalists (Independents), 2-5, 9, 13, 16, 29, 52, 60, 64, 66, 76f, 82-84, 90, 98f, 117, 128, 158-64, 171, 200, 202, 210-12, 214f, 219. *See also* Congregationalists by name
Conventicle Act (1664), 15, 59, 61, 73, 111, 129, 211, 213
Conventicle Act (1670), 59, 65, 73f, 213f
Conventicles, 14f, 72-74, 76f, 79, 99, 101, 103, 104n, 111, 144, 158f, 162, 200, 203, 208-20 *passim*
Cooper, Richard, 142
Cooper, Thomas, 73-75, 77f, 85
Coppe, Abiezer, 41
Corbet, John, 8n, 10, 19, 31, 130n
Corbyn, Samuel, 91f, 94, 161
Cornwall, 2, 14
Covenanters, 4, 131, 149, 170, 212, 217f
Cowley, Matthias, 48f
Cox, Nicholas, 215
Coxe, Nehemiah, 74f, 79, 85, 96
Cressener, Drue, 150
Crofton, Zachary, 20
Cromwell, Oliver, 142, 202
Crooke, John, 81
Crookshanks, John, 212
Crouch, John, 160
Cumberland, Martha, 157

Danvers, Henry, 9, 17, 40, 63, 66, 102, 150f, 153, 160, 164, 202f, 210
Davis, Colin, 41f
Day, James, 92
Declaration of Indulgence (1672), 1f, 63, 74f, 79, 89, 98, 158, 203, 216
Declaration of Indulgence (1687), 69, 221
Declaration of Rights (1689), 207
Delaune, Thomas, 63
Dell, William, 42, 134
Denne, Henry, 93, 95
Denne, John, 9, 63, 66
Dent, Edward, 78-80, 85
Devon, 2, 15
Diggers, 115, 122
Discipline, 10f, 80
Dod, John, 40
Doe, Charles, 185-87
Donne, John, 72-76, 78, 83-86, 93f, 96, 158
Dorset: Beaminster, 15; Weymouth, 209; Whitchurch, 15
Dover, Joan, 49
Drummond, Lieutenant-General William, 212
Durham, 210
Dyer, William, 22, 25, 29, 179, 195

Edinburgh, 212
Edward VI, 135, 137
Elizabeth I, 135, 137
Erbery, William, 121
Eston, John, 144
Evans, Katherine, 23
Excommunication, 10
Essex: Audley End, 92; Bocking, 97f; Braintree, 97f; Debden, 92; Thaxted, 92; other refs., 2
Essex, Arthur Capel, earl of, 43, 172
Eston, John, 202
Evans, Katherine, 179
Evelyn, John, 75

Farmer, Richard, 90
Farr, George, 75
Fell, Margaret, 23
Fenne, John, 74f, 77-79, 83, 85, 142f
Fenne, Samuel, 55, 73-75, 77-79, 83, 85-87, 96, 112
Ferguson, Robert, 8, 28f, 31, 44, 132, 136, 138, 170-72, 201, 221
Fifth Monarchists, 16f, 57, 101, 104, 106, 108, 111, 124, 141-53, 201-203, 208f, 213. *See also* Fifth Monarchists by name

Fitzhugh, Robert, 144
Fleming, Daniel, 111
Ford, Stephen, 161
Forrest, James, 134f
Foster, John, 96f
Foster, William, 74, 76f, 79
Fowler, Edward, 40, 42, 64, 113, 130n
Fowler, George, 76
Fownes, George, 162, 165f
Fox, George, 8, 107
Foxe, John, 102, 127f, 182
Friedman, Jerome, 42

Gammon, John, 70, 166
Gardner, John, 77
Geneva Bible, 46, 117n, 121f, 125n
Gibbs, John, 72, 77f, 83-85, 94, 158
Gibbs, Samuel, 83
Gifford, John, 39, 142
Gilpin, Richard, 215
Glasse, Thomas, 148
Gloucestershire: Bristol, 214, 216; Cirencester, 12; other refs., 219
Goodenough, Richard, 117
Goodman, Christopher, 105n, 201
Goodwin, John, 107, 113n, 210
Goodwin, Thomas, 19n, 160-64
Gordon, Alexander, of Earlston, 170
Gould, John, 6
Grantham, Thomas, 7f, 29, 31, 40, 176n
Greenhill, William, 19, 163f
Green Ribbon Club, 150
Grew, John, 202
Grew, Martha, 157
Griffith, George, 44, 64, 95f, 110, 117, 138, 148f, 153, 156-59, 161, 163, 165-67, 169-71, 201, 203
Griffith, John, 128
Guernsey, 15
Guy, William, 204

Hall, Thomas, 122n, 124n
Halliwell, Richard, 17, 203, 213
Hampden, Richard, 44
Hampshire: Winchester, 15
Harley, Edward, 132n, 200
Harper, John, 96
Harris, Benjamin, 49, 165
Harrison, F. M., 185n
Harrison, G. B., 185, 188n
Hartopp, Lady Elizabeth, 164
Hartopp, Sir John, 44
Haskin, Dayton, 40

Hawkins, Anne, 39
Hawthorne, Stephen, 81
Hayes, T. Wilson, 39
Haynes, Simon, 73-75, 78
Haynes, Thomas, 73, 75, 78
Hayward, Thomas, 95, 97
Helm, Paul, 190f
Helmes, Carnsew, 162
Henry, Matthew, 1n, 20, 26, 204
Henry, Philip, 6, 27, 196
Henry VIII, 134, 137
Henry family, 21, 25, 27
Hertfordshire: Ashwell, 81, 85f; Baldock, 97; Harpenden, 97; Hemel Hempstead, 97; Hertford, 215; Hitchin, 91, 95-97, 160; Pirton, 97; St. Albans, 97; St. Pauls Waldon, 91; Sandridge (Coleman Green), 97; Welwyn, 97; other refs., 2, 91f, 164
Hewling, William, 23
Hickeringill, Edmund, 34
Hicks, Thomas, 94
Hildyard, Sir Robert, 208
Hill, Christopher, 37, 41-49 *passim*, 55, 105, 115, 193
Hoare, Leonard, 163
Holcroft, Francis, 64, 72, 80, 84f, 90-96, 99, 161
Holloway, James, 6
Holmes, Nathaniel, 111
Holwey, Jeremy, 2
Holy Spirit: Nonconformist emphasis on, 28f, 54
Hone, William, 5
Honeyman, Andrew, bishop of Orkney, 213
Honylove, Thomas, 77
Hooke, William, 163
Horrockes, Thomas, 209
Howe, John, 7, 10, 26, 28f
Howell, Francis, 161
Howgill, Francis, 13n
Huguenots, 139
Hulton, Ann Henry, 22
Humfrey, John, 8, 123n
Hunt, Thomas, 6
Huntingdonshire: Eynesbury, 86; Ford End, 76, 85; Houghton, 92; Kimbolton (Wonditch), 77, 85; Somersham, 92; Warboys, 13; other refs, 15, 76, 91f

Inge, William, 89
Isaac, Edward, 74, 77, 85

James, duke of York, 44, 113, 131, 133, 170f, 175, 218; *see also* James II
James, John, 96
James II, 47, 69, 122, 124, 140f, 206, 220-22
Janeway, James, 3n
Janeway, Richard, 134
Jarvis, William, 77
Jelinger, Christopher, 23, 195
Jenkins, Leoline, 217
Jessey, Henry, 63f, 102, 143, 152, 157f, 160, 162, 164f
Johnson, Samuel, 138n
Jones, Captain Roger, 210f

Keach, Benjamin, 7, 67, 133
Keeble, Neil, 8, 31, 193
Keeling, Sir John, 53, 103, 104n
Keeling, Josiah, 171
Kelsey, Thomas, 96
Kent, Thomas, 77
Kestian, Nicholas, 89f
Kiffin, William, 9, 40, 63, 67, 160, 165, 204
King, Daniel, 67
Knollys, Hanserd, 67, 102
Knowles, John, 163
Knox, John, 105n, 201

Lacey, Douglas, 3
Lamb, Thomas, 67
Lancashire, 2, 214
Larke, Sampson, 221
Larkin, George, 49, 186f
Latham, George, 187
Latitudinarians, 64, 113, 130n
Lauderdale, John Maitland, earl of, 212
Lecky, William, 3, 16, 210
Lee, Samuel, 163
Leicestershire: Hucklescoate, 91; Leicester, 13, 89f
L'Estrange, Roger, 17, 48, 134, 209
Levellers, 122f
Lincolnshire, 2
Lindsay, Jack, 42
Literacy, 31
Lobb, Stephen, 5, 171
Lock, Thomas, 91
Lockyer, Nicholas, 20, 163, 212
Loddington, William, 94n
Loder, John, 161, 163
London: Bunyan's contacts in, 44, 63-67, 69-71, 79, 90, 96, 110f, 136, 143, 148-50, 153, 155-67, 169, 172-74, 201f; other

refs, 2, 4, 12, 14-16, 28, 58, 133f, 215f, 219, 221
Louis XIV, 120-22, 131, 175
Lovell, Thomas, 81
Luther, Martin, 32, 40, 53, 105

McCormack, Andrew, 16, 212
McGee, J. Sears, 41, 48
McGregor, Frank, 42
Machin, John, 7n, 23f
Magna Carta, 123
Maidwell, John, 13
Man, William, 72, 74f, 78-80
Marsden, Jeremiah, 16, 211
Marvell, Andrew, 8, 49, 130
Mary I, 120, 128
Mason, Colonel John, 211
Mason, William, 186
Mather, Increase, 150
Meade, Matthew, 44, 138, 148f, 153, 163f, 166f, 169-71, 176, 183, 203-206
Mede, Joseph, 40
Merchants' Lectures, 4
Merrill, Humphrey, 111
Middlesex, 2, 164
Midgley, Graham, 69
Millenarianism, 49f, 56f, 108f, 124f, 141-53 *passim*
Milton, John, 8, 105n, 138n, 201
Milward, John, 209
Milway, Thomas, 99
Mirabilis Annus tracts, 210
Mitchell, James, 213, 217
Monmouth, James, duke of, 44f, 47, 138, 150f, 167, 170-72, 175f, 218, 220f
Monmouthshire, 2, 219
More, Stephen, 70, 166
Morice, Sir William, 211
Mould, John, 24
Mugg, William, 89

Negus, Daniel, 81f
Nelson, Byron, 42
Nelthorpe, Richard, 170
Netherlands, 16f
Newey, Vincent, 48
Newman, Dorman, 172, 182
Nimrod, 46, 121f, 135
Nisbet, John, 149, 170f
Nonconformity: and liberty of conscience, 31-35; and spiritual experience, 18-28; and the underground press, 17f; debating tradition, 8f; ecumenical

concerns, 3-8; emphasis on the Holy Spirit, 28f, 54; literary culture, 8; number of Dissenters, 1f; organization and discipline, 9-11; responses to persecution, 11-17; urban strength of, 2f; views of the Bible, 29-31
Norfolk: Great Yarmouth, 16, 216; Norwich, 16
Northamptonshire: Bozeat, 82; Brafield on the Green, 82, 85; Hackleton, 82; Horton, 82; Rothwell, 83; Wellingborough, 82f; Wollaston, 82f, 85; other refs, 82-84
Northumberland: Berwick, 220; Newcastle upon Tyne, 214
Nye, Philip, 161, 163

Oates, Titus, 131
Oath against Transubstantiation, 207
Oath of Allegiance, 5, 207, 211
Oath of Supremacy, 5, 207
Oddy, Joseph, 91-94, 99
Offor, George, 102, 186
Ormond, James Butler, duke of, 17, 202f, 210, 213
Owen, Henry, 171
Owen, John: relations with Bunyan, 64, 99, 110, 117, 148f, 153, 160-69 *passim*, 182, 203, 206; views of, 8, 18-20, 22, 27-30, 33f, 50, 106n, 113n, 129-33, 136, 174n, 179, 195; other refs., 5, 44, 95f, 138, 156f, 170-72, 201, 204
Owens, W. Robert, 40, 49f

Palmer, Anthony, 64, 96, 110f, 117, 148f, 153, 155, 160-63, 165f, 169, 203
Palmer, Thomas, 211
Parker, Samuel, 8
Parnell, James, 93
Paul, Thomas, 9, 40, 63, 66, 160
Penington, Isaac, the younger, 8, 32
Penn, William, 2, 9, 40, 64, 94n, 177f
Pepys, Samuel, 129
Perkins, William, 40
Perrot, John, 18
Persecution of Nonconformists, 11-15, 211, 214f
Petto, Samuel, 99, 161
Philip II, 120
Phillips, John, 133
Pledger, Elias, 20f, 25, 27, 196, 204
Plots: Dublin Plot (1663), 16, 202, 210; Rathbone Plot (1665), 17, 58; Rye

House plotting (1682-83), 44, 139f, 149f, 169-73, 175f, 201, 203, 220; Tong Plot (1662), 16, 58, 111. *See also* Popish Plot
Ponder, John, 83
Ponder, Nathaniel, 49, 65, 83, 163, 165, 186
Ponder, Susannah, 83
Ponet, John, 105n
Pooley, William, 13
Popery, fear of, 4, 6, 17
Popish Plot, 4, 65f, 124, 131f, 135, 137, 139, 173, 216
Powell, Vavasor, 22, 102, 141-42n, 161, 178, 195
Preparation for salvation, 18-20
Presbyterians, 2-5, 9, 14-17, 29, 41, 53, 60, 89f, 98f, 111, 122n, 128, 130, 160, 162, 195, 203f, 209-20 *passim. See also* Presbyterians by name
Press, underground, 17f, 209f, 219
Printers and publishers, 48f, 117, 163-65, 171n, 172, 176, 186f, 201

Quakers, 2f, 8f, 12-15, 17-19, 23, 28-33, 41-43, 60, 64, 71, 74-76, 93f, 99, 121n, 143, 177, 179, 195, 207f, 211, 214. *See also* Quakers by name

Ranters, 41f, 60
Rathbone, Colonel, 17
Reade, John, 81f
Rebellions: Argyll (1685), 220f; Bothwell Bridge (1679), 218; Monmouth's (1685), 150f, 220f; Northern rebellion (1663), 16f, 58, 202, 210f
Reprobation Asserted, 185-91
Reresby, Sir John, 75
Resistance, theories of, 45-47
Reynolds, Edward, 98
Richardson, Edward, 16, 202, 210
Rivers, Isabel, 48
Rogers, James, 83
Rogers, John, 143, 152
Ross, Aileen, 47
Rowe, John, 163
Ruffhead, Josiah, 74, 77, 79
Russell, William Lord, 6, 140, 171-73, 176
Ryland, John, 186

Sabbath, 10, 66f, 162f
Sadler, Lynn, 39
Sanctification, doctrine of, 26-28
Savoy Conference (1661), 4

Savoy Declaration (1658), 4
Scott, Jonathan, 131
Scott, Oliver, 78, 80f, 85
Scott, Colonel Thomas, 210
Self-examination, duty of, 22-24, 194-96, 199
Semple, Gabriel, 212
Sensual imagery, 25f
Settle, Elkanah, 133
Sewster, John, 78
Shaftesbury, Anthony Ashley Cooper, earl of, 17, 43f, 47, 150, 170f, 201
Sharp, James, archbishop of St. Andrews, 213, 217
Sharrock, Roger, 37, 48f, 61, 66, 103, 134n, 185, 188, 189n, 193
Sheldon, Gilbert, 1f, 73, 87
Sidney, Algernon, 176
Simpson, John, 143f, 147f, 152, 158
Slater, Samuel, the elder, 22, 128
Smith, Francis, 49, 117, 165, 171n, 176, 182f, 219
Smith, Samuel, 80
Smith, William, 17-19
Solemn League and Covenant, 210, 218
Somersetshire: Taunton, 14, 219, 222; other refs, 2, 16, 209, 214, 216
Southwark, 70, 130, 135, 164, 166
Spiritual autobiographies, 20, 37-41, 195f
Spiritual diaries, 20f, 23f, 39, 195f
Spiritual experience: among Nononformists, 18-28; emphasis on the Holy Spirit, 28f
Staffordshire, 214
Stepney, 166
Stockton, Eleanor, 23f, 196, 200
Stockton, Owen, 20f, 24, 31, 196, 204
Strange, Nathaniel, 164, 202, 209
Strudwick, John, 166
Suffering, ethic of, 13f, 177-83
Suffolk: Pakefield, 15; Sudbury, 98f, 161; Wrentham, 16
Sunderland, Robert Spencer, earl of, 221
Sussex: Chichester, 218
Swinnock, George, 3, 177
Swinton, John, 28

Talon, Henri, 185
Taylor, Thomas, 75, 219
Ten Commandments, 27
Thirty-nine Articles, 4f, 7, 207
Tillinghast, John, 106, 146
Tillotson, John, 91
Tilney, Mary, 156f

Tindall, William York, 42, 45, 102, 109, 120, 124, 141, 193
Toleration: Nonconformist views of, 31-35; and James II, 221f; and the Revolution of 1688-89, 207f
Tombes, John, 9, 63
Tong, Israel, 131
Trevor, Sir John, 14, 216
Trosse, George, 21
Turner, Sir James, 49, 212
Tyndale, William, 32

Underwood, Ted L., 40

Venner, Thomas, 16, 57, 104, 141n, 144f, 152f, 202f, 208
Venning, Ralph, 163
Vernon, John, 148, 161, 163, 209
Vincent, Nathaniel, 14, 20, 130, 135

Wade, Nathaniel, 15, 219
Waite, John, 64, 78, 80f, 85, 91, 94f
Walcott, Captain Thomas, 5
Wallace, Lieutenant-Colonel James, 212
Waller, Lady Ann, 24
Waller, Sir William, 133
Wallis, Ralph, 217
Warren, Colonel Edward, 210
Warwickshire: Coventry, 111
Watson, Thomas, 3, 11, 22, 24f, 195, 199
Wavel, Richard, 66, 117, 162, 166, 169
Welch, John, 217

Wells, William, 90
Wesley, John, 209
West, Robert, 170f
Westminster Confession and Catechisms, 4
Westmorland, 15, 111, 210
Wharton, Philip Lord, 4f, 44
Wheeler, William, 72, 74, 78, 83-85, 94, 158
Whiston, Joseph, 9
Whitbread, William, 80
White, B.R., 39
Whitehead, George, 71, 74f, 94n
Whiteman, John, 55, 78f, 83
Wilkins, John, 164
William of Orange, 46f, 170, 205
Williamson, Joseph, 91, 111, 158-60, 162, 215
Wills, Obadiah, 9, 63
Wilson, John, 96f, 160
Wiltshire: Salisbury, 12; other refs, 16, 214, 216, 219
Wingate, Francis, 103, 202
Winstanley, Gerrard, 115
Wise, Laurence, 160, 162
Wolseley, Sir Charles, 26-30
Worcestershire: Worcester, 222
Wright, John, 72, 74f, 80, 155, 187
Wright, M., 155, 187
Wyclif, John, 104f

Yorkshire: Hull, 208; Whitby, 15; York, 111, 215; other refs, 2, 9, 209f